Library of Congress Cataloging in Publication Data

Harper, J. C. (Jacob Chandler), 1858-1939.
　Law of inter-state commerce.

　Reprint. Originally published: Cincinnati : R. Clarke, 1887.
　Includes index.
　1. Interstate commerce.　I. Title.
KF2289.3.H27　1983　　　　343.73'088　　　83-13789
ISBN 0-8377-0706-4　　　　347.30388

LAW

OF

INTER-STATE COMMERCE

ESPECIALLY AS APPLIED TO THE

"ACT TO REGULATE COMMERCE"

APPROVED FEBRUARY 4, 1887.

WITH NOTES OF DECISIONS

BY

J. C. HARPER

OF THE CINCINNATI BAR

CINCINNATI
ROBERT CLARKE & CO.
1887

COPYRIGHT
BY J. C. HARPER,
1887

TO

MY PRECEPTOR IN THE LAW.

THE HON. WARNER M. BATEMAN,

I GRATEFULLY INSCRIBE THIS WORK.

PREFACE.

General public interest has been awakened by the passage of the Act of Congress "to Regulate Commerce," popularly known as the Inter-State Commerce Act. The present work is not intended as a statement of individual views merely; but is, for the most part, a collection of the statutes and decisions, both in this country and in Great Britain, which bear upon the questions arising out of this law.

The commercial relations of the States among themselves and with foreign nations, and the necessity of vesting the power of regulating those relations in a national government, was one of the principal factors in bringing about the formation of the Constitution itself. The importance of the subject has since been fully demonstrated in the history of the nation. A large number of decisions have been rendered illustrating the character and scope of the power granted to Congress. All the decisions of the Supreme Court of the United States and some others, upon the subject, have been digested in this work in the belief that they would aid in properly comprehending the Act.

Some of the most important provisions of this law, including sections 2, 3, 7, and 16 of the Act, and the provision for the Commission, have been, in essential particulars, imported from the English statutes, which have been for many years in operation in England, and the subject of constant adjudication by the English courts. Similar statutes have also been enacted in the several States, varying in detail, and enforced in some instances by penalties, which have likewise been the subject of interpretation by the courts of those States. All of these decisions have been referred to as instructive in the construction of this Act, both in respect to the points of agreement and of divergence in their provisions.

Authorities defining the duties of common carriers at common law have also been collated to show how far the statute is declaratory of the common law and to what extent new duties have been imposed and new rights created.

There seemed to be a call for the early publication of the book, and, although I have digested and classified the material in the best way that the limited time and the encroachments of practice would permit, the matter is not altogether in the form I would prefer. The chief object has been to make it serviceable, capable of ready reference, and full enough in statement for actual use rather than mere reference, as many of the authorities cited are not accessible except in the large cities.

With these observations I submit the work to the indulgent consideration of the profession. If it shall prove an aid to the proper interpretation and enforcement of the Act, I shall be repaid.

I desire to acknowledge the many courtesies extended to me in the preparation of this work by M. W. Myers, Esq., the Librarian of the Cincinnati Law Library.

CINCINNATI, *May* 2, 1887.   J. C. HARPER.

CONTENTS.

PART I.

PROVISIONS OF THE CONSTITUTION OF THE UNITED STATES.

	PAGE.
The Purpose of the Grant of Power to Congress to Regulate Commerce,	1
The Nature and Scope of the Power,	1
Commerce—Its Meaning,	2
Commerce—A Natural Right,	3
Commerce with Foreign Nations,	3
Commerce among the Several States,	3
Commerce with the Indian Tribes,	5
Acts of Congress which have been held to be Valid Exercises of the Power,	6
In National Matters, the Power of Congress is Exclusive,	6
Subjects, Local in their Nature, may be Regulated by the States in the Absence of Legislation by Congress,	10
Questions of Domestic Concern Reserved to the States,	11
The Power of Congress to make all Laws Necessary and Proper for carrying into Execution the Powers granted it,	14
No Tax or duty to be levied on Articles Exported from a State,	14
No Preference shall be given to the Ports of one State over those of another,	14
State Inspection Laws,	16
Tonnage Duties,	16
Regulations respecting the Territories,	17
The Pacific Railroads.	18

PART II.

AN ACT TO REGULATE COMMERCE.

SEC. 1, PAR. 1.	Carriers subject to the Act,	19
	Notes.—Introductory—Constitutionality of the Act,	19
	Common Carriers,	29
	Common Control, Management or Arrangement,	33
SEC. 1, PAR. 2.	"Railroad" and "Transportation" defined,	36

(vii)

CONTENTS.

			PAGE.
Sec. 1, Par. 3.	Unjust and Unreasonable Charges Prohibited,		36
	Note.—Obligation of Common Carriers at Common Law,		37
Sec. 2.	Equality in Rates required,		40
	Notes.—At Common Law and under English Statutes,		41
	Like kind of Traffic,		46
	Similar Circumstances and Conditions,		47
	Other English Decisions,		59
	State Statutes and Decisions,		64
Sec. 3, Par. 1.	Undue Preferences Prohibited,		65
	Notes.—English Statutes and Decisions,		66
	At Common Law,		94
Sec. 3, Par. 2.	Reasonable and Equal Facilities for the Interchange of Traffic must be given, and Discriminations between connecting Lines Forbidden,		96
	Notes.—English Statutes and Decisions,		96
	Powers of Company,		103
	Facilities for Receiving, Forwarding, and Delivering Traffic,		105
	Discriminations in Charges between Connecting Lines,		113
	Drawing Cars of other Roads,		114
	At Common Law and under State Statutes,		115
Sec. 4.	Greater Charge in the Aggregate for Shorter than for Longer Haul Forbidden—Commission authorized to relieve Carriers in special cases from Operation of this Section,		118
	Notes.—Introductory—English and State Statutes and Decisions,		119
	Greater Compensation in the *Aggregate*,		125
	Like Kind of Property,		126
	Substantially Similar Circumstances and Conditions.		126
	Over the Same Line,		130
	In the Same Direction,		130
	Same Charge for Shorter as for Longer Distance,		130
	Power of Commission to Suspend the Section,		130
Sec. 5.	Pooling Arrangements Prohibited,		134
	Note.—Railway Pools,		134
Sec. 6, Par. 1.	Printed Schedule of Freight Rates and Passenger Fares must be kept in every Depot and Station.		139
	Notes.—Terminal Charges and Rules affecting the Aggregate Charge,		140
	Depots and Stations—What are,		143

CONTENTS.   ix

			PAGE.
Sec. 6, Par. 2.	Special Provision as to Freight shipped from United States through Foreign Country into United States,		144
Sec. 6, Par. 3.	No Advance in Rates, Fares, or Charges so Published shall be made without Ten Days' Notice—Reductions shall be posted Immediately,		145
Sec. 6, Par. 4.	All Charges Greater or Less than those named in Schedule Forbidden,		145
Sec. 6, Par. 5.	Schedules, Contracts, Joint Tariffs, etc., to be filed with the Commission, to be Published when Directed by it,		146
Sec. 6, Par. 6.	Remedies for Violations of this Section,		147
Sec. 7.	Combinations to Prevent Carriage being Continuous Forbidden—Break of Bulk, etc., shall not Prevent Carriage being Continuous,		147
	Notes.—Duties of Connecting Carriers,		148
	Continuous Shipment in Same Cars		150
	Place of Shipment to Place of Destination,		151
	Through Traffic—Cases under Section 11, Regulation of Railways Act, 1873,		152
Sec. 8.	Carrier Liable in Damages to Persons Injured by Violations of Act—Costs, Including Counsel Fee,		156
	Notes.—English Decisions,		156
	Actions against Carriers for Damages,		158
	Counsel or Attorney's Fee,		160
Sec. 9.	Actions for Damages: Where to be Brought—Criminating Evidence,		163
	Note.—Statutes Requiring the Giving of Criminating Evidence,		164
Sec. 10.	Penalty for Violation of Act—Directors, Officers, and Employes Liable to Prosecution,		166
Sec. 11.	Inter-State Commerce Commission Established—Appointment, Terms, Removal, and Qualification of Commissioners,		167
Sec. 12, Par. 1.	Powers of the Commission,		168
Sec. 12, Par. 2.	United States Circuit Court may Compel Obedience to Subpœna,		169

CONTENTS.

		PAGE.
SEC. 13, PAR. 1.	Complaints of Violations of Act and Procedure thereon by the Commission,	170
	Note.—The Duties of the Commission—Nature and Scope of the Act, and the Obligation of Carriers Subject to it,	170
SEC. 13, PAR. 2.	Investigation at the Request of State or Territorial Commissioners, or upon its own Motion,	175
SEC. 13, PAR. 3.	Want of Direct Damage to the Complainant,	175
SEC. 14, PAR. 1.	Written Reports of Investigations to be made; and Findings of Fact therein to be *Prima Facie* Evidence,	175
	Note.—*Prima Facie* Evidence—Constitutionality of such Statutes,	176
SEC. 14, PAR. 2.	Reports of Investigations to be Entered of Record, and Copies Furnished,	179
SEC. 15.	Orders of the Commission to Carriers found Violating the Act,	179
SEC. 16.	Procedure in Circuit Court to Enforce Obedience to Orders—Appeal to Supreme Court,	180
	Note.—English Statutes and Decisions as to Procedure,	182
SEC. 17.	Regulation of the Proceedings of the Commission,	183
SEC. 18.	Salaries of Commissioners, Secretary, etc.,	184
SEC. 19.	Principal Office of the Commission—Sessions Elsewhere,	185
SEC. 20.	Carriers to make Annual Reports to the Commission,	185
	Note.—As to the Constitutionality of this Requirement,	186
SEC. 21.	Annual Reports of the Commission,	187
SEC. 22.	Savings from the Operation of the Act,	187
	Note.—Mileage, Excursion, and Commutation Passenger Tickets,	188
SEC. 23.	Appropriation for Purposes of this Act,	192
SEC. 24.	Time at which the Act takes Effect,	192

APPENDIX.

ENGLISH STATUTES.

The Railway and Canal Traffic Act, 1854,	193
The Regulation of Railways Act, 1868,	197
The Regulation of Railways Act, 1873,	198

TABLE OF CASES.

                                                                                   PAGE.

Aberdeen Co. v. Gt. North. Ry. Co., 3 Nev. & Mac. 205 .... 68, 113
Almy v. California, 24 How. 169 14
Am. Ins. Co. v. Canter, 1 Peters, 511 17
—— v. Pinckney, 29 Ills. 392 31
Allen v. Hawks, 11 Pick. 359 176
—— v. Parish, 3 Ohio, 193 191
Atchison, etc., R. Co. v. Harper, 19 Ks. 529 161
—— v. D. & N. O. R. Co., 110 U. S. 667 .... 32, 42, 94, 115, 116, 148
Attorney-Gen. v. Bingham Ry. Co., 2 Eng. Ry. Cas. 89 .... 64, 122
—— v. Gt. North. Ry. Co. 183
Audendried v. P. & R. R. Co., 68 Pa. St. 370 .... 37, 41, 65
Ayr Harbor Trustees v. Glasgow Ry. Co., 4 Ry. & Can. Traf. Cas. 81..35, 80, 82

Babcock v. R. Co., 49 N. Y. 491 149
Barrett v. Gt. North. Ry. Co., 1 Nev. & Mac. 38 .... 97, 107
Bartmeyer v. Iowa, 18 Wall. 129 13
Baxendale v. Bristol Ry. Co., 1 Nev. & Mac. 229 87
—— v. East Cos. Ry., 4 C. B. (N. S.) 63 .... 37, 40, 41, 53, 61
—— v. Gt. W. Ry. Co., 16 C. B. (N. S.) 1 60
—— v. G. W. Ry. Co., 5 C. B. 336 (Reading Case) 45, 49
—— v. ——, 5 C. B. 336 .... 58, 66, 78, 85, 95
—— v. London & S. W. Ry. Co., 12 C. B. (N. S.) 758 85
—— v. N. Devon Ry. Co., 3 C. B. (N. S.) 324 88
—— v. S. W. Ry. Co., 35 L. J. 108 .... 61, 63
—— v. West Mid. Ry. Co., 3 Giff. 650 183
Beadell v. East. Cos. Ry. Co., 2 C. B. (N. S.) 509 88
Beer Co. v. Massachusetts, 97 U. S. 25 13
Belfast, etc., Ry. Co. v. G. N. Ry. Co., 3 Nev. & Mac. 419 29
—— v. ——, 4 Ry. & Can. Traf. Cas. 379 .... 29, 35
Belger v. Dinsmore, 51 N. Y. 166 31
Bell v. London, etc., Ry. Co., 2 Nev. & Mac. 185 .... 48, 49, 66, 87
Belisdyke Coal Co. v. North B. Ry. Co., 2 Nev. & Mac. 105 ...48, 49, 58, 79, 80
Bennett v. Manchester Ry. Co., 6 C. B. (N. S.) 707 183
Bintnall v. R. Co., 32 Vt. 673 149
Birdsall v. Coolidge, 93 U. S. 64 162
Blumenthal v. Brainard, 38 Vt. 402 30
Board v. Merchant, 103 N. Y. 143 .... 177, 179

(xi)

TABLE OF CASES.

	PAGE.
B. & O. R. Co. v. Maryland, 21 Wall. 456	21
Bond v. Wabash, etc., Ry. Co., 67 Iowa, 712.	163
Boston & M. R. v. Wentworth, 20 N. H. 406	161
Boyd v. U. S., 116 U. S. 616	165
Boyle v. Wiseman, 19 Ex. 647	164
Branley v. S. E. Ry., 12 C. B. (N. S.) 63	37, 41. 44
Bridge Co. v. U. S., 105 U. S. 470	6, 7
Broughton Coal Co. v. G. W. Ry. Co., 4 Ry. & Can. Traf. Cas. 191	72
Brown v. Adams Exp. Co., 15 W. Va., 831.	37
—— v. Houston, 114 U. S. 622.	6, 16, 151
—— v. Kemball, 12 Vt. 617	177
—— v. Manchester S. & L. Ry. Co., 10 L. R. Q. B. Div. 250.	40
—— v. Maryland, 12 Wheat. 419.	1, 4, 7, 13, 20, 21
Buckland v. Adams Exp. Co., 97 Mass. 124	31
Budd v. Lond. Ry. Co., 36 L. T. (N. S.) 802	55, 76, 120, 126, 128, 133
Burkholder v. Union Trust. Co., 82 Mo. 572	160
Burlington R. Co. v. Chicago Lumber Co., 15 Neb. 390	38
Burroughs v. R. Co., 100 Mass. 26.	149
Bussey v. Memphis, etc., R. Co., 13 Fed. Rep. 330	149
Cairns v. N. E. Ry. Co., 4 Ry. & Can. Traf. Cas. 221	142
Caledonia Ry. Co., etc., v. Greenock, etc., 4 Ry. & C. T. Cas. 135	35
—— v. N. B. Ry. Co., 3 Nev. & Mac. 403	29, 110
Callanan v. Hurley, 93 U. S. 387	177
Camden R. Co. v. Briggs, 1 Zab. (N. J.) 406	31
Canal Co. v. Birmingham, etc., Canal Co., 3 Nev. & Mac. 113	121
Canada S. Ry. Co. v. Bridge Co., 8 Fed. Rep. 190	6, 23, 39
Cardwell v. Bridge Co., 113 U. S. 205	10
Carton v. Ill. Cent. R. Co., 59 Iowa, 148	22
C. & A. R. Co. v. Chicago, etc., Coal Co., 79 Ill. 127	24, 25, 26, 27, 159
—— v. People, 67 Ill. 11.	28, 37, 39, 41, 42, 48, 55, 122, 159, 179
Caterham Ry. Co. v. London Ry. Co., 1 C. B. (N. S.) 410	63, 97, 107, 110, 150
Cathcart v. Robinson, 5 Pet. 264	29, 97
C. B. & Q. R. Co. v. Iowa, 94 (U. S.) 155	22
—— v. Parks, 18 Ill. 460	37, 41
—— v. People, 77 Ill. 443	38, 47, 159
Cent. B. U. P. R. Co. v. Nichols, 24 Kans. 242	163
Cen. Ry. Co. v. Collins, 40 Ga. 582	139
Cen. Ohio Salt Co. v. Guthrie, 35 Ohio St. 666	136, 137
Cen. Wales, etc., Ry. Co v. Gt. West. Ry. Co., 4 Ry. & Can. Traf. Cas. 110.	29
—— v. Gt. W. Ry. Co., 2 Nev. & Mac. 191	80
Cen. Wales & Can. Junc. Ry. Co. v. London & N. W. Ry. Co., 4 Ry. & Can. Traf. Cas. 211	153, 155
Charlton v. Newcastle, etc., R. Co., 5 Jur. (N. S.) 1100	136
Chatterley Iron Co. v. North S. Ry. Co., 3 Nev. & Mac. 205	113
Chicago Dock Co. v. Garrity, 115 Ill. 155.	116
Chicago, etc., R. Co. v. Iowa, 94 U. S. 155	23, 25, 30, 38
—— v. Moss, 60 Miss. 641	162

TABLE OF CASES. xiii

	PAGE.
Chicago R. v. Thompson, 19 Ill. 578	30
Childs v. Dolan, 5 Allen, 319	178
Chy Lung v. Freeman, 92 U. S. 275	3, 8, 14
Cin'ti Stock Yards Co. v. U. R. Stock Yards Co., 7 Cin'ti W. L. Bul. 295	94, 118
Citizens' Bank v. Nantucket Steamboat Co., 2 Story C. C. 32	30
Clonmel Traders v. Waterford Ry. Co., 4 Ry. & Can. Traf. Cas. 92	83, 143
C. & N. W. R. R. Co. v. Fuller, 17 Wall. 560	13, 22
Coates v. Ex. Co., 45 Mo. 238	169
Coe v. Errol, 116 U. S. 517	4, 6, 9, 16, 20, 33, 151
—— v. L. & N. R. Co., 3 Fed. Rep. 775	94
Coggs v. Bernard, 2 Ld. Raym. 909	30
Colman v. G. E. Ry. Co., 4 Ry. & Can. Traf. Cas. 108	140
Com'rs v. Carlisle, Brightly, 40	139
—— v. Portland, etc., R. Co., 63 Me. 269	28
Commonwealth v. Carpenter. 100 Mass. 204	178
—— v. Eastern Ry. Co., 103 Mass. 254	24, 118, 131, 169
—— v. Kelly, 10 Cush. 69	178
—— v. Latry, 8 Gray 459	178
—— v. Parker, 2 Pick. 550	177
—— v. Rowe, 16 Gray, 47	178
—— v. Wallace, 7 Gray 15	178
—— v. W. & N. R. Co., 124 Mass. 561	123
—— v. Williams, 6 Gray, 1	178
Concord & P. R. v. Forsaith, 59 N. H. 122	42, 51, 54
Conn. v. New Haven, etc., Co., 37 Conn. 153	118
Converse v. Trans. Co., 33 Conn. 166	149
Conway v. Taylor's Ex'r, 1 Black, 603	11
Cook v. Pennsylvania, 97 U. S. 566	7, 13, 21
Cooley v. Wardens of Phila., 12 How. 299	10, 16
Cooper v. London, etc., Ry. Co., 4 Jur. (N. S.) 762	183
—— v. S. W. Ry. Co., 1 Nev. & Mac. 185	86
Cooper Mfg. Co. v. Ferguson, 113 U. S. 727	9, 21
Copp v. Heninker, 55 N. H. 179	177
Corbett v. Greenlaw, 117 Mass. 167	177
Council Bluffs v. Kansas City, etc., R. Co., 45 Iowa, 338	24, 151
County of Mobile v. Kimball, 102 U. S. 691	2, 3, 6, 10
Cowdrey v. Railroad Co., 1 Woods (U. S. C. C.) 331	41
Crandall v. Nevada, 6 Wall. 35	10, 11
Crawford v. Wick, 19 Ohio St. 190	136
Crouch v. G. N. Ry. Co., 9 Exch. 557	46, 59, 60
—— v. London Ry. Co., 7 Ry. Cas. 717	61

Denaby, etc., Co., v. Manchester, Ry. Co., L. R. 11 App. Cas. (H. L.) 97.
47, 48, 49, 50, 57, 58, 63, 66, 67, 68, 71, 125, 127, 128, 130, 156, 157
—— v. ——, 3 Nev. & Mac. 426; 4 Ry. & Can. Traf. Cas. 23...67, 69, 70, 94, 130
Diphwys, etc., Co. v. Festiniog Ry. Co., 2 Nev. & Mac. 73.
38, 58, 67, 77, 78, 93, 95, 108, 142

TABLE OF CASES.

	PAGE.
Doyle v. Doyle, 56 N. H. 567	177
Dred Scott v. Sandford, 19 How. 393	17
Dublin Whis. Dis. Co. Lim., etc., v. Midland G. W. Ry. Co., 4 Ry. & Can. Traf. Cas. 32	155
Dublin R. Co. v. Midland R. Co., 3 Nev. & Mac. 379	107
Dublin Steam Pack. Co. v. London Ry. Co., 4 Ry. & Can. Traf. Cas. 10	82
Durkee v. Janesville, 28 Wis. 464	162
Dwight v. Brewster, 1 Pick. 50	29
Dwyer v. Gulf, etc., R. Co., 23 Am. & Eng. R. Cas. 656	160
East., etc., Ry. Co. v. Gt. West., etc., Ry. Co., 1 Nev. & Mac. 331	154
Eclipse Towboat Co. v. Ponchartrain R. R. Co., 24 La. Ann. 1	118
Edmonds v. Gt. West. Ry. Co., 11 C. B. 588	60
Ellis v. Drake, 8 Allen, 161	178
Erie Ry. Co. v. New Jersey, 2 Vroom, 531	8
Escanaba Co. v. Chicago, 107 U. S. 678	10
Evershed v. London & N. W. R. Co., 3 L. R. Q. B. Div. 134	56, 157
Express Co. v. Rush, 24 Ind. 403	149
Fair v. Manhattan Ins. Co., 112 Mass. 320	177
Fales v. Wadsworth, 23 Maine, 553	178
Fanning v. Chadwick, 3 Pick. 420	176
—— v. Gregoire, 9 How. 534	12
Field v. Gooding, 106 Mass. 310	178
Finnie v. S. W. R. Co., 2 Macq. 177	63, 64
Fishbourne v. G. S. & W. Ry. Co., 2 Nev. & Mac. 224	83
Fisher v. N. Y. C. & H. R. R. Co., 46 N. Y. 644	158
Fitchburg R. Co. v. Gage, 12 Gray, 393	37, 41
Foreman v. G. W. Ry. Co., 2 Nev. & Mac. 202	48, 55, 57
Foster v. Com'rs of Mobile, 22 How. 244	8
Foster, etc., v. G. W. Ry. Co., 4 Ry. & Can. Traf. Cas. 58	158
Foster v. Master & Wardens, 94 U. S. 246	8
Fuller v. Chicago, etc., Ry. Co., 31 Iowa, 187	158, 167, 192
Galena & Chicago U. R. R. Co. v. Rae, 18 Ills. 488	95, 198
Garton v. Bristol, etc. Ry. Co., 1 Nev. & Mac. 218; 6 C. B. (N. S.) 639.	49, 52, 62, 78, 79, 85
—— v. ——, 30 L. J., Q. B. 273	62
—— v. Gt. W. Ry. Co., 1 Nev. & Mac. 214; 5 C. B. (N. S.) 669	86
Georgia R. R. v. Railroad Com'rs, 70 Ga. 674	24, 132, 169
—— v. ——, 71 Ga. 863	24, 132
Gibbons v. Dist. of Col., 116 U. S. 404	17
—— v. Ogden, 9 Wheat. 1	1, 2, 3, 4, 7, 11, 20, 21, 35
Gilman v. Phila., 3 Wall. 713	10
Girardot v. Midland Ry. Co., 4 Ry. & Can. Traf. Cas. 291	48, 51, 92
Gisborn v. Hurst, 1 Salk. 249	29
Gloucester Ferry Co v. Pennsylvania, 114 U. S. 196	3, 6, 7, 8, 10, 11, 12, 21, 22
Goddard v. London, etc., Ry. Co., 1 Nev. & Mac. 308	142
Gordon v. Hutchinson, 1 Watts & S. 285	29

TABLE OF CASES.

Goshen v. Richmond 4 Allen, 458. 177
Greenock Ry. Co. v. Caledonian Ry. Co., 2 Nev. & Mac. 227. ....35, 152
Greenop v. S. E. Ry. Co., 2 Nev. & Mac. 319. ....54, 128
Gt. West. Ry. Co. v. Burns, 60 Ill. 284. 95
—— v. Ry. Com'rs, 7 L. R. Q. B. Div. 182 ....113, 114
—— v. Sutton, L. R. 4 Eng. & Ir. App. 226 ...37, 41, 45, 46, 47, 59, 60, 64, 133, 157

Hall v. De Cuir, 95 U. S. 485 ....8, 21
Hammans v. G. W. Ry. Co., 4 Ry. & Can. Traf. Cas. 181. 155
Hand v. Ballou, 2 Kernan, 541.. 177
Harborne Ry. Co. v. London, etc., Ry. Co., 2 Nev. & Mac. 169 144
Hardy v. A. T. & S. F. R. Co., 32 Kan. 698 .... 1, 21, 24, 33, 151
Hare v. London, etc., R. Co., 2 Johns. & H. 80... 136
Harris v. Cockermouth Ry. Co., 1 Nev. & Mac. 97; 3 C. B. (N. S.) 693.
49, 50, 53, 56, 57, 58, 74, 77, 127
Harris v. London R. Co., 3 Nev. & Mac. 331 ....104, 113
Haslem v. Adams Ex. Co., 6 Bosw. 235 31
Hastings Town Council v. S. E. Ry. Co., 2 Nev. & Mac. 179....................... 98
Hawkes v. Bingham, 16 Gray, 561... 178
Hays v. Pa. Co., 12 Fed. Rep. 309 ....27, 37, 41, 51, 54, 55, 188
Heisermann v. Burlington Ry. Co., 63 Iowa, 732................................38, 158
Henderson v. Mayor, 92 U. S. 260 ....2, 3, 6, 10, 14, 21
Herrimann v. Burlington, etc., R. Co., 57 Iowa, 187.................................. 163
Hersh v. North C. Ry. Co., 74 Pa. St. 181.. 124
Higgins v. Casks Lime, 130 Mass. 1... 9
Hilliard v. Goold, 34 N. H. 230... 46
Hillme v. Railroad Co., 100 N. Y. 395 157
Holland v. Festiniog Ry. Co., 2 Nev. & Mac. 278 ....49, 78
Hollister v. Nowlen, 19 Wend. 239 37
Holmes v. Hunt, 122 Mass. 505 ....164, 176
Howard v. Moot, 64 N. Y. 262 177
Holyhead Local Board v. London Ry. Co., 4 Ry. & Can. Traf. Cas. 37..... 112
Hozier v. Caledonian Ry. Co., 1 Nev. & Mac. 27 ....89, 121
Huddersfield v. Ry. Co., 4 Ry. & Can. Traf. Cas. 44................................. 29
Huse v. Glover, 119 U. S. 543... 16

Ilfracombe Co. v. London, etc., Co., 1 Nev. & Mac. 58............................. 88
Ill. Cen. R. Co. v. Stone, 20 Fed. Rep. 468 ....5, 9, 23
Indianapolis R. Co. v. Rinard, 46 Ind. 293... 66
Indiana v. Pullman Pal. Car Co., 16 Fed. Rep. 193................................9, 31
International Bridge Co. v. Canada South. Ry. Co., 8 App. Cas. 723......... 39

James, etc. v. Taff Vale, etc., R. Co., 3 Nev. & Mac. 540 109
Johnson v. Chicago, etc., Elevator Co., 119 U. S. 388............................... 16
—— v. R. Co., 16 Fla. 623 ....37, 41, 158
Johnston v. Midland R., 6 Eng. Ry. Cas. 47... 31
Jones v. Eastern Cos. Ry. Co., 3 C. B. (N. S.) 718; 1 Nev. & Mac. 45....89, 121
—— v. North-eastern Ry. Co., 2 Nev. & Mac. 208...................................... 143
Junction City Ry. Co. v. G. W. Ry. Co., 1 Nev. & Mac. 331 130

TABLE OF CASES.

	PAGE.
Kaeiser v. Ill. Cent. R. Co., 18 Fed. Rep. 151	21
Kansas v. Bradley, 26 Fed. Rep. 289	13
Kansas Pac. Ry. Co. v. Mower, 16 Kan. 573	160, 161
Kendall v. Kingston, 5 Mass. 524	164, 177
Killmer v. N. Y. C. & H. R. R. Co., 100 N. Y. 395	37, 41
Kimball v. Rutland R., 26 Vt. 249	30
Lancashire R. Co. v. Gidlow, 7 H. L. 517	45, 157
Lazarus v. Commonwealth Ins. Co., 19 Pick. 81	176
Lee v. Tillotson, 24 Wend. 337	177
Lees v. Lancashire Ry. Co., 1 Nev. & Mac. 352	93
Liverpool Ins. Co. v. Mass., 10 Wall. 566	14
Lloyd v. Northampton R. Co., 3 Nev. & Mac. 259	73
L. & N. R. Co. v. Railroad Com'rs of Tenn., 19 Fed. Rep. 679	23, 25, 27, 38, 39
Local Board v. N. E. R. Co., 3 Nev. & Mac. 306	112
—— v. London Ry. Co., 2 Nev. & Mac. 214	108
Lock v. Bennett, 7 Cush. 445	176
Locke v. N. E. Ry. Co., 3 Nev. & Mac. 44	93, 141
Logan v. Central R., 74 Ga. 684	117, 151
Lowe v. Pimental, 115 Mass. 44	177
London & N. W. R. Co. v. Evershed, L. R. 3 App. Cas. 1029.	43, 44, 50, 55, 56, 67, 68, 75, 128, 133
London Ry. Co. v. Staines Ry. Co., 3 Nev. & Mac. 48	103, 104, 110, 113
Lotspeich v. Cent. R. Co., 73 Ala. 306	48, 124, 149
Lowell Wire Fence Co. v. Sargeant, 8 Allen, 189	31
Magar v. Grima, 8 How. 490	13
Machine Co. v. Gage, 110 U. S. 676	13
Mackin v. Boston, 135 Mass. 201	30, 114, 151
Manchester, etc., Ry. Co. v. Brown, L. R. 8 App. Cas. 703	30, 40
—— v. Denaby Co., 4 Ry. & Can. Traf. Cas. 450	71
Marriott v. London Ry. Co., 1 C. B. (N. S.) 449; 1 Nev. & Mac. 47	88, 183
Matthews v. Offley, 3 Sumner, 115	178
Mattingly v. Dist. of Col., 97 U. S. 687	17
Mayor, etc., of N. Y. v. Miln, 11 Peters, 102	14
Mayor, etc., v. S. E. Ry. Co., 1 Nev. & Mac. 349	175
Meeker v. Winthrop Iron Co., 17 Fed. Rep. 48	162
Menacho v. Ward, 27 Fed. Rep. 529	27, 37, 41, 53, 58, 78, 136
Mercantile Mut'l Ins. Co. v. Chase, 1 E. D. Smith, 115	31
Merry v. Glasgow Ry. Co., 4 Ry. & Can. Traf. Cas. 383	47, 125
Messenger v. Penn. R. Co., 36 N. J. L. 407	37, 41, 42
Miller v. Mayor of N. Y., 10 Fed. Rep. 513; affirmed, 109 U. S. 385	24, 131, 168
Miners' Bank. v. Iowa, 12 How. 1	17
Mineral Springs Mfg. Co. v. Mich. C. R. Co., 16 Wall. 318	33
Minis v. U. S. 15 Pet. 423	35
Mobile v. Kimball, 102 U. S. 691	1
Mobile R. Co. v. Sessions, 28 Fed. Rep. 592	5, 9, 23
Monson v. Palmer, 8 Allen, 551	177

TABLE OF CASES. xvii

	PAGE
Mo. Pac. Ry. Co. v. Texas & Pac. Ry. Co., 30 Fed. Rep. 2.	24, 51, 55, 114, 122, 132, 136
—— v. ——, 1 Ry. & Corp. L. J. 428	134
Moore v. Ill. Cent. R. Co., 68 Ill. 385	38
Mo. Riv., etc., R. Co. v. Shirley, 20 Kan. 660	163
Morgan v. Morse, 13 Gray, 150	176
—— v. Louisiana, 118 U. S. 455	13, 16
Munhall v. Penn. R. Co., 92 Pa. St. 150	56, 57, 118
Munn v. Illinois, 94 U. S. 113	14, 16, 22, 25, 37, 38
Murray v. Glasgow Co., 11 Court Sess. Cas. 4 (Ser.) 205.	64, 130, 157
Murphy v. Ramsey, 114 U. S. 15	17, 18
Myrick v. Mich. Cent. Ry. Co., 107 U. S. 102	30, 149
Macfarlane v. Ry. Co. (No. 2), 4 Ry. & Can. Traf. Cas. 269	68, 94, 145
McCool v. Smith, 1 Black, 459	29, 97
McCoy v. C. I., etc., R. Co., 13 Fed. Rep. 3	94, 115
McDonald v. Hovey, 110 U. S. 619	29, 67, 97
McDuffie v. Railroad Co., 52 N. H. 430	37, 54
—— v. P. & R. R. R., 52 N. H. 430	42, 158
McMillan v. R. Co., 10 Mich. 119	149
Nathan v. Louisiana, 8 How. 73	13
National Bank. v. County of Yankton, 101 U. S. 129	17
Napier v. Glasgow Ry. Co., 1 Nev. & Mac. 292	82, 116
Nashua, etc., Corp. v. Boston, etc., R. Corp., 19 Fed. Rep. 804	137
Nevin v. Pullman Co., 11 Am. & E. R. Cas. 92	31
N. E. Exp. Co. v. M. C. R. Co., 57 Me. 188	37, 41, 42, 95
Nichols v. Smith, 115 Mass. 332	30
N. J. R. v. Penn. R., 3 Dutch. 100	30
Nicholson v. G. W. Ry. Co. (No. 1), 5 C. B. 366; 1 Nev. & Mac. 121.	45, 48, 49, 51, 52, 68, 80, 89, 127
—— v. —— (No. 2), 1 Nev. & Mac. 143	52
Nitshill Coal Co. v. Caledonian Ry. Co., 2 Nev. & Mac. 39	46, 48, 74, 80
Nolan v. Collins, 112 Mass. 12	177
Norfolk & W. R. Co. v. Commonwealth (Pa.), 26 Am. & Eng. R. Cas.	489, 24
N. Pa R. Co. v. Adams, 54 Pa. St. 94	161
Ogden v. Saunders, 12 Wheat. 213	164, 177
Ogdensburg, etc., R. Co. v. Min. Springs Mfg. Co., 16 Wall. 318	149
—— v. Pratt, 22 Wall. 123	33
Oxlade v. N. E. Ry. Co., 3 Nev. & Mac. 35	144
—— v. —— (No. 1), Nev. & Mac. 72.	57, 77, 79, 92, 126, 133
Pace v. Burgess, 92 U. S. 372	14
Pacific, etc., Co. v. R. R. Com'rs, 9 Sawyer, 253	7, 8, 20, 23
Packard v. Richardson, 17 Mass. 122	177
Packet Co. v. Aiken, 16 Fed. Rep. 890	10
—— v. Catlettsburg, 105 U. S. 559	11, 16
—— v. Keokuk, 95 U. S. 80	11
Packet Co. v. St. Louis, 100 U. S. 423	11, 16

TABLE OF CASES.

	PAGE
Page v. Smith, 99 Mass. 395	29
Painter v. London Ry. Co., 1 Nev. & Mac. 58; 2 C. B. (N. S.) 702	88
Palmer v. London Ry. Co., 1 Nev. & Mac. 271	84
—— v. ——, 1 Nev. & Mac. 243	84
Parker v. Gt. W. Ry. Co., 3 Ry. Cas. 563 (Exch.)	59, 60
—— v. ——, 6 E. & B. 77	60
—— v. ——, 11 C. B. 545	62
—— v. ——, 6 Ry. Cas. 776	157
Parkinson v. Gt. W. Ry. Co., 1 Nev. & Mac. 280	83, 84
Paul v. Virginia, 8 Wall. 168	9, 14
Paxon v. Ills. Cent. R. Co, 56 Iowa, 427	47, 59, 159, 160
Peet v. Chicago R. Co., 20 Wis. 594	95
Peik v. C. & N. W. R. Co., 94 U. S. 164	22, 38
Pennock v. Dialogue, 2 Pet. 1	29, 97
Penn. v. Wheeling Bridge Co., 13 How. 518	7, 16
Penn. R. Co. v. Canfield, 46 Pa. St. 211	124, 151
Pensacola Tel. Co. v. W. U. Tel. Co., 96 U. S. 1	2, 6, 9, 20, 23
People v. Campagnie, 107 U. S. 59	8, 13
—— v. Kelly, 24 N. Y. 76	165
—— v. Lyon, 27 Hun, 180	178
Peoria R. Co. v. Chicago, R. Co., 109 Ill. 135	30, 115, 151
Perkins v. Railroad Co., 47 Me. 573	149
—— v. Scott, 57 N. H. 55	177
Phila. Fire Ass'n v. New York, 119 U. S. 110	14
Pickard v. Pullman South. Car Co., 117 U. S. 34	9, 21, 22, 23, 31
Pickford v. Caledonian Ry. Co., 1 Nev. & Mac. 252	84
—— v. Grand J. Ry. Co., 10 M. & W. 399; 3 Eng. Ry. Cas. 144	62
Pierce v. New Hampshire, 5 How. 504	7
Pillow v. Roberts, 13 How. 472	177
Plimpton v. Somerset, 33 Vt. 283	179
Portland, etc., R. v. Grand Tr. Ry. Co., 46 Me. 69	131
Prov. Coal Co. v. P. & W. R. Co., 26 Am. & Eng. R. Cas. 42	9
Pullman Palace Car Co. v. Mo. Pac. Ry. Co., 11 Fed. Rep. 634	34
Pullman, etc., Co. v. Texas, etc., Ry. Co., 11 Fed. Rep. 625	136

Rae v. Grand Trunk Ry. Co., 14 Fed. Rep. 401	13
Ragan v. Aiken, 9 B. J. Lea (Tenn.) 609	58
Railroad Com'rs v. Portland, etc., R. Co., 63 Maine, 260	24, 38, 118, 131, 169
—— v. Railroad Co. 22 S. Car. 220	5, 6, 9, 23
Railroad Co. v. Berry, 68 Pa. St. 272	149
—— v. Boyes, 9 Cox, 32	164
—— v. Brown, 8 App. Cas. 703	39
—— v. Fuller, 17 Wall. 560	11
—— v. Hammersley, 104 U. S. 1	118
—— v. Hill, 14 Bradw. (Ill. App.) 579	41, 65, 123, 125
Railroad Co. v. Husen, 95 U. S. 465	9, 13, 14, 21
—— v. Richmond, 19 Wall. 584	14, 24, 26, 27

TABLE OF CASES. xix

	PAGE.
Ransome v. Eastern Cos. Ry. Co. (No. 1), 1 C. B. (N. S.) 437.	45, 48, 50, 53, 56, 57
—— v. —— (No. 2), 4 C. B. (N. S.) 135	73, 75, 133
—— v. —— (No. 3), 4 C. B. (N. S.) 159	75, 121
—— v. —— (No. 4), 1 Nev. & Mac. 155	73, 75
Reynolds v. U. S., 98 U. S. 145.	17, 18
Richardson v. Midland Ry. Co., 4 Ry. & Can. Traf. Cas. 1	89, 92
Riley v. Horne, 5 Bing. 217.	39
Robertson v. Great S. & W. Ry. Co., 2 Nev. & Mac. 374	141
—— v. Midland, etc., Ry. Co., 2 Nev. & Mac. 409	87
Rowland v. Penn. R. Co., 52 Pa. St. 250	124, 152
Ruggles v. Illinois, 108 U. S. 526	25, 38
Sandford v. Railroad Co., 24 Pa. St. 381	31, 37, 42, 65, 95
Sargent v. B. & L. R., 115 Mass. 416	42, 65, 95
Scofield v. Ry. Co., 43 Ohio St. 571	27, 37, 41, 51, 56, 55, 58, 78, 95
Scott v. Erie Ry. Co., 34 N. J. Eq. 354	159
S. E. Ry. Co. v. Ry. Com'rs, 3 Nev. & Mac. 464; 6 Q. B. Div. 586	98
Sherlock v. Alling, 93 U. S. 99	4, 11, 21, 33
Sherman v. Am. Ex. Co., 23 Ills. 197; 26 Ills. 504	31
Shipper v. Penn. R. Co., 47 Pa. St. 338	37, 41, 95, 124
Sinnot v. Com'rs of Mobile, 22 How. 227	8
Smith v. Chicago R. Co., 5 N. W. Rep. 309	37
—— v. Maryland, 18 How. 71	13
S. & N. Ala. R. Co. v. Morris, 65 Ala. 193	162
South Carolina v. Georgia, 93 U. S. 4	6, 16, 23
Southern Ex. Co. v. Newby, 36 Ga. 635	31
South Sea Ferry Co. v. London Ry. Co., 2 Nev. & Mac. 341	82
Spofford v. Boston & M. R., 128 Mass. 326	65
Sprague v. Thompson, 118 U. S. 90	11
Starin v. New York, 115 U. S. 709	11
State v. Beswick, 18 R. I. 211	178
—— v. Chicago, etc., R. Co., 19 Neb. 476	24, 118, 131, 164, 169
—— v. Furbush, 72 Me. 493	9
—— v. Higgins, 13 R. I. 330	178
—— v. Mellor, 13 R. I. 211	178
—— v. Nebraska Tel. Co., 17 Neb. 126	41, 42
—— v. New Haven, etc., Co., 42 Conn. 56	118
—— v. North, 27 Mo. 464	9
—— v. Nowell, 58 N. H. 514	165, 166
—— v. Noyes, 47 Me. 189	28
—— v. Republican V. R. Co., 17 Neb. 647	38, 41, 95
—— v. Telephone Co., 36 O. S. 296	42
—— v. Thomas, 47 Conn. 546	178
—— v. Vanderbilt, 37 O. S. 590	135
—— v. Warner, 13 La. 52	165
State of Penn. v. Wheeling, etc., Bridge Co., 18 How. 241	15
Staunton v. Allen, 5 Denio, 440	136

TABLE OF CASES.

	PAGE.
Steamship Co. v. Portwardens, 6 Wall. 31	8, 11
Steever v. Ill. Cent. Ry. Co., 62 Iowa, 371	158
Stewart v. Laird, 1 Cranch, 299	177
—— v. Terre Haute R. Co., 3 Fed. Rep. 768	33, 149
St. Louis & Cairo R. R. v. Blackwood, 14 Ill. App. 503	140
St. Louis, etc., Ry. Co. v. Hill, 14 Bradw. 579	25, 124, 160, 163, 179
Stockwell v. U. S., 13 Wall. 531	147, 163
Stoddard v. Chapin, 15 Vt. 443	177
Stone v. Farmers' Loan and Trust Co., 116 U. S. 307	23, 24, 25, 27, 38, 39
Strict v. Swansea Canal Co., 16 C. B. (N. S.) 245	57
Sutton v. G. W. Ry. Co., L. R. 4 H. L. 226	51
Swan v. Railroad, 132 Mass. 116	46
Swindon Ry. v. Gt. W. Ry., 4 Ry. & Can. Traf. Cas. 349	110
Telegraph Co. v. Texas, 105 U. S. 460	2, 6, 8, 9, 21, 23
Telephone Co. v. B. & O. Tel. Co., 35 Alb. L. J. 271	42
Tharsis v. London Ry. Co., 3 Nev. & Mac. 455	103, 104, 106
Thomas v. Boston & Prov. R. Co., 10 Met. 472	30
Thompson v. Kenyon, 100 Mass. 108	178
—— v. London & N. W. Ry. Co., 2 Nev. & Mac. 115	55, 56, 77, 128
Thomas v. N. Staff Ry. Co., 3 Nev. & Mac. 1	105, 111
Toomer v. London R. Co., 3 Nev. & Mac. 79	79, 105, 107, 108
Thurlow v. Mass., 5 How. 504	13
Transportation Co. v. Parkersburg, 607 U. S. 691	11
Turpin v. Burgess, 117 U. S. 507	14, 16
Turner v. Maryland, 107 U. S. 38	13
Twells v. Penn. R. Co., 3 Am. L. Reg. (N. S.) 728	59, 78, 132
U. S. Ex. Co. v. Backman, 28 O. S. 144	31
U. S. v. Boston & A. R. Co., 15 Fed. Rep. 209	23
—— v. Brown, 1 Sawy. 531	165
—— v. Claypool, 14 Fed. Rep. 127	167
—— v. Coombs, 12 Pet. 72	4, 6, 18, 23
—— v. Dickson, 15 Pet. 165	189
—— v. E. T. V. & G. R. Co., 13 Fed. Rep. 642	24
—— v. 43 Gallons Whisky, 93 U. S. 188	5
—— v. Holliday, 3 Wall. 407	5
—— v. Louisville & N. R. Co., 18 Fed. Rep. 480	23
—— v. McCarthy, 18 Fed. Rep. 87	164, 165
—— v. Peniston, 98 U. S. 569	18
Union Pac. R. Co. v. Peniston, 18 Wall. 5	18
—— v. U. S. 117 U. S. 355	122
U. S. v. Union Pacific R. Co., 91 U. S. 72	29
—— v. Saline Bank, 1 Pet. 100	164
—— v. Stephens, 12 Fed. Rep. 52	18
—— v. Williams, 15 Int. Rev. Rec. 199	165
Veazie v. Moor, 14 How. 568	121
Victoria Co. v. Neath, etc., Ry. Cos., 3 Nev. & Mac. 37	109

TABLE OF CASES.

	PAGE
Vincent v. Chicago & A. R. Co., 49 Ill. 33	94
Vt. & M. R. v. Fitchburg R., 14 Allen, 462	30, 114, 151
—— v. ——, 9 Cush. 369	169

Wabash, etc., Ry. Co. v. Illinois, 118 U. S. 557.
              2, 5, 6, 7, 9, 11, 12, 13, 21, 22, 35, 38

—— v. People, 105 Ill. 236	124
Walling v. Michigan, 116 U. S. 446	6, 9, 21
Wannan v. Scottish Cent. Ry. Co., 2 Sess. Cas. 1373; 1 Nev. & Mac. 237	84
Waring v. The Mayor, 8 Wall. 110	7
Warwick Canal Co. v. Birmingham Canal Co., 5 L. R. Exch. Div. 1	156
Watkinson v. Wrexham R. Co., 3 Nev. & Mac. 5	67, 103, 104, 106, 141, 143, 147
Webb v. Den., 17 How. 376	178
Webber v. Virginia, 103 U. S. 344	9, 21
Weil v. Calhoun, 25 Fed. Rep. 865	9
Welton v. Missouri, 91 U. S. 275	1, 2, 9, 21
Welch v. Cook, 97 U. S. 541	17
West v. London & N. W. Ry. Co., L. R. 5 C. P. 622	111
W. Va. Transp. Co. v. Sweetser, 25 W. Va. 634	159
White's Bank v. Smith, 7 Wall. 646	6
Wiggins Ferry Co. v. E. St. Louis, 107 U. S. 365	12
Wilson v. Blackbird Creek Marsh Co., 2 Pet. 245	10
—— v. McNamee, 102 U. S. 572	10
Wood v. Wood, 1 Carr & P. 59	189
Woodger v. Gt. East. Ry. Co., 2 Nev. & Mac. 102	44
Woodruff v. Parham, 8 Wall. 129	7, 13
Worcester v. Georgia, 6 Pet. 575	5
Wormsley v. Dalby, 26 L. J. (Exch.) 219	189
Young v. Gwendraeth Val. Ry., 4 Ry. & Can. Traf. Cas. 247	114
Zuns v. S. E. Ry. Co., 4 L. R. Q. B. 539	44

LAW OF INTER-STATE COMMERCE.

PART I.

PROVISIONS OF THE CONSTITUTION OF THE UNITED STATES.

Congress shall have power . . . to regulate commerce with foreign nations, and among the several states and with the Indian tribes. [Art. 1, § 8, cl. 3.]

§ 1. THE PURPOSE OF THE GRANT TO CONGRESS.

"**The design and object** of that power, as evinced in the history of the constitution, was to establish a perfect equality amongst the several states as to commercial rights, and to prevent unjust and invidious distinctions, which local jealousies, or local and partial interests, might be disposed to introduce and maintain." *Veazie* v. *Moor*, 14 How. 568, 574; The Federalist. Nos. 7, 11; *Gibbons* v. *Ogden*, 9 Wheat. 1, 224 et seq.; *Mobile* v. *Kimball* 102 U. S. 691; *Welton* v. *Missouri*, 91 U. S. 275.

"It may be doubted whether any of the evils proceeding from the feebleness of the federal government contributed more to that great revolution which introduced the present system, than the deep and general conviction that commerce ought to be regulated by congress. It is not therefore, matter of surprise, that the grant should be as extensive as the mischief, and should comprehend all foreign commerce and all commerce among the states." Marshall, C. J., in *Brown* v. *Maryland*, 12 Wheat. 419, 446.

§ 2. THE NATURE AND SCOPE OF THE POWER.

"**The power to regulate** . . . is to prescribe the rule by which the commerce is to be governed. This power, like all others vested in congress, is complete in itself, may be exercised to its utmost extent, and acknowledges no limitations other than are prescribed in the constitution. . . . If, as has always been understood, the sovereignty of congress, though limited to specified objects, is plenary as to those objects, the power over commerce with foreign nations, and among the several states, is vested in congress as absolutely as it would be in a single government, having in its constitution the same restrictions on the exercise of the power as are found in the constitution of the United States. The wisdom and the discretion of congress, their identity with the people, and the influence which their constituents possess at elections, are, in this, as in many other instances, as that, for example, of declaring war, the sole restraints on which they have relied to secure them from its abuse. They are the restraints on which the people must often rely solely in all representative governments." Marshall, C. J., in *Gibbons* v. *Ogden*, 9 Wheat. 1, 197.

"It is obvious that the government, in regulating commerce with foreign nations and among the states, may use means that may also be employed by a state, in the exercise of its acknowledged powers; that, for example, of regulating commerce within a state." Marshall, C. J., in *Gibbons* v. *Ogden*, 9 Wheat. 204.

"The 'power to regulate commerce,' here meant to be granted, was that power to regulate commerce which previously existed in the states." Johnson, J., in *Gibbons* v. *Ogden*, 9 Wheat. 227.

Whenever the subjects in regard to which a power to regulate commerce is asserted are in their nature national, or admit of one uniform system or plan of regulation, they are exclusively within the regulating control of congress. *The Case of the State Freight Tax*, 15 Wall. 232; *Henderson* v. *Mayor*, 92 U. S. 260; *County of Mobile* v. *Kimball*, 102 U. S. 691; *Wabash, etc., Ry. Co.* v. *Illinois*, 118 U. S. 557.

The power conferred upon congress to regulate commerce with foreign nations and among the several states, is not confined to the instrumentalities of commerce known, or in use when the constitution was adopted, but keeps pace with the progress of the country, and adapts itself to the new developments of time and circumstances. It was intended for the government of the business to which it relates, at all times and under all circumstances; and it is not only the right, but the duty, of congress to take care that intercourse among the states and the transmission of intelligence are not obstructed or unnecessarily incumbered by state legislation. *Pen. Tel. Co.* v. *W. U. Tel. Co.*, 96 U. S. 1, 9, Waite, C. J.; *Telegraph Co.* v. *Texas*, 105 U. S. 460.

"A telegraph company occupies the same relation to commerce, as a carrier of messages, that a *railroad company does as a carrier of goods.*" *Telegraph Co.* v. *Texas*, 105 U. S. 460, 464, Waite, C. J.

"It covers property which is transported as an article of commerce from foreign countries, or among the states, from hostile or interfering state legislation until it has mingled with and become a part of the general property of the country, and protects it even after it has entered a state from any burdens imposed by reason of its foreign origin." *Welton* v. *Missouri*, 91 U. S. 275.

§ 3. COMMERCE: ITS MEANING.

"**Commerce,** undoubtedly, is traffic, but it is something more; it is intercourse. It describes the commercial intercourse between nations, and parts of nations, in all its branches, and is regulated by prescribing rules for carrying on that intercourse." Marshall, C. J., in *Gibbons* v. *Ogden*, 9 Wheat. 1, 189-190; 12 Wheat. 446, 447; *Gloucester Ferry Co.* v. *Pennsylvania*, 114 U. S. 196; *Henderson* v. *Mayor*, 92 U. S. 259, 270, in which Miller, J., says that the opinion of Chief Justice Marshall, in *Gibbons* v. *Ogden, supra,* "has become the accepted canon of construction of this clause of the constitution, as far as it extends."

"Commerce is intercourse; one of its most important ingredients is traffic. . . . Congress has a right not only to authorize importation, but to authorize the importer to sell." Marshall, C. J., in 12 Wheat. 446-7.

"Commerce with foreign countries and among the states, strictly considered, consists in intercourse and traffic, including in these terms navigation and the transportation and transit of persons and property, as well as the purchase, sale, and exchange of commodities. To regulate it, as thus defined, there must be only one system of rules applicable alike to the whole country, which congress alone can prescribe. *County of Mobile* v. *Kimball*, 102 U. S. 691.

§ 4. COMMERCE A NATURAL RIGHT.

"The constitution does not confer the right of intercourse between state and state. That right derives its source from those laws whose authority is acknowledged by civilized man throughout the world. . . . The constitution found it an existing right, and gave to congress the power to regulate it." Marshall, C. J., in *Gibbons* v. *Ogden*, 9 Wheat. 211.

§ 5. COMMERCE WITH FOREIGN NATIONS.

"No sort of trade can be carried on between this country and any other to which this power does not extend." Marshall, C. J., 9 Wheat. 194.

"The passage of laws which concern the admission of citizens and subjects of foreign nations to our shores belongs to congress and not to the states. It has the power to regulate commerce with foreign nations; the responsibility for the character of those regulations and for the manner of their execution belongs solely to the national government." Miller, J., in *Chy Lung* v. *Freeman*, 92 U. S. 275, 280

§ 6. COMMERCE AMONG THE SEVERAL STATES.

"The word 'among' means intermingled with. A thing which is among others is intermingled with them. Commerce among the states can not stop at the external boundary line of each state, but may be introduced into the interior. It is not intended to say that these words comprehend that commerce which is completely internal, which is carried on between man and man in a state, or between parts of the same state, and which does not extend to or affect other states. It may very properly be restricted to that commerce which concerns more states than one." Marshall, C. J., in *Gibbons* v. *Ogden, supra,* 194.

"Commerce among the states must, of necessity, be commerce with the states." *Ib.* 196.

"The power is co-extensive with the subject on which it acts, and can not be stopped at the external boundary of a state, but must enter its interior." Marshall, C. J., in *Brown* v. *Maryland,* 12 Wheat. 446.

"It does not stop at the mere boundary line of a state. . . . It extends to such acts done on land which interfere with, obstruct, or prevent the due exercise of the power to regulate commerce and navigation with foreign nations, and among the states." (Story, J.)

So held, in a prosecution under the act of March 3, 1825, punishing thefts of goods belonging to vessels in distress, though the offense was committed above high-water mark, within the State of New York. The act was within the grant to congress to regulate commerce. *U. S.* v. *Coombs,* 12 Pet. 72.

"Whenever a commodity has begun to move as an article of trade from one state to another, commerce in that commodity between the states has commenced. The fact that several different and independent agencies are employed in transporting the commodity, some acting entirely in one state, and some acting through two or more states, does not in any respect affect the character of the transaction. To the extent which each agency acts in that transportation, it is subject to the regulation of commerce." Field, J., in *The Daniel Ball,* 10 Wall. 557, 565.

So held, in the case of a steamer plying upon Grand River, Michigan, entirely within the bounds of that state, but employed in transporting goods destined for other states. *The Daniel Ball, supra; Coe* v. *Errol,* 116 U. S. 517.

"It authorizes legislation with respect to all the subjects of . . . inter-state commerce, the persons engaged in it, and the instruments by which it is carried on." Field, J., in *Sherlock* v. *Alling,* 93 U. S. 99, 103.

A statute of Illinois enacted that, if any railroad company shall, within that state, charge or receive for transporting passengers or freight, of the same class, the same or a greater sum, for any distance, than it does for a longer distance, it shall be liable to a penalty for unjust discrimination. The defendant in this case made such discrimination in regard to goods transported over the same road or roads, from Peoria, in Illinois, and from Gilman, in Illinois, to New York, charging more for the same class of goods carried from Gilman than from Peoria, the former being eighty-six miles nearer to New York than the latter, this difference being in the length of the line within the State of Illinois.

Held: 1. This court follows the Supreme Court of Illinois in holding that the statute of Illinois must be construed to include a transportation of goods under one contract and by one voyage from the interior of the State of Illinois to New York.

2. This court holds further that such a transportation is "commerce among the states," even as to that portion of the voyage which lies within

the State of Illinois; while it is not denied that there may be a transportation of goods which is begun and ended within its limits, and disconnected with any carriage outside of the state, which is *not* commerce among the states.

3 The latter is subject to regulation by the state, and the statute of Illinois is valid as applied to it. But the former is national in its character, and its regulation is confided to congress exclusively by that clause of the constitution which empowers it to regulate commerce among the states.

4. That a statute of a state, intended to regulate or to tax, or to impose any other restriction upon the transmission of persons or property, or telegraphic messages from one state to another, is not within that class of legislation which the states may enact in the absence of legislation by congress; and that such statutes are void even as to that part of such transmission which may be within the state.

5 It follows that the statute of Illinois, as construed by the supreme court of the state, and as applied to the transaction under consideration, is forbidden by the Constitution of the United States, and the judgment of that court is reversed. *Wabash, St. L. & P. Ry. Co.* v. *Illinois*, 118 U. S 557; 1 Ry & Corp. L. J. 3; 26 Am. & Eng. R. Cas. 1, reversing 105 Ill. 236

See *L. & N. R. Co.* v. *Railroad Com'rs of Tenn.*, 19 Fed. Rep. 679, where, under a similar statute and state of facts, Baxter and Hammond, JJ. reached the same result as in the Wabash case. Also, *Railroad Com'rs* v. *Railroad Co.*, 22 S. Car. 220; *s. c.*, 26 Am. & Eng. R. Cas. 29; *Mobile, etc., R. Co.* v. *Sessions*, 28 Fed. Rep. 592; *Ill. Cent. R. Co.* v. *Stone*, 20 Fed. Rep. 468.

§ 7. Commerce with the Indian Tribes.

"In the regulation of trade with the Indian tribes, the action of the law, especially when the constitution was made, was chiefly within a state." Marshall, C. J., in 9 Wheat. 196.

The law of Georgia, subjecting white persons, residing in the Cherokee nation, to arrest and punishment, and authorizing their removal from the nation, held unconstitutional. *Worcester* v. *Georgia*, 6 Pet. 515.

This power extends to the regulation of commerce with the Indian tribes and with the individual members of such tribes, though the traffic, and the Indian with whom it is carried on, are wholly within the territorial limits of a state. *U. S.* v. *Holliday*, 3 Wall. 407; *U. S.* v. *43 Gallons Whisky*, 93 U. S. 188.

No state can withdraw the Indians within its limits from the operation of the laws of congress regulating trade with them, notwithstanding any rights it may confer upon them as electors or citizens. *U. S.* v. *Holliday, supra*.

The act of February 12, 1862, punishing the sale of spirituous liquors to Indians is constitutional. *Ib.*

And congress may extend its prohibition to territory in proximity to that occupied by Indians. *U. S.* v. *43 Gallons Whisky, supra.*

§ 8. Acts of Congress which have been held to be Valid Exercises of the Power.

Telegraph. The act of congress approved July 24, 1866 (14 Stat. 221; Rev. Stat., § 5263 et seq.), entitled "An act to aid in the construction of telegraph lines, and to secure to the government the use of the same for postal, military, and other purposes," so far as it declares that the erection of telegraph lines shall, as against state interference, be free to all who accept its terms and conditions, and that a telegraph company of one state shall not, after accepting them, be excluded by another state from prosecuting its business within her jurisdiction, is a legitimate regulation of commercial intercourse among the states. *Pen. Tel. Co.* v. *W. U. Tel. Co.*, 96 U. S. 1; *Telegraph Co.* v. *Texas*, 105 U. S. 460.

Larceny of goods. That congress may enact laws punishing thefts of goods while they constitute a part of the commerce under its control, see *U. S.* v. *Coombs*, 12 Pet. 72; *Coe* v. *Errol*, 116 U. S. 517.

Maritime conveyances and liens. The act of congress of July 20, 1850, providing for the effect of recording conveyances of vessels, held constitutional. *White's Bank* v. *Smith*, 7 Wall. 646. See *The Lottawanna*, 21 Wall. 558.

Bridges and navigable rivers. Congress may declare bridges over navigable rivers lawful structures. *The Wheeling Bridge*, 18 How. 429; *The Clinton Bridge*, 10 Wall. 454. Or, devolve that power upon some officer. *Miller* v. *City of N. Y.*, 10 Fed. Rep. 513; affirmed, 109 U. S. 385.

And congress may require the alteration of a bridge, which it had previously authorized, without incurring any liability to the bridge company. *Bridge Co.* v. *U. S.*, 105 U. S. 470.

That congress may, in the exercise of its power to regulate commerce, prescribe the charges for use of a bridge over a navigable stream, see *Canada S. Ry. Co.* v. *Bridge Co.*, 8 Fed. Rep. 190.

Congress has power to close one of several channels in a navigable stream. *South Carolina* v. *Georgia*, 93 U. S. 4.

§ 9. In National Matters the Power of Congress is Exclusive.

As to matters which are in their nature national, or admit of a uniform system or plan of regulation, the power to regulate is exclusively vested in congress. *Henderson* v. *Mayor*, 92 U. S. 260; *County of Mobile* v. *Kimball*, 102 U. S. 692; *Gloucester Ferry Co.* v. *Pennsylvania*, 114 U. S. 196; *Wabash, etc., Ry. Co.* v. *Illinois*, 118 U. S. 557.

Non-action by congress as to this character of commerce, is a declaration that it shall be free and untrammeled. *Walling* v. *Michigan*, 116 U. S. 446, 455; *Brown* v. *Houston*, 114 U. S. 622; *Railroad Com'rs* v. *Railroad Co.*, 22 S. Car. 220; *s. c.*, 26 Am. & Eng. R. Cas. 29, 41.

"The commerce with foreign nations and between the states, which consists in the transportation of persons and property between them, is a subject of national character, and requires uniformity of regulation." *Gloucester Ferry Co.* v. *Pennsylvania, supra; Wabash, etc., Ry. Co.* v. *Illinois, supra; Pacific, etc., Co.* v. *Railroad Com'rs.* 9 Sawyer, 253; 18 Fed. Rep. 10.

Tax—License. A state law requiring an importer to take and pay for a license before he should be permitted to sell a package of imported goods is in conflict with the power of congress to regulate commerce. *Brown* v. *Maryland,* 12 Wheat. 419. See *Cook* v. *Pennsylvania,* 97 U. S. 566.

"It may be proper to add that we suppose the principles laid down in this case to apply equally to importations from a sister state." Marshall, C. J., in *Brown* v. *Maryland,* 12 Wheat. 449. But see *Woodruff* v. *Parham,* 8 Wall. 129, 131.

The statute of Pennsylvania, requiring every auctioneer to collect and pay into the state treasury a tax on his sales, is, when applied to imported goods in the original packages, by him sold for the importer, in conflict with sections 8 and 10 of article 1 of the Constitution of the United States, and therefore void, as laying a duty on imports and being a regulation of commerce. *Cook* v. *Pennsylvania,* 97 U. S. 566.

This immunity does not extend to the purchaser of goods from an importer. *Waring* v. *The Mayor,* 8 Wall. 110, 123.

In *Pierce* v. *New Hampshire,* 5 How. 504, a law of New Hampshire was upheld which prohibited the sale of distilled spirits in any quantity without a license. In that case the plaintiff in error had purchased and brought a barrel of gin from Massachusetts and sold it in the cask in which they received it. In the opinion of Taney, C. J., the case was not within *Brown* v. *Maryland, supra,* because congress had not legislated upon the subject of commerce between states, while it had as to commerce with foreign nations (p. 578).

Obstructions and burdens upon navigation. The laws of New York granting to Livingston and Fulton the exclusive right to navigate the waters within that state with steam vessels for a term of years are in conflict with article 1, section 8, clause 3. *Gibbons* v. *Ogden,* 9 Wheat. 1.

The law of Virginia authorizing the Wheeling bridge is in conflict with legislation of congress regulating commerce among the states upon the Ohio river, and the bridge was found to be a nuisance and its abatement decreed. *Pennsylvania* v. *Wheeling, etc., Bridge Co.,* 13 How. 518.

The act of congress, declaring the bridge to be a lawful structure, was a valid exercise of its power to regulate commerce, and annulled the decree of the supreme court adjudging it to be a nuisance and requiring its abatement. *The Wheeling Bridge Case,* 18 How. 429; *The Clinton Bridge,* 10 Wall. 454; *Bridge Co.* v. *U. S.,* 105 U. S. 470.

The statute of Alabama requiring all steamboats engaged in navigating the waters of that state, before they shall leave the port of Mobile, to file in the office of the probate judge of Mobile a written statement of the name of the vessel, also of the owners, their place of residence, and their relative interest in her, and imposing a fine for failing to do so, is in conflict with the act of congress regulating the coasting trade. *Sinnot* v. *Com'rs of Mobile*, 22 How. 227.

The same rule was extended to a towboat licensed to engage in the coasting trade, and employed in lightering and towing in aid of vessels engaged in foreign commerce. *Foster* v. *Com'rs of Mobile*, 22 How. 244.

A state statute requiring payment to port-wardens of a fee of five dollars, whether called upon to perform any service or not, is a regulation of commerce and unconstitutional. *Steamship Co.* v. *Portwardens*, 6 Wall. 31.

A state law which requires the masters of vessels engaged in foreign commerce to pay a certain sum to a state officer, on account of every passenger brought from a foreign country into the state, or before landing any alien passenger in the state, is invalid, as a regulation of foreign commerce. *Passenger Cases*, 7 How. 283 (1848), four judges dissenting; *People* v. *Campagnie*, 107 U. S. 59.

A state statute imposing a burdensome and almost impossible condition on a ship-master, as a prerequisite to landing his passengers, or an alternative payment of a small sum of money for each one of them, is a regulation of commerce and void. *Henderson* v. *Mayor*, 92 U. S. 259; *Chy Lung* v. *Freeman*, *Ib.* 275; *People* v. *Campagnie*, 107 U. S. 59.

A state board of railroad commissioners has no power to regulate or interfere with the transportation of persons or merchandise by a steamship company between ports within that state and in other states. *Pacific, etc., Co.* v. *Board of R. Com'rs*, 18 Fed. Rep. 10.

The act of Louisiana, in relation to survey of hatches of every seagoing vessel arriving at New Orleans, is a regulation of commerce and void. *Foster* v. *Master and Wardens*, 94 U. S. 246.

A state can not levy a tax upon a corporation, when the only business it does within the state is the landing and receiving of freight and passengers ferried across a river from another state. *Gloucester Ferry Co.* v. *Pennsylvania*, 114 U. S. 196.

A state law forbidding discriminations on account of race or color by railroads, steamboats, and other public conveyances, in carrying passengers, is, when applied to inter-state commerce, unconstitutional. *Hall* v. *De Cuir*, 95 U. S. 485.

Taxation and regulation of railroads, telegraphs, goods, etc. A state statute imposing a tax upon freight carried out of it or brought within it is void as a regulation of commerce among the states. *Case of the State Freight Tax*, 15 Wall. 232; *Telegraph Co.* v. *Texas*, 105 U. S. 460; *Erie Ry. Co.* v. *New Jersey*, 2 Vroom, 531.

Distinction drawn between such a tax and one upon gross receipts of railroad companies. *State Tax on Railway Gross Receipts*, 15 Wall. 284.

Section 6 of the act of the legislature of Tennessee, passed March 16, 1877 (Laws of 1877, ch. 16, p. 26), which imposes a privilege tax of $50 per annum on every sleeping car or coach used or run over a railroad in Tennessee, and not owned by the railroad on which it is run or used, is void so far as it applies to the inter-state transportation of passengers carried over railroads in Tennessee, into or out of or across that state, in sleeping cars owned by a corporation of Kentucky and leased by it, for transportation purposes, to Tennessee railroad corporations, the latter receiving the transit fare and the former the compensation for the sleeping accommodations. *Pickard* v. *Pullman Southern Car Co.*, 117 U. S. 34. See *Wabash Case*, § 6, pp. 4, 5.

State statutes granting exclusive rights of establishing and maintaining telegraph lines, or imposing a tax on every message sent, are regulations of commerce in conflict with the constitution. *Pensacola Telegraph Co.* v. *W. U. Tel. Co.*, 96 U. S. 1; *Telegraph Co.* v. *Texas*, 105 U. S. 460.

When goods, the product of a state, have begun to be transported from that state to another, and not till then, have they become the subjects of inter-state commerce, and, as such, are subject to a national regulation, and cease to be taxable by the state of their origin. Goods on their way through a state from a place outside thereof, to another place outside thereof, are in course of inter-state or foreign transportation, and are subjects of inter-state or foreign commerce, and not taxable by the state through which they are passing, even though detained within that state by low water or other temporary cause. But property brought to a depot for purpose of transportation outside of the state, while remaining there, is still liable to state taxation. *Coe* v. *Errol*, 116 U. S. 517.

State laws regulating commerce between the states, by fixing fares or imposing other restrictions, are in conflict with article 1, section 8, clause 3, and void. *Wabash, St. L. & P. R. Co.* v. *Illinois*, 118 U. S. 557; 1 Ry. & Corp. L. J. 3; 26 Am. & Eng. R. Cas. 1; reversing *s. c.*, 104 Ill. 476, 105 Ill. 236; *Railroad Com'rs* v. *Railroad Co.*, 22 S. Car. 220; *s. c.*, 26 Am. & Eng. R. Cas. 29; *Mobile & O. R. Co.* v. *Sessions*, 28 Fed. Rep. 592; *Ill. Cent. R. Co.* v. *Stone*, 20 Fed. Rep. 468. Contra, *Providence Coal Co.* v. *P. & W. R. Co.*, 26 Am. & Eng. R. Cas. 42.

Foreign corporations—Contracts. A state can not impose limitations upon foreign corporations making contracts for carrying on commerce between the states. *Cooper Manufacturing Co.* v. *Ferguson*, 113 U. S. 727; *Paul* v. *Virginia*, 8 Wall. 168. See *Norfolk & W. R. Co.* v. *Commonwealth* (Pa.), 26 Am. & Eng. R. Cas. 48.

A state can not exclude a foreign corporation engaged in inter-state commerce. *Indiana* v. *Pullman Palace Car Co.*, 16 Fed. Rep. 193.

Discriminations against products of other states. A state license or tax discriminating against the products of other states or countries is void. *Welton* v. *Missouri*, 91 U. S. 275; *Webber* v. *Virginia*, 103 U. S. 344; *Walling* v. *Michigan*, 116 U. S. 446; *State* v. *Furbush*, 72 Me. 493; *Higgins* v. *Casks Lime*, 130 Mass. 1; *State* v. *North*, 27 Mo. 464; *In re Watson*, 15 Fed. Rep. 511.

A state "local option" law can not discriminate between domestic and other wines. *Weil* v. *Calhoun*, 25 Fed. Rep. 865.

Same—Texas and Mexican cattle. The statute of Missouri, prohibiting the driving of Texas, Mexican, or Indian cattle into the state between March 1st and November 1st of each year, is in conflict with the commerce clause of the constitution. *Railroad Co.* v. *Husen*, 95 U. S. 465.

§ 10. Subjects, Local in their Nature, may be Regulated by the States in the Absence of Legislation by Congress.

"Now, the power to regulate commerce, embraces a vast field, containing not only many, but exceedingly various subjects, quite unlike in their nature; some imperatively demanding a single uniform rule, operating equally on the commerce of the United States in every part, and some, like the subject now in question (pilotage), as imperatively demanding that diversity, which alone can meet the local necessities of navigation.

"Either absolutely to affirm or deny that the nature of this power requires exclusive legislation by congress, is to lose sight of the nature of the subjects of this power, and to assert, concerning all of them, what is really applicable but to a part. Whatever subjects of this power are in their nature national, or admit only of one uniform system, a plan of regulation may justly be said to be of such a nature as to require exclusive legislation by congress. That this can not be affirmed of laws for the regulation of pilots and pilotage is plain." Curtis, J., in *Cooley* v. *Wardens of Philadelphia*, 12 How. 299, 319; *Gilman* v. *Philadelphia*, 3 Wall. 713; *Ex parte McNeil*, 13 Wall. 236; *Crandall* v. *Nevada*, 6 Wall. 35; 16 Wall. 482; *Packet Co.* v. *Aiken*, 16 Fed. Rep. 890; *Wilson* v. *McNamee*, 102 U. S. 572; *The Lottawanna*, 21 Wall. 558, 581; *County of Mobile* v *Kimball*, 102 U. S. 691. See *Henderson* v. *Mayor, etc.*, 92 U. S. 272, 273.

"As to those subjects of commerce which are local or limited in their nature or sphere of operation, the state may prescribe regulations until congress assumes control of them." *Gloucester Ferry Co.* v. *Pennsylvania*, 114 U. S. 196.

Dams. Thus, in the absence of all legislation by congress, a state has power to improve its lands, and promote the public health, by authorizing a dam to be built across a creek, though it was previously navigable from the sea by vessels enrolled and licensed for the coasting trade. *Willson* v. *Blackbird Creek Marsh Co.*, 2 Pet. 245; *Cardwell* v. *Bridge Co.*, 113 U. S. 205.

Bridges. In the absence of legislation by congress, the State of Pennsylvania may authorize the construction of a bridge across the Schuylkill river at Philadelphia, although the river is tidal and navigable. *Gilman* v. *Philadelphia*, 3 Wall. 713; *Escanaba Co.* v. *Chicago*, 107 U. S. 678; *Cardwell* v. *Bridge Co.*, 113 U. S. 205. See, also, *The Passaic Bridges*, 3 Wall. 782.

Harbors. The act of the State of Alabama for the improvement of Mobile harbor is valid. *County of Mobile* v. *Kimball*, 102 U. S. 691.

Pilotage. A regulation of pilots and pilotage is a regulation of commerce within the grant of congress, but, in the absence of congressional legislation, the states may regulate the subject. *Cooley* v. *Board of Wardens*, 12 How. 299; *Ex parte McNeil*, 13 Wall. 236; *Wilson* v. *McNamee*, 102 U. S. 572.

State statutes in conflict with acts of congress are void (statutes of Georgia as to pilotage). *Sprague* v. *Thompson*, 118 U. S. 90.

Wharfage. A municipality owning improved wharves is authorized to charge reasonable wharfage fees. *Packet Co.* v. *Keokuk*, 95 U. S. 80; *Packet Co.* v. *St. Louis*, 100 U. S. 423; *Packet Co.* v. *Catlettsburg*, 105 U. S. 559; *Transportation Co.* v. *Parkersburg*, 107 U. S. 691.

And in the absence of legislation by congress, a suit for relief against unreasonable wharfage, can not be maintained in the United States courts, as arising under the constitution or laws of the United States. *Transportation Co.* v. *Parkersburg*, 107 U. S. 691.

Liens—Material-men. State laws creating liens in favor of material-men for supplies furnished to a vessel in her home port are valid. *The Lottawanna*, 21 Wall. 558.

Marine torts. Until congress has made some regulation as to the liability for marine torts resulting in death, a state statute, giving a right of action to the personal representatives of the deceased, where his death is caused by the wrongful act or omission of another, applies to a tort committed within the territorial limits of the state; and, as thus applied, is no encroachment upon the commercial power of congress. *Sherlock* v. *Alling*, 93 U. S. 99.

Tax on inter-state commerce. Likewise, a state tax upon railroad and stage companies for every passenger carried out of the state by them is a regulation of commerce of such a local character that in the absence of congressional action will be valid. *Crandall* v. *Nevada*, 6 Wall. 35; Chase, C. J., and Clifford, J., dissenting on the ground that "commerce is secured against such legislation in the states by the constitution, irrespective of congressional action" (p. 49). See this case commented on. *Case of the State Freight Tax*, 15 Wall. 232, 281. See, also, *Gloucester Ferry Co.* v. *Pennsylvania*, 114 U. S. 196; *Wabash, etc., Ry. Co.* v. *Illinois*, 118 U. S. 557.

§ 11. QUESTIONS OF DOMESTIC CONCERN RESERVED TO THE STATES.

"They (state inspection laws) form a portion of an immense mass of legislation which embraces every thing within a territory of a state not surrendered to the general government; all which can be most advantageously exercised by the states themselves. Inspection laws, quarantine laws, health laws of every description, as well as laws for regulating the internal commerce of a state, and those which respect turnpike roads, ferries, etc., are parts of this mass." Marshall, C. J., in *Gibbons* v. *Ogden*, 9 Wheat. 1, 203; *Steamship Co.* v. *Portwardens*, 6 Wall. 31, 33; *Railway Co.* v. *Fuller*, 17 Wall. 560, 568.

Ferries. Accordingly, it has been held that a state may grant an exclusive ferry right, and, while it can not prevent a vessel from making the customary landings in the usual pursuit of commerce, it can prevent a vessel from exercising the ordinary business of ferrying goods and passengers across the river between two points for pay. *Conway* v. *Taylor's Ex'r*, 1

Black, 603; *Fanning* v. *Gregoire*, 9 How. 534; *Starin* v. *New York*, 115 U. S. 709.

And may license, tax, and regulate ferries. *Wiggins Ferry Co.* v. *E. St. Louis*, 107 U. S. 365, 374–5. But see *Gloucester Ferry Co* v. *Pennsylvania*, 114 U. S. 196, § 9, p. 8.

Domestic commerce, etc. The phrase [to regulate commerce among the states], can never be applied to transactions wholly internal, between citizens of the same community, or to a polity and laws whose ends and purposes and operations are restricted to the territory and soil and jurisdiction of such community. Nor can it properly be concluded that, because the products of domestic enterprise in agriculture or manufactures, or in the arts, may ultimately become the subjects of foreign commerce; that the control of the means, or the encouragements by which enterprise is fostered and protected, is legitimately within the import of the phrase, foreign commerce, or fairly implied in any investiture of the power to regulate such commerce. A pretension as far reaching as this would extend to contracts between citizen and citizen of the same state, would control the pursuits of the planter, the grazier, the manufacturer, the mechanic, the immense operations of the collieries and mines and furnaces of the country; for there is not one of these avocations, the results of which may not become the subjects of foreign commerce, and be borne either by turnpikes, canals, or railroads, from point to point within the several states, toward an ultimate destination like the one above mentioned. Such a pretension would effectually prevent or paralyze every effort at internal improvement by the several states; for it can not be supposed that the states would exhaust their capital and their credit in the construction of turnpikes, canals, and railroads, the remuneration derivable from which, and all control over which, might be immediately wrested from them, because such public works would be facilities for a commerce which, whilst availing itself of those facilities, was unquestionably internal, although intermediately or ultimately it might become foreign. The rule here given, with respect to the regulation of foreign commerce, equally excludes from the regulation of commerce between the states and the Indian tribes the control over turnpikes, canals, or railroads, or the clearing and deepening of water-courses exclusively within the states, or the management of the transportation upon and by means of such improvements." Daniel, J., in *Veazie* v. *Moore*, 14 How. 568, 573–4, in which a state law, granting to an individual an exclusive right to navigate the upper waters of the Penobscot river, lying wholly within the state, separated from tide water by falls impassable for purposes of navigation, and not forming a part of any continuous track of commerce between two or more states, or with a foreign country, was held not repugnant to the constitution or any law of the United States. See *Wabash, etc., Ry. Co.* v. *Illinois*, 118 U. S. 557.

A state law requiring railroads annually to fix their rates, publish the same, and punishing the charging of a higher rate, held, in the case of a railroad running through several states, that it was the exercise of the

§ 8.]　　　　　　TO REGULATE COMMERCE.　　　　　　13

police power reserved to the states. *C. & N. W. Railroad Co.* v. *Fuller,* 17 Wall. 560; *Rae* v. *Grand Trunk Ry. Co.,* 14 Fed. Rep. 401. But see *Wabash St. Louis & P. Ry. Co.* v. *Illinois,* 118 U. S. 557, and pp. 4, 5, 9 *supra.*

Inspection laws. The statute of Maryland requiring the inspection of tobacco and prescribing charges therefor is not a regulation of commerce. *Turner* v. *Maryland,* 107 U. S. 38. In notes to this case (pp. 51, 53) the legislation by the colonies and states of this character is fully collected.

Inspection laws have exclusive reference to personal property. *People* v. *Campagnie,* 107 U. S. 59, 61.

Quarantine laws. The Louisiana quarantine laws are a rightful exercise of the police power for the protection of health. *Morgan* v. *Louisiana,* 118 U. S. 455.

As to what are proper quarantine, inspection, and health laws, see *R. Co.* v. *Husen,* 95 U. S. 465; *Turner* v. *Maryland,* 107 U. S. 38.

License and tax laws. The states have complete control of their internal and domestic affairs, and their laws, although they may indirectly affect foreign and inter-state commerce, are not, therefore, in conflict with the national constitution, providing such laws do not discriminate against the people or products of other states and countries. Thus liquor license laws affecting all alike have been held to be valid. *License Cases,* 5 How. 504. Or, prohibitory laws. *Bartemeyer* v. *Iowa,* 18 Wall. 129; *Beer Co.* v. *Massachusetts,* 97 U. S. 25; *Kansas* v. *Bradley,* 26 Fed. Rep. 289.

So licenses upon occupations, as upon a broker, although he may deal entirely in foreign securities. *Nathan* v. *Louisiana,* 8 How. 73. Upon peddlers of sewing machines. *Machine Co.* v. *Gage,* 110 U. S. 676. Upon traveling salesmen. *In re Rudolph,* 2 Fed. Rep. 65. But a state law requiring a license to sell imported goods in the original package is unconstitutional. *Cook* v. *Pennsylvania,* 97 U. S. 566; *Brown* v. *Maryland,* 12 Wheat. 419.

The liquor license laws of Massachusetts and Rhode Island are not in conflict with article 1, section 8. They act altogether upon the retail or domestic traffic within their respective borders. *Thurlow* v. *Massachusetts* 5 How. 504, 577.

A state law which imposes a tax on exchange and money brokers is not repugnant to the power of congress to regulate commerce. *Nathan* v *Louisiana,* 8 How. 73.

A state tax upon legacies payable to aliens is not a regulation of commerce. *Mager* v. *Grima,* 8 How. 490.

A uniform state tax upon all sales, whether made by a citizen of that state or some other state, and whether the goods sold are the produce of that state or some other state, is valid. *Woodruff* v. *Parham,* 8 Wall. 123; *Machine Co.* v. *Gage,* 100 U. S. 676.

Protection of oysters. The law of Maryland to prevent the destruction of oysters and forfeiting a vessel violating the same, is not in conflict with the power of congress to regulate commerce. *Smith* v. *Maryland,* 18 How. 71.

Private contracts. The power of congress to regulate commerce was not intended to interfere with private contracts not designed to create impediments to free commercial intercourse. *Railroad Co.* v. *Richmond*, 19 Wall. 584.

Insurance. The issuing of a policy of insurance is not a transaction of commerce within the meaning of the constitution, although the parties be domiciled in different states; and a state may prescribe the terms upon which a foreign insurance company may do business within its borders. *Paul* v. *Virginia*, 8 Wall. 168; *Liverpool Ins. Co.* v. *Massachusetts*, 10 Wall. 566; *Phila. Fire Ass'n* v. *New York*, 119 U. S. 110.

Tax on railway receipts. A tax upon the gross receipts of railways, although such receipts are made up in part from freights received on goods transported from and to other states, is not a regulation of interstate commerce. *State Tax on Railway Gross Receipts*, 15 Wall. 234; *The Delaware Railroad Tax*, 18 Wall. 206; *B. & O. R. Co.* v. *Maryland*, 21 Wall. 456.

Police powers. The act of New York, which inflicts a penalty upon the master of a vessel arriving from a foreign port, who neglects to report to the mayor, or recorder, an account of his passengers, is not a regulation of commerce, but of police. *Mayor, etc., of N. Y.* v. *Miln*, 11 Peters, 102, Story, J., dissenting; criticised in *Henderson* v. *Mayor, etc.*, 92 U. S. 259.

Whether the states possess the power to prevent criminals, paupers, and diseased persons coming from abroad, *quaere*. *Henderson* v. *Mayor*, 92 U. S. 259, 275; *Chy Lung* v. *Freeman*, *id.* 275; *Railroad Co.* v. *Husen*, 94 U. S. 465.

§ 12. Congress shall have power . . . to make all laws which shall be necessary and proper for carrying into execution the foregoing powers, and all other powers vested by this constitution in the government of the United States, or in any department or officer thereof. [Art. 1, § 8, cl. 18.]

§ 13. No tax or duty shall be laid on articles exported from any state. [Art. 1, § 9, cl. 5.]

A stamp required upon packages of tobacco intended for exportation, as a means of preventing fraud and of identifying the same, and the proper fees for the same, is not a tax or duty within the foregoing provision. *Pace* v. *Burgess, Collector*, 92 U. S. 372; *Turpin* v. *Burgess*, 117 U. S. 504. See also *Almy* v. *California*, 24 How. 169.

That this clause is a limitation only upon congress, see *Munn* v. *Illinois*, 94 U. S. 113, 135.

§ 14. No preference shall be given by any regulation of

§ 8, 9.] TO REGULATE COMMERCE. 15

commerce or revenue to the ports of one state over those of another; nor shall vessels bound to or from one state be obliged to enter clear or pay duties in another. [Art. 1, § 9, cl. 6.]

The history of this clause and the purpose which the framers of the constitution had in view in its adoption are fully set out by Mr. Justice Nelson, in his opinion in the case of *State of Pennsylvania* v. *Wheeling and Belmont Bridge Co.*, 18 How. 421, 434 et seq. In the opinion in that case, he said: "The history of the provision, as well as its language, looks to a prohibition against granting privileges or immunities to vessels entering or clearing from the ports of one state over those of another. That these privileges and immunities, whatever they may be in the judgment of congress, shall be common and equal in all the ports of the several states. Thus much is undoubtedly embraced in the prohibition; and it may, certainly, also embrace any other description of legislation looking to a direct privilege or preference of the ports of any particular state over those of another. Indeed, the clause, in terms, seems to import a prohibition against some positive legislation by congress to this effect, and not against any incidental advantages that might possibly result from the legislation of congress upon other subjects connected with commerce, and confessedly within its power." . . .

"It is urged that the interruption of the navigation of the steamboats engaged in commerce and in conveyance of passengers upon the Ohio river at Wheeling from the erection of the bridge, and the delay and expense arising therefrom, virtually operate to give a preference to this port over that of Pittsburgh; that the vessels to and from Pittsburgh navigating the Ohio and Mississippi rivers are not only subjected to this delay and expense in the course of the voyage, but that the obstruction will necessarily have the effect to stop the trade and business at Wheeling, or divert the same in some other direction or channel of commerce. Conceding all this to be true, a majority of the court are of the opinion that the act of congress is not inconsistent with the clause of the constitution referred to; in other words, that it is not giving a preference to the ports of one state over those of another, within the true meaning of that provision. There are many acts of congress passed in the exercise of this power to regulate commerce, providing for a special advantage to the port or ports of one state, and which very advantage may incidentally operate to the prejudice of the ports in a neighboring state, which have never been supposed to conflict with this limitation upon its power. The improvement of rivers and harbors, the erection of light-houses, and other facilities of commerce, may be referred to as examples. It will not do to say that the exercise of an admitted power of congress conferred by the constitution is to be withheld, if it appears or can be shown that the effect and operation of the law may incidentally extend beyond the limitation of the power. Upon any such interpretation, the principal object of the framers of the instrument in conferring the power would be sacrificed to the subordinate consequences resulting from its exercise. These consequences and incidents are very proper considerations to be urged upon congress for the purpose of dissuading that body from its exercise, but afford no ground for denying the power itself, or the right to exercise it." *Pennsylvania* v. *Wheeling Bridge*, 18 How. 421, 434; *South Carolina* v. *Georgia*, 93 U. S. 4, 13.

A state law requiring payment of pilotage fees is not within this clause. *Cooley* v. *Board of Wardens*, 12 How. 299, 314. Nor quarantine fees. *Morgan* v. *Louisiana*, 118 U. S. 455. Nor wharfage fees. *Packet Co.* v. *St. Louis*, 100 U. S. 423, *Packet Co.* v. *Catlettsburg*, 105 U. S. 559. Nor the diversion of the channel of a navigable stream. *South Carolina* v. *Georgia*, 93 U. S. 4.

This provision operates only as a limitation of the powers of congress, and in no respect affects the states in the regulation of their domestic affairs. *Munn* v. *Illinois*, 94 U. S. 113, 135; *Morgan* v. *Louisiana*, 118 U. S. 455; *Johnson* v. *Chicago, etc., Elevator Co.*, 119 U. S. 388, 400.

§ 15. No state shall, without the consent of the congress, lay any imposts or duties on imports or exports, except what may be absolutely necessary for executing its inspection laws; and the net produce of all duties and imposts, laid by any state on imports or exports, shall be for the use of the treasury of the United States; and all such laws shall be subject to the revision and control of the congress. [Art. 1, § 10, cl. 2.] See *supra*, § 11.

The terms "imports" and "exports" in this clause has reference to goods brought from or carried to foreign countries alone, and not to goods transported from one state to another. *Brown* v. *Houston*, 114 U. S. 622; *Coe* v. *Errol*, 116 U. S. 517; *Turpin* v. *Burgess*, 117 U. S. 507.

"The prohibition has reference to the imposition of duties on goods by reason or because of their exportation, or intended exportation, or whilst they are being exported." *Turpin* v. *Burgess, supra*.

§ 16. No state shall, without the consent of congress, lay any duty on tonnage. [Art. 1, § 10, cl. 3.]

A "duty on tonnage," within the meaning of the constitution, is a charge upon a vessel, according to its tonnage, as an instrument of commerce, for entering or leaving a port, or navigating the public waters of the country. *Huse* v. *Glover*, 119 U. S. 543.

§ 17. Regulations Respecting the Territories.

The Congress shall have power to dispose of and make all needful rules and regulations respecting the territory or other property belonging to the United States. (Art. 4, § 3, cl. 2.)

Whether the power of congress to govern the territories is derived from the right of the United States to acquire territory, or from that clause in the constitution which empowers congress " to make all needful rules and regulations concerning the territory and other property of the United States," the possession of the power is unquestioned. *American Ins. Co.* v. *Canter*, 1 Peters, 511.

In the Dred Scott case it was held by the majority of the court that this clause of the constitution is confined to the territory which, at that time, belonged to or was claimed by the United States, and can have no influence on territory afterwards acquired from a foreign government. *Dred Scott* v. *Sandford*, 19 How. 393. It is doubtful whether this decision can now be regarded as an authority upon this point any more than upon some other questions passed upon in that celebrated case. *Slaughter House Cases*, 16 Wall. 94, Field, J.

But whatever clause of the constitution may be the source of the power of congress over the territories, the existence of the power is now settled beyond all dispute. *National Bank* v. *County of Yankton*, 101 U. S. 129; *Gibbons* v. *District of Columbia*, 116 U. S. 404; *Murphy* v. *Ramsey*, 114 U. S. 15; *Reynolds* v. *U. S.*, 98 U. S. 145; *Miners' Bank* v. *Iowa*, 12 How. 1; 2 Story on Constitution, 1322–1330; Cooley Const. Lim. (5th ed.) p. 34, note.

Subject to the limitations expressly or by implication imposed by the constitution, congress has full and complete authority over a territory, and may directly legislate for the government thereof. It may declare a valid enactment of the territorial legislature void or a void enactment valid, although it reserved in the organic act no such power. *National Bank* v. *County of Yankton*, 101 U. S. 129.

The scope and character of the power vested in congress in legislating for the territories and other places under its jurisdiction are shown specially in the legislation of congress concerning the District of Columbia and the Mormons.

It is within the constitutional power of congress, acting as the local legislature of the District of Columbia, to tax different classes of property within the district at different rates. *Gibbons* v. *District of Columbia*, 116 U. S. 404. It may abolish the local government of the district and institute a new government and prescribe rules for its regulation. *Welch* v. *Cook*, 97 U. S. 541. And it may confirm and make valid the unauthorized acts of the officers of the district, so as to make invalid street assessments enforceable. *Mattingly* v. *District of Columbia, Ib.* 687.

The stringent legislation directed against polygamy in Utah and affecting nearly every relation of life, private as well as public, has been upheld as within the legislative power of congress over the territories. *Reynolds* v. *United States*, 98 U. S. 145, 166; *Murphy* v. *Ramsey*, 114 U. S. 15.

Congress has prohibited the introduction of spirituous liquors into Alaska. Act of March 3, 1873. *United States* v. *Stephens*, 12 Fed. Rep. 52.

So that congress, in respect to commerce in the territories, possesses all the power that any sovereignty could possess, subject to the limitations imposed by the constitution.

Sec. 18. The Pacific Railroads and other railroad companies incorporated by congress are peculiarly subject to any rules or regulations that congress may prescribe. In the charter of the Union Pacific Railroad Company, congress expressly reserved the right to reduce, fix, and regulate rates of fare thereon when the net earnings of the road should exceed ten per cent of its cost, and also to amend its charter. See *Union Pacific R. Co.* v. *Peniston*, 18 Wall. 5; *United States* v. *Same*, 98 U. S. 569, 616.

PART II.

AN ACT TO REGULATE COMMERCE.(1)

Carriers subject to the Act.

Sec. 1. Par. 1. *Be it enacted by the Senate and House of Representatives of the United States of America in Congress assembled,* That the provisions of this act shall apply to any common carrier or carriers(2) engaged in the transportation of passengers or property wholly by railroad, or partly by railroad and partly by water(3) when both are used, under a common control, management, or arrangement,(4) for a continuous(5) carriage or shipment, from one state or territory of the United States, or the District of Columbia, to any other state or territory of the United States, or the District of Columbia, or from any place in the United States to an adjacent foreign country, or from any place in the United States through a foreign country to any other place in the United States, and also to the transportation in like manner of property shipped from any place in the United States to a foreign country and carried from such place to a port of transshipment, or shipped from a foreign country to any place in the United States and carried to such place from a port of entry either in the United States or an adjacent foreign country: *provided, however,* that the provisions of this act shall not apply to the transportation of passengers or property, or to the receiving, delivering, storage, or handling of property, wholly within one state, and not shipped to or from a foreign country from or to any state or territory as aforesaid.(6)

(1) Introductory Note.

Constitutionality of the act. The statement has been made, speaking of this act, that when "its constitutionality is challenged, it will be found that outside of some disjected *dicta* of judges, there is no precedent for it in the decisions of the United States courts" (Dos Passos, Inter-state Commerce Act, p. xii.); and again, that the language of Mr. Justice Miller, in the *Wabash case*, "should be regarded as *obiter dictum*, and used only in a most general sense." (*Ibid.*, p. 8.) In view of these surprising declarations, a more detailed statement of the authorities bearing directly upon the constitutionality of this act will be made.

Probably no power granted to congress is more plenary than that "to regulate commerce with foreign nations and among the several states and with the Indian tribes." (Constitution U. S., art. 1, § 8, cl. 3.) Chief Justice Marshall said it comprehended "all foreign commerce and all commerce among the states." (*Brown* v. *Maryland*, 12 Wheat. 419, 446.) The same great jurist again said that the power of congress over that commerce "is vested in congress as absolutely as it would be in a single government having in its constitution the same restrictions on the exercise of the power as are found in the Constitution of the United States." (*Gibbons* v. *Ogden*, 9 Wheat. 1, 197.) Justice Johnson, in the same case, said: "The 'power to regulate commerce' here meant to be granted was that power to regulate commerce which previously existed in the states." (9 Wheat. 227.)

The power is not confined to the instrumentalities of commerce known or in use when the constitution was adopted, but keeps pace with the progress of the country and adapts itself to the new developments of time and circumstances. It was intended for the government of the business to which it relates at all times and under all circumstances. (Chief Justice Waite, in *Pensacola Telegraph Co.* v. *Western Union Telegraph Co.*, 96 U. S. 1, 9.) An instance of the almost unlimited power of congress, when acting upon subjects within this clause, is found in the *Wheeling Bridge case*. The supreme court found that the bridge was in fact an obstruction to navigation and ordered its abatement as a nuisance. (13 How. 518.) Congress subsequently passed an act declaring the bridge to be a lawful structure. The supreme court recognized it as a valid exercise of the power to regulate commerce; that the bridge was in law no longer a nuisance, and the decree for its abatement as such was not enforceable. (18 How. 421.)

Inter-state commerce. The power of congress does not stop at the mere boundary line of a state; it must enter the interior; it is coextensive with the subject on which it acts. (*Brown* v. *Maryland*, 12 Wheat. 446; *U. S.* v. *Coombs*, 12 Pet. 72.)

"Whenever a commodity has begun to move as an article of trade from one state to another, commerce in that commodity between the states has commenced." (Field, J., *The Daniel Ball*, 10 Wall. 557, 565; *Coe* v. *Errol*, 116 U. S. 517; *Pacific, etc., Co.* v. *R. Com'rs*, 9

Sawy. 253; 18 Fed. Rep. 10; *Hardy* v. *Railroad Co.*, 32 **Kan 698**, 717.)

The grant to congress "authorizes legislation with respect to all the subjects . . . of inter-state commerce, the persons engaged in it, and the instruments by which it is carried on." (Field, J., *Sherlock* v. *Alling*, 93 U. S. 99, 103; *The Daniel Ball, supra; Pacific, etc., Co.* v. *R. Com'rs*, 9 Sawy. 253.) "Nearly all the railroads in the country are, or may be, used to a greater or less extent as links in through transportation." (Bradley, J., in *B. & O. R. Co.* v. *Maryland*, 21 Wall. 456, 469.)

The power of congress extends, then, not only to goods moving from state to state and the traffic in them (*Brown* v. *Maryland*, 12 Wheat. 419; *Cook* v. *Pennsylvania*, 97 U. S. 566; *Welton* v. *Missouri*, 91 U. S. 275; *Webber* v. *Virginia*, 103 U. S. 344; *Walling* v. *Michigan*, 116 U. S. 446; *Railroad Co.* v. *Husen*, 95 U. S. 465), but also to the instruments and persons transporting them (*Gibbons* v. *Ogden*, 9 Wheat. 1; *The Daniel Ball*, 10 Wall. 557; *Henderson* v. *Mayor*, 92 U. S. 259; *Case of State Freight Tax*, 15 Wall. 232; *Telegraph Co.* v. *Texas*, 105 U. S. 460; *Pickard* v. *Pullman Palace Car Co.*, 117 U. S. 34; *Cooper Manufacturing Co.* v. *Ferguson*, 113 U. S. 727).

From these premises, does it not follow logically and irresistibly, that the transportation of persons and property from one state to another is "commerce among the states?"

Regulation of inter-state commerce. "The 'power to regulate' . . . is to prescribe the rule by which the commerce is to be governed." (*Gibbons* v. *Ogden*, 9 Wheat. 1, 197, Marshall, C. J., whose opinion in this case "has become the accepted canon of construction of this clause of the constitution," Miller, J., 92 U. S. 270.)

What more has congress done in the present act than "to prescribe the rule by which the commerce" therein specified "is to be governed?"

Thus much to show how the act of February 4, 1887, stands upon principle. Nor does the case of *Wabash, St. Louis and Pacific Railway Co.* v. *Illinois*, 118 U. S. 557, announce any novel doctrine.

Transportation of persons and property between and through the several states has long been recognized as commerce among the states; that it is a subject of national concern admitting of and requiring a single, uniform system; and, therefore, by the constitution, exclusively confided to congress. (*Case of State Freight Tax*, 15 Wall. 232; *Hall* v. *DeCuir*, 95 U. S. 485; *Gloucester Ferry Co.* v. *Pennsylvania*, 114 U. S. 196; *Pickard* v. *Pullman, etc., Car Co.*, 117 U. S. 34.)

If it had not been for the decisions of the supreme court in *C. & N. W. R. Co.* v. *Fuller*, 17 Wall. 560, and the *Granger cases* (*Munn* v. *Illinois*, 94 U. S. 113; *C. B. & Q. R. Co.* v. *Iowa*, *Ib.* 155; *Peik* v. *C. & N. W. R. Co.*, *Ib.* 164), no doubt would probably ever have existed on the subject.

But the true construction of the commercial clause of the constitution, and the fact that other questions obscured this in the *Granger cases*, were as clearly apprehended and stated by the supreme courts of Iowa and Kansas, in 1882 and 1884, as by the Supreme Court of the United States in the *Wabash case*. (*Carton* v. *Ill. Cent. R. Co.*, 59 Iowa, 148; *Hardy* v. *A. T. & S. F. R. Co.*, 32 Kan. 698, 715.) In the former, where the property was transported from Ackley, Iowa, to Chicago, Illinois, the court said that "any regulation of the transportation of goods from one state to another, upon railroads, operates as a regulation of commerce, and a state statute prescribing such a regulation is unconstitutional." In the latter case, involving the transportation of goods from St. Louis, Missouri, to Hutchinson, Kansas, the Supreme Court of Kansas considered and disapproved the opinion of the Supreme Court of Illinois in the *Wabash case* (104 Ills. 476), and held that the statute of Kansas regulating the charges of railroads did not apply to any case where goods were transported from one to another state. It was a stronger case than the *Wabash case*. In that case, the contract was an entire one for the voyage from Illinois to New York, the Wabash railroad carrying the goods through two other states beside Illinois in their journey. In the Kansas case, the defendant road performed its entire service within that state, there was a separate way bill for that part of the transportation, and the quota of the freight it received was shown. The court said: "That each railroad company in the case before us issued its own way bill to and from the connecting point with the defendant, and that each company was liable for the loss and damage occurring on its road only, does not affect the question of inter-state commerce. From the time the goods began to be moved from St. Louis, Missouri, until they were delivered at Hutchinson, in this state, they were the subjects of commerce, and commerce among the states, and therefore inter-state commerce." (Horton, C. J., 32 Kans. 717.)

All the decisions holding that state statutes, similar in scope and purpose to the present act, were regulations of inter-state commerce, and, as such, unconstitutional, because the power to prescribe rules on the subject was vested solely in congress, are direct authorities for the constitutionality of congressional legislation of this character. (*Wabash, etc., Ry. Co.* v. *Illinois*, 118 U. S. 557; *Gloucester Ferry Co.* v.

Pennsylvania, 114 U. S. 196; *Pickard* v. *Pullman, etc., Car Co.*, 117 U. S. 34; *Railroad Com'rs* v. *Railroad Co.*, 22 S. Car. 220; *Mobile & Ohio R. Co.* v. *Sessions*, 28 Fed. Rep. 592; *Ill. Cent. R. Co.* v. *Stone*, 20 Fed Rep. 468; *L. & N. R. Co.* v. *Railroad Com'rs of Tenn.*, 19 Fed. Rep. 679; *Pacific Coast Steamship Co.* v. *R. Com'rs of Cal.*, 9 Sawy. 253; *s. c.*, 18 Fed. Rep. 10; *Kaeiser* v. *Ill. Cent. R. Co.*, 18 Fed. Rep. 151.

As further recognition that such legislation is a regulation of commerce within the power of congress, see *Pensacola Tel. Co.* v. *W. U. Tel. Co.*, 96 U. S. 1; *Telegraph Co.* v. *Texas*, 105 U. S. 460; *U. S.* v. *Coombs*, 12 Pet. 72; *South Carolina* v. *Georgia*, 93 U. S. 4; *Stone* v. *Farmers' Loan and Trust Co.*, 116 U. S. 307.

That congress has the right to fix the rates of fare, or, at least, the maximum compensation for transportation of persons and property between the states and with foreign countries, see *Canada S. Ry. Co.* v. *International Bridge Co.*, 8 Fed. Rep. 190; *L. & N. R. Co.* v. *R. Com'rs*, 19 Fed. Rep. 679.

Previous acts of congress regulating commerce. Congress has already passed several acts regulating commerce between the states. The act of March 3, 1873, regulating the transportation of live stock, is one of them. It is now incorporated into the Revised Statutes, sections 4386 to 4390, and provides that "no railroad company within the United States whose road forms any part of a line of road over which cattle, sheep, swine, or other animals are conveyed from one state to another, or the owners or masters of steam, sailing, or other vessels carrying or transporting cattle, sheep, swine, or other animals from one state to another, shall confine the same in cars, boats, or vessels of any description, for a longer period than twenty-eight consecutive hours, without unloading the same for rest, water and feeding, for a period of at least five consecutive hours, unless prevented from so unloading by storm or other accidental causes. In estimating such confinement, the time during which the animals have been confined without such rest on connecting roads from which they are received shall be included, it being the intent of this section to prohibit their continuous confinement beyond the period of twenty-eight hours, except upon contingencies hereinbefore stated." (§ 4386.) This legislation has been held to be a constitutional exercise of the power of congress to regulate commerce among the several states (*U. S.* v. *Boston & A. R. Co.*, 15 Fed. Rep. 209; *U. S.* v. *Louisville & N. R. Co.*, 18 Fed. Rep. 480), and not to apply to transportation from a point within a state to another point therein, but only to transportation from one state to another. (*U. S.* v. *E. T. V. & G. R. Co.*, 13 Fed. Rep. 642.)

The act of June 15, 1866 (Rev. Stats. § 5258), provides that railroad companies transporting property from one state to another may "connect with roads of other states so as to form *continuous lines* for the transportation of the same to the place of destination." This has also been recognized as constitutional. (*Railroad Co.* v. *Richmond*, 19 Wall. 584; *Council Bluffs* v. *Kansas City, etc., R. Co.*, 45 Iowa, 338, 351; *Hardy* v. *Atchison, etc., R. Co.*, 32 Kans. 698, 717.) See note 38 to § 7, *post*; see, also, *Mo. Pac. Ry. Co.* v. *Texas & Pac. Ry. Co.*, 30 Fed. Rep. 2; also, the acts incorporating the several Pacific railroads.

The question has been raised whether a railroad wholly within a state which chartered it, is subject to the regulation of congress at all (see *Norfolk & W. R. Co.* v. *Commonwealth*, S. C. Penn., Oct. 4, 1886, 1 Ry. & Corp. L. J. 134), but the *ratio decidendi* of the cases is, I submit, that if such railroads are in fact engaged in carrying goods to or from points outside the state, they become instrumentalities of inter-state commerce, and, as such, subject to the control of congress.

Commission features of the act. Congress undoubtedly has power under the commerce clause of the constitution, if not restricted by some other provision of that instrument, to create the Commission and give it the powers enumerated in the act, as it had to devolve upon the Secretary of War the determination of the question whether the East River suspension bridge, between New York and Brooklyn, was an obstruction to navigation. (*Miller* v. *Mayor of New York*, 109 U. S. 385.) See also *Georgia Railroad* v. *Railroad Com'rs*, 70 Ga. 674; 71 Ga. 863; *Stone* v. *Farmer's L. & T. Co.*, 116 U. S. 307, 332 et seq.; *R. Com'rs* v. *Portland, etc., R. Co.*, 63 Me. 269, 285; *Commonwealth* v. *Eastern R. Co.* 103 Mass. 254; *State* v. *Chicago, etc., R. Co.*, 19 Neb. 476; and see note 27 to § 4.)

"An act of incorporation, which confers upon the directors of a railroad company the power to make by-laws, rules and regulations touching the disposition and management of the company's property and all matters pertaining to its concerns, confers no right which is violated by the creation of a state railroad commission, charged with the general duty of preventing the exaction of unreasonable or discriminating rates upon transportation done within the limits of the state, and with the enforcement of reasonable police regulations for the comfort, convenience, and safety of travelers and persons doing business with the company within the state." (*Stone* v. *Farmers' L. & T. Co.*, 116 U. S. 307.)

Fourteenth amendment—Due process of law. A government may regulate the conduct of its citizens toward each other, and, when necessary for the public good, the manner in which each shall use his own property; and it has, in the exercise of these powers, been customary in England from time immemorial, and in this country from its first colonization, to regulate common carriers and others engaged in public employment. When the owner of property devotes it to a use in which the public has an interest, he in effect grants to the public an interest in such use, and must, to the extent of that interest, submit to be controlled by the public. The adoption of the Fourteenth Amendment does not change the law in this particular. (*Munn* v. *Illinois*, 94 U. S. 113.)

Railroad companies are carriers for hire and engaged in a public employment affecting the public interest, and are, unless protected by their charter, subject to legislative control. (*Chicago, etc., R. Co.* v. *Iowa*, 94 U. S. 155.)

Charter rights. In view of the decisions heretofore referred to, it probably will not be questioned that the charters of railroad companies, or any other statutory provisions made by the states, can not interfere with the control of congress over such corporations, in so far as they are engaged in commerce subject to the control of congress. While a railroad corporation may have a contract with the state relieving it of state supervision and direction in the conduct of its affairs, such contract can not affect the power of congress. The law of congress is supreme, and if any state statute or contract conflicts with it, the latter must yield.

Upon the question of what words will amount to an exemption from the legislative control of the state, it has been decided that a grant of immunity from such control will never be presumed. It must clearly and unequivocally appear by words of positive grant. (*Ruggles* v. *Illinois*, 108 U. S. 526; *Stone* v. *Farmers' L. & T. Co.*, 116 U. S. 307.)

A charter granting to a railroad company the right "from time to time to fix, regulate, and receive the tolls and charges by them to be received for transportation," does not deprive the state of its power to act upon the reasonableness of the tolls and charges so fixed and regulated. (*Stone* v. *Farmers' L. & T. Co., supra.*)

A charter right to fix rates with discriminations "conducive to interests of road" is subject to the limitation that the discriminations shall be reasonable and not extortionate. (*St. Louis, etc., Ry. Co.* v. *Hill*, 14 Bradw. 579.)

Existing contracts. The question will no doubt arise whether the act interferes with existing contracts. The rule, I take it, is that if the contracts were valid when made they still remain valid. In other words, if the contracts were not in conflict with any statute, public policy, or rule of the common law, or were not designed at the time they were entered into, to create impediments to the freedom and equality of commercial intercourse, they will remain valid, notwithstanding they may be in conflict with some provision of the present act. (*Railroad Co.* v. *Richmond*, 19 Wall. 584; *C. & A. R. Co.* v. *Chicago, etc., Coal Co.*, 79 Ill. 127.)

The act of congress of June 15, 1866, authorizing every railroad company in the United States whose road was operated by steam, and its successors and assigns, to carry upon and over its road, boats, bridges, and ferries, all passengers, troops, government supplies, mails, freights, and property, on their way from one state to another state, and to receive compensation therefor, and to connect with roads of other states so as to form continuous lines for the transportation of the same to their place of destination; and the act of July 25, 1866, authorizing the construction of certain bridges over the Mississippi river, and among others a bridge connecting Dubuque with Dunleith, in the State of Illinois, and providing that the bridges, when constructed, should be free for the crossing of all trains of railroads terminating on either side of the river, for reasonable compensation, were designed to remove trammels upon transportation between different states, interposed by state enactments or by existing laws of congress, and were not intended to interfere with private contracts and annul such as had been made on the basis of existing legislation and existing means of inter-state communication.

Accordingly, a contract between a railroad company and an elevator company, that the latter company, in consideration of erecting and using for that purpose an elevator, should have for a prescribed term the handling, at a stipulated price, of all grain brought by the railroad company in its cars to the city of Dubuque, on the Mississippi river, to be transmitted to a place beyond, did not cease to be valid and binding upon the parties, because afterward, by the construction of a railroad bridge across the Mississippi river at Dubuque, it became unnecessary for the railroad company or its lessee, and a useless expense to it, to have the grain brought by it to Dubuque handled at that place. The enforcement of the contract, after the construction of the bridge, was not an interference with the power of congress to regulate commerce between the states. (*Railroad* v. *Richmond, supra.*)

The Illinois act of 1873, to prevent extortion and unjust discrimination by railroads, was not designed to reach a case where a contract existed prior to its passage, to carry on certain terms. It was not intended to interfere with or abrogate existing contracts fairly made prior to its passage. (*C. & A. R. Co.* v. *Chicago, etc., Coal Co.*, 79 Ill. 121.)

Since writing the foregoing, I have examined the admirable discussion by Mr. Phelps of the question whether congress has the power to abrogate or impair the validity of contracts. (1 Ry. & Corp. L. J. 362, April 16, 1887.) The authorities which he collects would seem to show that congress does not—as it certainly should not—have such power, except in bankruptcy matters. (*Sinking Fund cases*, 99 U. S. 737.)

The courts will assuredly not give the act an interpretation conflicting with vested legal rights, if its language will reasonably bear any other construction. (*Railroad Co.* v. *Richmond*, 19 Wall. 584.)

And it is, in my judgment, not only capable of a construction which would except valid contracts from its operation, but that such construction ought to be given to it, as was done by the Supreme Court of Illinois in construing a similar statute. (*C. & A. R. Co.* v. *Chicago, etc., Coal Co.*, 79 Ill. 127; see also *Railroad Co.* v. *Richmond, supra*.)

It is to be borne in mind that some existing contracts probably could not be upheld at common law, being of a character similar to those held invalid in *Scofield* v. *Ry. Co.*, 43 Ohio St. 571; *Hays* v. *Pa. Co.*, 12 Fed. Rep. 309; *Menacho* v. *Ward*, 27 Fed. Rep. 529, and other cases hereafter cited. All such contracts would be invalid now and afford no ground for making discriminations.

State statutes held invalid as destroying vested rights of railroad companies. The Tennessee railroad commission bill, approved March 30, 1883, held to be invalid because its provisions are too indefinite, vague, and uncertain to sustain a suit for the penalties imposed. It leaves to the jury to say whether, upon the proof, the difference in rates amounted to discrimination, or whether the charges were unjust and unreasonable, thus making the guilt or innocence of the accused depend upon the finding of a jury, and not upon a construction of the act. It relegates the administration of the law to the unrestrained discretion of the jury, and there can be, therefore, no approximation to uniform results, but verdicts would be as variant as their prejudices, and inevitably lead to inequalities and injustice. (*Louisville & N. R. Co.* v. *Railroad Commission of Tenn.*, 19 Fed Rep. 679; see *Stone* v. *Farmers' L. & T. Co.*, 116 U. S. 307, 336.)

"That no railroad corporation . . . shall charge or collect for the transportation of goods, merchandise or property on its road, for any distance, the same or any larger or greater amount as toll or compensation than is at the same time charged or collected for the transportation of similar quantities of the same class of goods, merchandise or property over a greater distance upon the same road; nor shall such corporation charge different rates for receiving, handling, or delivering freight at different points on its road, or roads connected therewith, which it has a right to use. Nor shall any such railroad corporation charge or collect for the transportation of goods, merchandise or property, over any portion of its road, a greater amount as toll or compensation than shall be charged or collected by it for the transportation of similar quantities of the same class of goods, merchandise or property over any other portion of its road of equal distance; and all such rules, regulations, or by-laws of any such railroad corporation as fix, prescribe or establish any greater toll or compensation than is hereinbefore prescribed, are hereby declared to be void." (Act, Ills., July 1, 1871, § 1; Laws 1871-2, p. 635.)

§ 2 defined a "railroad corporation."

§ 3 prescribed the standard of rates.

§ 4 prescribed a penalty of $1,000, and a reasonable attorney's fee to be taxed by court.

§ 5 authorized forfeiture of franchise for "any willful violation of the act."

The constitution authorized the general assembly to "pass laws to correct abuses and prevent *unjust* discrimination and extortion in the rates of freight," etc.

Held, that the act is unconstitutional, as it "forbids any discriminations whatever, under any circumstances, whether just or unjust, in charges for transporting the same class of freight over equal distances, even though moving in opposite directions, and does not permit the companies to show that the discrimination is not unjust, but infers guilt as a conclusive presumption from the mere fact of a difference of rates, without any opportunity of rebutting such presumption, is in violation" of the constitutional guaranties for the protection of life, liberty and property, of trial by jury, etc.

An act prohibiting *unjust* discriminations, and the making of a greater charge for the same or less distance, *prima facie* evidence of unjust discrimination, would be constitutional. (*C. & A. R. Co.* v. *People*, 67 Ill. 11.)

The law of Maine, March 26, 1858, requiring railroad trains to stop at crossings twenty minutes for arrival of train on the other road, *held* to impose a new duty upon the railroad, and to be in conflict with charter of the Penobscot and Kennebec railroad. (*State* v. *Noyes*, 47 Me. 189; but see this decision explained and limited in *Railroad Com'rs* v. *Portland, etc. R. Co.*, 63 Me. 269, 285-6.)

Sources of the act—Decisions under similar statutes—Rules of construction. An examination of the notes to the various sections of the present act will reveal that many of its provisions have been copied almost literally from other statutes, notably the English Railway and Canal Traffic Act, 1854, and the Regulation of Railways Act, 1873.

In determining questions under the English acts of 1854 and 1873, the paramount consideration is held to be the convenience of the public. (*Caledonian Ry. Co.* v. *N. B. Ry. Co.*, 3 Nev. and Mac. Ry. Cas. 403; *Belfast, etc., Ry. Co.* v. *G. N. Ry. Co., Ib.* 419; *Huddersfield* v. *Ry. Co.*, 4 Ry. and Can. Traf. Cas. 44; *Cent Wales, etc., Ry. Co.* v. *Gt. West. Ry. Co.*, 4 *Ib.* 110; *Belfast, etc., Ry. Co.* v. *G. N. Ry. Co., Ib.* 159.)

The decisions under the English statutes, have additional value from the fact that the Supreme Court of the United States has repeatedly recognized the rule that where English statutes have been adopted into our own legislation, the known and settled construction of those statutes by courts of law has been considered as silently incorporated into the acts or has been received with all the weight of authority. (*McDonald* v. *Hovey*, 110 U. S. 619; *Cathcart* v. *Robinson*, 5 Pet. 264; *Pennock* v. *Dialogue*, 2 Pet. 1; *McCool* v. *Smith*, 1 Black, 459; *The Abbotsford*, 98 U. S. 440.) But English decisions rendered subsequently to the adoption of the statute in this country, have not the same weight. (*Cathcart* v. *Robinson, supra.*)

As considerable stress is being laid upon the debates in congress upon the act, it is perhaps well to keep in view the rule that in construing an act of congress the court may recur to the history of the times when it was passed in order to ascertain the reason for, as well as the meaning of, particular provisions in it, but the views of individual members in debate can not be considered. (*U. S.* v. *Union Pacific R. Co.*, 91 U. S. 72.)

(2) COMMON CARRIERS.

A common carrier has been defined to be "one who undertakes for hire to transport the goods, of such as choose to employ him, from place to place." (Parker, C. J., in *Dwight* v. *Brewster*, 1 Pick. 50.) In *Gisborn* v. *Hurst*, 1 Salk. 249, he is said to be one "undertaking for hire to carry the goods of all persons indifferently." And this is said by Gibson, C. J., in *Gordon* v. *Hutchinson*, 1 Watts & S. 285, to be "the best definition of a common carrier in its application to the business of this country." Hutchinson, in his work on Carriers, § 47, says: "A common or public carrier is one who undertakes, as a business, for hire or reward, to carry from one place to another, the goods of all persons who may apply for such carriage, provided the goods be of the kind which he professes to carry, and the person so applying will agree to have them carried upon the lawful terms prescribed by the carrier." He must exercise the business of carrying as a "public employment." (*Coggs* v. *Bernard*, 2 Ld. Raym. 909, Holt, C. J.) "He must undertake to carry goods for persons generally, and he must hold himself out as ready to engage in the transportation of goods for hire as a business and not as a casual occupation *pro hac vice*." (Story on Bailments, § 495; *Citizens' Bank* v. *Nantucket Steamboat Co.*, 2 Story C. C. 32; see, also, Angell on Carriers, § 68 et seq.; Wood's Brown on Carriers, § 42 et seq.)

Railroad companies are engaged in a public employment affecting the public interest, and are common carriers for hire. (*Chicago, etc., R. Co.* v. *Iowa*, 94 U. S. 155; Angell on Carriers, § 78; *Chicago R.* v. *Thompson*, 19 Ills. 578; Hutchinson on Carriers, § 67; Redfield on Carriers, § 37.)

"They advertise for freight; they make known the terms of the carriage; they provide suitable vehicles and select convenient places for receiving and delivering goods; and as a legal consequence of such acts, they have become common carriers of merchandise and are subject to the provisions of the common law which are applicable to carriers." (*Thomas* v. *Boston & Prov. R. Co.*, 10 Met. 472.)

Receivers operating a railroad are liable as common carriers. (*Blumenthal* v. *Brainerd*, 38 Vt. 402; *Page* v. *Smith*, 99 Mass. 395; *Nichols* v. *Smith*, 115 Mass. 332.)

If one railroad transports a car for another railroad for hire, it is liable as a common carrier although the car is on its own trucks. (*N. J. R.* v. *Penn. R.*, 3 Dutch, 100; *Vt. & M. R.* v. *Fitchburg R.*, 14 Allen, 462; *Mackin* v. *Boston & A. R.*, 135 Mass. 201, 206; *Peoria, etc., R. Co.* v. *Chicago, etc., R. Co.*, 109 Ill. 135; s. c., 19 Cent. L. J. 111 and note; 18 Am. & E. R. Cas. 506 and note.)

"Railroad companies that transport cattle and live stock for hire for such persons as choose to employ them thereby assume and take upon themselves the relation of common carriers." (Angell on Carriers, § 78.) But a railroad company is not a common carrier of live animals in the same sense that it is a carrier of goods. (*Myrick* v. *Mich. Cent. R. Co.*, 107 U. S. 102, 107; 2 Rohrer on Rail. 1299, § 27.)

A railroad company may make one rate to carry cattle as common carriers, and a lower rate merely to furnish cars and let the owner of the cattle take charge of them, and in the latter case the company is not liable as a common carrier. (*Kimball* v. *Rutland R.*, 26 Vt. 249; *Manchester, etc., Ry. Co.* v. *Brown L. R.*, 8 App. Cas. (H. L.) 703.)

In the case of a private railroad constructed on the land of the proprietors "the public have no more interest in it or control over it than they have in any other improvements which men make on their own lands." (*Sandford* v. *Railroad Co.*, 24 Pa. St. 381.)

Transportation companies, despatch companies, and fast freight lines, and the like, are common carriers. (*Mercantile Mut. Ins. Co.* v. *Chase*, 1 E. D. Smith, 115; Angell on Carriers, § 76; Redfield on Carriers, § 197; Hutchinson on Carriers, § 72.)

Express companies are common carriers. (*Sherman* v. *Am. Ex. Co.*, 23 Ills. 197; 26 Ills. 504; *Am. Ins. Co.* v. *Pinckney*, 29 Ilis. 392; *Belger* v. *Dinsmore*, 51 N. Y. 166; *Haslam* v. *Adams Ex. Co.*, 6 Bosw. 235; *Lowell Wire Fence Co.* v. *Sargent*, 8 Allen, 189; *Buckland* v. *Adams Ex. Co.*, 97 Mass. 124; *Southern Ex. Co.* v. *Newby*, 36 Ga. 635; *U. S. Ex. Co.* v. *Backman*, 28 O. S. 144; Hutchinson on Carriers, § 68.)

The fact that express and transportation companies and other carriers do not own the vehicles in which the goods are transported, does not affect the question of whether they are common carriers. (*U. S. Ex. Co.* v. *Backman*, 28 O. S. 144; *Buckland* v. *Adams Ex. Co.*, 97 Mass. 124; Hutchinson on Carriers, § 69 et seq.)

As to whether **sleeping-car companies** are within the act, see *Pickard* v. *Pullman Co.*, 117 U. S. 34; *Nevin* v. *Pullman Co.*, 11 Am. & E. R. Cas. 92; *Indiana* v. *Pullman Co.*, 16 Fed. Rep. 193; 11 Biss. 561.

It has been suggested that carriers might limit their business to carrying to and from the two termini of the road, and to the carriage of a particular description of goods. (Mr. Easley, Ry. Age, March 11, 1887; *Johnston* v. *Midland R.*, 6 Eng. Ry. Cas. 47.) But would not this be giving an undue preference to a particular "locality," or to a "particular description of traffic," within section 3 of the act?

(3) The Railway and Canal Trafic Act, 1854, § 2 (see Appendix), provides for the combination of railway and canal transportation; and by the Regulation of Railways Act, 1868, § 16 (see Appendix), the provision is extended to steam vessels of every description worked by a railway or canal company, and the traffic carried on thereby. It is further extended by § 11 of the Regulation of Railways Act, 1873 (see Appendix).

Where a charter authorized a railroad company to charge a certain rate per mile, it was held to apply to the entire line of communication—to the conveyance by water as well as by rail. (*Camden, etc., R. Co.* v. *Briggs*, 1 Zab. (N. J.) 406; Angell on Carriers, § 128; 2 Zab. 623.)

(4) COMMON CONTROL, MANAGEMENT, ETC.

The phrase "under a common control, management, or **arrangement**," it would seem, has reference to the preceding clause, "or partly by railroad and partly by water when both are used;" so that the statute applies to two classes of carriers: (1) those "engaged in the transportation of passengers and property wholly by railroad, . . . for a continuous carriage or shipment from one state or territory," etc., and (2) to "carriers engaged in the transportation of passengers or property . . . partly by railroad and partly by water, when both are used under a common control, management, or arrangement, for a continuous carriage or shipment from one state or territory," etc.

The second paragraph of section 3, and section 7 of the act, relating to the duties of connecting carriers, were certainly intended to create other obligations than those existing at common law, as defined by the supreme court in the case of the *Atchinson T. & S. F. R. Co.* v. *The Denver & N. O. R. Co.*, 110 U. S. 667.

In section 11 of the Regulation of Railways Act, 1873 (see Appendix), it is provided that, "where a railway company or canal company use, maintain, or work, or are party to an *arrangement* for using, maintaining, or working, steam vessels for the purpose of carrying on a communication between any towns or ports, the provisions of this section shall extend to such steam vessels, and to the traffic carried thereby;" and in section 2 of the Railway and Canal Traffic Act, 1854, that "every railway company and canal company, and railway and canal company, having or working railways or canals, which form part of a continuous line of railway or canal or railway and canal communication, . . . shall afford," etc.

It seems probable that the framers of this act used the word "arrangement" in the same sense in which it is used in the English act of 1873. And it is to be noted that the word is used in the English act only in connection with the combination of railway and water transportation, and, in view of the similarity of the present act to the English statutes, which will be more apparent from an examination of the succeeding notes, it affords an additional reason for concluding that the word was intended to apply only in the same connection in the section now under consideration.

As is well said by Mr. Easley, "These words in this paragraph have some other meaning than the fact that two lines are used or operated by the same company by virtue of ownership under a lease, contract, or agreement, because two lines so situated are, by the next paragraph of the act, defined to be a 'railroad.'" (Railway Age, March 11, 1887.)

But I do not think that the act can be confined to the two classes mentioned by Mr. Easley. It applies, in my judgment, to—

1. All carriers engaged in transportation wholly by railroad for a continuous carriage or shipment between states, territories, and to and from foreign countries.

2. All carriers engaged in transportation partly by railroad and partly by water, when both are used, under a common control, management, or arrangement, for a continuous carriage between states, territories, and to and from foreign countries.

The first class includes all roads "in use by any corporation operating a railroad, whether owned or operated under a contract, agreement, or lease," and also "all bridges or ferries used or operated in connection with any railroad" (paragraph 2, section 1), and also carriers engaged in the transportation of passengers or property by railroad for a continuous carriage or shipment between states, territories, etc., *i. e.*, to the continuous carriage when wholly by railroad, of persons and property between states, territories, etc., as mentioned in the act, without reference to whether it is by virtue of a contract or arrangement between the connecting lines. (*Coe* v. *Errol*, 116 U. S. 517; *The Daniel Ball*, 10 Wall. 557, 565; *Sherlock* v. *Alling*, 93 U. S. 99, 103; *Pacific, etc., Co.* v. *R. Commissioners*, 9 Sawy. 253; 18 Fed. Rep. 10; *Hardy* v. *Atchison, etc., R. Co.*, 32 Kan. 717.)

In other words, if railroad companies are engaged in the carriage of persons or property between points included within the act, which is in fact intended to be continuous, the companies may be compelled to afford facilities for making the carriage continuous and thus meeting public convenience, as has been done under the English acts of 1854 and 1873. Section 7, and the second paragraph of section 3 are intended to accomplish, to some extent at least, the same purpose, with reference to inter-state, foreign and territorial commerce, that the English acts of 1854 and 1873 have accomplished with reference to all transportation in Great Britain.

There is a vast difference between compelling a railroad company to contract for the carriage of individuals or goods beyond its own line, and thus assuming the liability of a common carrier for transportation over other lines, and compelling a railroad company to afford facilities by which the transportation over its own and connecting lines shall be continuous. The first can not be done. (*Mineral Springs Mfg. Co.* v. *Mich. C. R. Co.*, 16 Wall. 318; *Ogdensburg, etc., R. Co.* v. *Pratt*, 22 Wall. 123; *Stewart* v. *Terre Haute, etc., R. Co.*, 3 Fed. Rep. 768, and cases cited on *Ib.*, p. 769.)

The supreme court in the *Atchison case* recognized that the latter could be done by statute, and intimated the opinion that such a statute as the present would require railways to afford such facilities. (110 U. S. 667, 684-5.)

As to the second class, it has already been held by Judge Deady, on the application of a receiver for instructions under the act, that " the mere fact that a railway wholly within a state, and a vessel running between said state and another meet at a point within the railway state, and thus form a continuous line of transportation between the two states, by the one taking up the goods delivered by the other, at its terminus, and carrying them thence to their destination does not bring the carriers who so use the railway and steamer within the act. So long as the railway and steamer are each operated under a separate and distinct control, making its own rates and only liable for the carriage and safe delivery of the goods at the end of its own route, the act does not apply to the transaction. To make these carriers subject to the act, the railway and vessel must, as therein provided, be operated or used under a 'common control'—a control to which each is alike subject and by which rates are prescribed and bills of lading given for the carriage of goods over both routes as one." (*Ex parte Koehler*, Chicago Legal News, April 16, 1887, p. 251.)

Common control or management. Where a railroad company made a contract concerning all roads which it then did or might thereafter control, by ownership, lease, or otherwise, and thereafter acquired more than a majority of the stock of B., another railway company, and by voting such stock elected B.'s board of directors; and where certain persons were members of the board of directors of both A. and B., and the same persons were respectively presidents and vice-presidents of both companies: *Held*, that A. had not acquired "control" of B. within the meaning of the terms of the contract, and that the meaning of the word "control," as used in said contract, meant an immediate or executive control exercised by the officers and agents chosen by and acting under the direction of A.'s board of directors. (*Pullman Palace Car Co.* v. *Missouri Pac. Ry. Co.*, 11 Fed. Rep. 634, McCrary, J.; Mr. Justice Miller concurring.)

"Arrangement"—What is? Section 11 of the Regulation of Railways Act, 1873, enacts (*inter alia*) that " where a railway company use, maintain, or work, or are party to an arrangement for using, maintaining, or working steam vessels for the purpose of carrying on a communication between any towns or ports, the provisions of this section shall extend to such steam vessels and to the traffic carried thereby." Upon objection that this clause only applies where the arrangement as to the steam vessels was made by the company to whom the railway with which the steam vessels directly communicated belonged: *Held*, that such clause extended the whole provisions of section 11, and took effect whenever there was an arrangement with the proprietors of steam vessels for the conveyance of passengers or goods to and from any port or town with which there was railway communication, provided the railway company party to the arrangement owned or worked, or was otherwise immediately interested in, some portion or other of the line of railway communication. (*Caledonian Ry. Co., etc.*, v. *Greenock, etc., Ry. Co.*, 4 Ry. & Can. Traf. Cas. 135; see *Greenock Ry. Co.* v. *Caledonian Ry. Co.*, 2 Nev. & Mac. Ry. Cas. 227.)

An agreement between a steamboat company and a railway company that the steam vessels belonging to the former shall ply between two ports "for one year and thereafter until written notice to terminate the agreement six months from the date of such notice," "daily or at least upon alternate days of each week, the hours of departure of the boats to be determined by the steamboat company, regard being had, however, to the convenience of the railway company and to the times of the arrival and departure of their trains," and containing also a clause that any dispute or difference as to the provisions of the agreement should be referred to the decision of an arbitrator to be appointed by the board of trade, whose decision was to be binding, is an *arrangement* for using, maintaining, or working steam vessels within the meaning of section 11 of the Regulation of Railways Act, 1873. (*Belfast, etc., Ry. Co.* v. *G. N. Ry. Co.*, 4 Ry. & Can. Traf. Cas. 379.)

— **Through booking.** The existence of through bookings between A. and B. for the carrying of traffic by a certain steam vessel for the sea part of the through journey between these places is not such an *arrangement* for the "use" of these vessels as to make section 11 apply to them, and to enable the owners to require a through rate between A. and C. under that section. (*Ayr Harbour Trustees* v. *Glasgow Ry. Co.*, 4 Ry. & Can. Traf. Cas. 81.)

(5.) As to **continuous** carriage or shipment see section 3, par. 2, and section 7, and the notes thereto.

(6.) **Domestic commerce.** The office of a proviso generally is either to except something from the enacting clause, or to qualify its generality, or to exclude some possible ground of misinterpretation. (*Minis* v. *U. S.*, 15 Pet. 423.)

The subject-matter excepted by this proviso has, in all the decisions, from *Gibbons* v. *Ogden*, 9 Wheat. 1, to *Wabash, etc., Ry. Co.* v. *Illinois*, 118 U. S. 557, been recognized as reserved by the constitution to the several states. See the cases collected in Part I, p. 11 to 14, *supra*.

The public and many of our railroad officers seem to assume that the act regulates and controls the entire railroad transportation of the country. Accordingly, railroad companies are posting rates and conforming to the requirements of the law with reference to transportation wholly within the states. It is true that, in the debates in congress, claims were made for it that can have no foundation in the constitutional right of congress to regulate commerce. It must be borne in mind that the power of congress exists only with reference to commerce between the states, with foreign nations and with the Indian tribes; and in and through the territories. The regulation of commerce wholly within the states still remains solely within the jurisdiction of the several states. Such commerce is still controlled by state statutes where they exist, or by the common law where no statutory regulation has been attempted. The authorities are fully collected in Part I, sections 1 to 11, *supra*.

The only way in which the legislation of congress can affect commerce entirely within a state, is to see that it shall not obstruct or defeat the operation of the present law upon the commerce subject to it. For instance, I take it to be clear that, so far as the present act is concerned, a railroad company can discriminate in rates of freight between points in the state, can give passes and other advantages to control such business, provided such advantages are not a "device" used to prejudice or prefer shipments between the states, to and from foreign countries, etc.

"Railroad" and "Transportation" Defined.

Sec. 1, Par. 2. The term "railroad"(7) as used in this act shall include all bridges and ferries used or operated in connection with any railroad, and also all the road in use by any corporation operating a railroad, whether owned or operated under a contract, agreement, or lease;(8) and the term "transportation"(9) shall include all instrumentalities of shipment or carriage.

(7.) See "Railway," defined in the Railway and Canal Traffic Act, 1854, § 1, and Regulation of Railways Act, 1873, § 3, Appendix.
(8.) See note 4, "Common Control," etc., *supra*, p. 32.
(9.) See "Traffic," defined in the Railway and Canal Traffic Act, 1854, § 1, and Regulation of Railways Act, 1873, § 3, Appendix.

Unjust and Unreasonable Charges Prohibited.

Sec. 1, Par. 3. All charges made for any service rendered or

§ 1, PAR. 3.] INTER-STATE COMMERCE ACT. 37

to be rendered in the transportation of passengers or property as aforesaid, or in connection therewith, or for the receiving, delivering, storage, or handling of such property, shall be reasonable and just; and every unjust and unreasonable charge for such service is prohibited and declared to be unlawful.(10)

10. The obligation resting upon a common carrier at common law was to carry goods for a reasonable compensation. (*Gt. West. Ry. Co.* v. *Sutton*, L. R. 4 Eng. & Ir. App. 226, 237; Angell on Carriers, § 124; *Johnson* v. *R. Co.*, 16 Fla. 623; *Baxendale* v. *Eastern Cos. Ry.*, 4 C. B. (N. S.) 63; *Branley* v. *S. E. Ry.*, 12 C. B. (N. S.) 63; *Fitchburg R. Co.* v. *Gage*, 12 Gray, 393; *Exp. Benson*, 18 S. Car. 38; *Menacho* v. *Ward*, 27 Fed. Rep. 531; *s. c.*, 23 Am. & E. R. Cas. 647; 34 Alb. L. J. 44; *Messenger* v. *Penn R. Co.*, 36 N. J. L. 407; *McDuffie* v. *Railroad Co.*, 52 N. H. 430; *Munn* v. *Illinois*, 94 U. S. 113, 134; *Sandford* v. *R. Co.*, 24 Pa. St. 378; *Shipper* v. *Penn. R. Co.*, 47 Pa. St. 338, 341; *Audenried* v. *P. & R. R. Co.*, 68 Pa. St. 370; *C. B. & Q. R. Co.* v. *Parks*, 18 Ill. 460; *C. & A. R. Co.* v. *People*, 67 Ill. 11; *Scofield* v. *Lake Shore, etc., Ry. Co.*, 43 O. S. 571; *N. E. Exp. Co.* v. *M. C. R. Co.*, 57 Me. 188; *Hays* v. *Penna. Co.*, 12 Fed. Rep. 309; *Hollister* v. *Nowlen*, 19 Wend. 239; *Smith* v. *Chicago, etc., R. Co.*, 5 N. W. Rep. 242; *Brown* v. *Adams Exp. Co.*, 15 W. Va. 821.)

The above paragraph is, then, merely declaratory of the common law.

The common law duty imposed upon common carriers to carry goods for a reasonable compensation does not preclude special contracts regulating freight charges. After long continued acquiescence an action to recover back excessive charges can not be maintained. (*Killmer* v. *N. Y. C. & H. R. R. Co.*, 100 N. Y. 395.)

If the shipper was compelled to pay more than was reasonable, he might recover back, in an action for money had and received, the excess over a reasonable charge. A lower rate made to another was *evidence* that the higher rate was unreasonable. (*Gt. Western Ry. Co.* v. *Sutton*, L. R. 4 Eng. & Ir. App. 226, 237 (H. L.); Angell on Carriers, § 124; *Johnson* v. *R. Co.*, 16 Fla. 623.) See also notes 41 and 42 to § 8, *post.*

In the circumstances of their origin, and in their powers, uses, and duties, railroad corporations are clearly distinguishable from other merely private corporations. They must be conducted in furtherance of the public objects of their creation. (*R. Com'rs* v. *Portland, etc., R.*

Co., 63 Me. 269, 277; *State* v. *Republican V. R. Co.*, 17 Neb. 647; *L. & N. R. Co.* v. *R. Com'rs*, 19 Fed. Rep. 679.)

Railways are engaged in a public employment. As common carriers they exercise a sort of public office, and have duties to perform in which the public are interested. (*Chicago, etc., R. Co.* v. *Iowa*, 94 U. S. 155; *Munn* v. *Illinois*, 94 U. S. 113; *Peik* v. *Chicago, etc., Ry. Co.*, 94 U. S. 164; *L. & N. R. Co.* v. *R. Com'rs, supra.*)

Accordingly, "in countries where the common law prevails, it has been customary from time immemorial for the legislature to declare what shall be a reasonable compensation under such circumstances, or, perhaps, more properly speaking, to fix a maximum beyond which any charge made would be unreasonable." (Waite, C. J., in *Munn* v. *Illinois, supra; Chicago, etc., R. Co.* v. *Iowa*, and *Peik* v. *Chicago R. Co., supra.*)

A state may limit the amount of charges made by railroad companies, unless restrained by charter. (*Ibid.*)

But such statutes can not in any way extend to inter-state commerce. (*Wabash, etc., Ry. Co.* v. *Illinois*, 118 U. S. 557, and cases cited in note 1, *supra.*)

Where a statute fixes maximum charges for transportation, it determines conclusively that charges in excess of those so fixed are unreasonable; and evidence to prove the excessive charges to be reasonable is immaterial. (*Heiserman* v. *Burlington, etc., Ry. Co.*, 63 Iowa, 732; see *Ruggles* v. *Illinois*, 91 Ill. 256; *s. c.*, 108 U. S. 526; *Stone* v. *Farmers' L. & T. Co.*, 116 U. S. 307.)

To recover the penalties prescribed by Illinois act approved May 2, 1873, for unreasonable and extortionate charges, it is not enough to show that the charges are more than fair and reasonable rates, but the charges must exceed the maximum rates fixed by the railroad commissioners. (*C. B. & Q. R. Co.* v. *People*, 77 Ill. 443.) Under act of 1871, see *Moore* v. *Ill. Cent. R. Co.*, 68 Ill. 385.

A common carrier by rail can not legally increase the charges for transportation by wrongfully diverting freight from its proper course in transit. (*Burlington, etc, R. Co.* v. *Chicago Lumber Co.*, 15 Neb. 390.)

The use of cars upon other lines is a service incidental to the receiving, forwarding, and delivering of traffic, and is within the provisions of the act. (*Diphwys, etc., Co.* v. *Festiniog Ry. Co.*, 2 Nev. & Mac. 73.)

The elements entering into a reasonable charge for the transportation of persons or property are:

1st. The cost of performing the service.

§ 1, PAR. 3.]   INTER-STATE COMMERCE ACT.   39

2d. A fair return upon the capital invested. (*Louisville & N. R. Co.* v. *Rail. Com'rs*, 19 Fed. Rep. 679; *Canada South. Ry. Co.* v. *International Bridge Co.*, 8 Fed. Rep. 190.)

In considering the question of the reasonableness of charges, the principle is not what profit it may be reasonable for a railway company to make, but what is reasonable to charge to the person who is charged. (*International Bridge Co.* v. *Canada South. Ry. Co.*, 8 App. Cas. 723.)

3d. A premium covering the liability a common carrier assumes as an insurer. (*Riley* v. *Horne*, 5 Bing. 217; Angell on Carriers, § 127; see *Railroad Co.* v. *Brown*, 8 App. Cas. 703; Ivatt on Carriers, 199.)

As to the delicacy and difficulty of determining what are reasonable charges for railroad transportation, see *Canada South. Ry. Co.* v. *International Bridge Co.*, 8 Fed. Rep. 190; *C. & A. Ry. Co.* v. *People*, 67 Ill. 11; *L. & N. R. Co.* v. *Rail. Com'rs*, 19 Fed. Rep. 679.

As to the constitutionality of statutes which leave to the determination of a jury the question of whether charges are reasonable: *L. & N. Ry. Co.* v. *Rail. Com'rs*, 19 Fed. Rep. 679 (cited in *Stone* v. *Farmers L. & T. Co.*, 116 U. S. 307, 336); *C. & A. R. Co.* v. *People*, 67 Ill. 11.

Small parcels—Increased expense of handling. A railway company was empowered to charge certain tonnage rates or tolls for all articles, matters, and things carried or conveyed along the line, and to provide locomotive or other power for the carriage and conveyance of passengers, cattle, goods, etc., and to make reasonable charges for such carriage and conveyance, in addition to the tonnage rates. The company might, from time to time, make such orders for fixing, and by such orders fix the sum to be charged by them in respect of small parcels, not exceeding one hundred weight each, as to them should seem proper. And the aforesaid rates and tolls should at all times be charged equally, and after the same rate per ton throughout the whole of the railway in respect of the same description of articles, matters, or things, and no reduction or advance in the rates and tolls should, either directly or indirectly, be made partially, or in favor of or against any particular person or company. The company framed a scale of charges for the carriage of parcels not exceeding one hundred weight each, with charges higher than the tonnage rates, but which included a reasonable charge for the use of their carriages and locomotive power. Under this scale where a number of separate parcels (each weighing less than one hundred weight, but exceeding one hundred weight, if taken in the aggregate) was brought to the railway by the same person, and containing the same article, and all directed to the same person at their place of destination, the company charged tonnage or lower rate; but if similar parcels were brought addressed to several different persons, they were charged the higher or parcel rate. *Held*, that there was nothing to induce the court (or which ought to induce a jury) to infer that the charges so made were unreasonable, regard being had to the additional trouble incurred by the company. (*Baxendale* v. *Eastern Counties Railway Company*, 4 C. B. (N. S.) 63; 27 L. J. C. P. 137.)

Reasonableness of contract limiting liability of carriers. A fish merchant delivered fish to a railway company to carry upon a signed contract relieving the company as to all fish delivered by him "from all liability for loss or damage by delay in transit, or from whatever other cause arising," in consideration of the rates being one-fifth lower than where no such undertaking was granted; the contract to endure for five years. The servants of the company accepted the fish, although from the pressure of business they could not carry it in time for the intended market, and the fish lost the market. *Held*, that upon the facts the merchant had a *bona fide* option to send the fish at a reasonable rate with liability on the company as common carriers, or at the lower rate upon the terms of the contract; that the contract was in point of fact just and reasonable within the Railway and Canal Traffic Act, 1854 (17 & 18 Vict., c. 31, s. 7), and covered the delay; and that the company were not liable for the loss. (*Manchester, etc., Ry. Co.* v. *Brown*, 8 L. R. App. Cas. 703; 53 L. J. Q. B. Div. 124; 50 L. T. (N. S.) 281; 32 W. R. 207; 48 J. P. 388, reversing *s. c., nom. Brown* v. *Manchester S. & L. Ry. Co.*, 10 L. R. Q. B. Div. 250; 52 L. J. Q. B. Div. 132; 48 L. T. (N. S.) 473; 31 W. R. 491; 47 J. P. 436.)

EQUALITY IN RATES REQUIRED(11).

Sec. 2. That if any common carrier, subject to the provisions of this act shall, directly or indirectly, by any special rate, rebate, drawback, or other device, charge, demand, collect, or receive from any person or persons a greater or less compensation for any service rendered, or to be rendered, in the transportation of passengers or property, subject to the provisions of this act, than it charges, demands, collects, or receives from any other person or persons for doing for him or them a like and contemporaneous service in the transportation of a like kind of traffic(12) under substantially similar circumstances and conditions,(13) such common carrier shall be deemed guilty of unjust discrimination, which is hereby prohibited and declared to be unlawful (14).

(11) Equality in Rates.

At common law. In England, it is well settled that at common law a common carrier was not obliged to transport goods for all persons for the same compensation. (*Great Western Ry.* v. *Sutton*, L. R. 4 Eng. & Ir. App. (H. L.) 226, 237; *Baxendale* v. *Eastern Cos. Ry.*, 4 C. B. (N. S.) 63; *Branley* v. *S. E. Ry. Co.*, 12 C. B. (N. S.) 63; followed in this country in *Fitchburg R. Co.* v. *Gage*, 12 Gray, 393 (1859); see 128 Mass. 326; 115 Mass. 422; *Johnson* v. *R. Co.*, 16 Fla. 623 (1878); *Ex parte Benson*, 18 S. Car. 38 (1882); *Menacho* v. *Ward*, 27 Fed. Rep. 529, 531; *s. c.*, 23 Am. & E. Ry. Cas. 647; 24 Alb. L. J. 44 (1886). See *Killmer* v. *R. Co.*, 100 N. Y. 395.

A contract by a railroad company to pay a rebate upon all cotton shipped over the road by certain persons is not inequitable or against public policy; and, after shipment made, is binding on the company and its creditors. (*Ex parte Benson*, 18 S. Car. 38; *Cowdrey* v. *Railroad Co.*, 1 Wood (U. S. C. C.) 331, 335.)

"Whatever objections to these rebatements might be made by the state, or by planters and others who did not obtain as favorable terms, it does not lie in the mouths of stockholders or creditors who reap positive benefits from the arrangement to complain of it." (*Cowdrey* v. *Railroad Co.*, *supra*, Bradley, Justice.)

But it said that "the weight of American authority, however, is that the common law requires that charges must be *equal* to all, for the same service of transportation under like circumstances." (*Railroad Co.* v. *Hill*, 14 Bradwell (Ill. App.) 579 (1884); *Messenger* v. *Penn. R. Co.*, 36 N. J. L. 407; *s. c.*, 37 N. J. L. 531; *Shipper* v. *Penn. Ry. Co.*, 47 Pa. St. 338, 341; *Cumberland, etc., R. Co's Appeal*, 62 Pa. St. 218; *Audenreid* v. *P. & R. R. Co.*, 68 Pa. St. 370; *C. B. & Q. R. Co.* v. *Parks*, 18 Ill. 460, 464; *C. & A. R. Co.* v. *People*, 67 Ill. 11 (1873); *Scofield* v. *Railway Co.*, 43 O. S. 571 (1885); *N. Eng. Exp. Co.* v. *M. C. R. Co.*, 57 Me. 188; *Hays* v. *Penn. Co.*, 12 Fed. Rep. 309; *State* v. *Nebraska Telephone Co.*, 17 Neb. 126; *State* v. *R. Co.*, 17 Neb. 647 (1885.)

"The railroad company has the right, by its charter, to fix the tariff or fare, which it shall receive for carrying passengers or freight upon its road. These charges, however, must be uniform; that is, the charge should be the same for all persons similarly situated, and for all freights of a like kind and quality, for a given service. They may divide passengers and freights into classes, with descriptive distinctions, and charge different rates for different classes, for a given service, but the charge should be uniform upon all persons and freights embraced within each class." (*C. B. & Q. R. Co.* v. *Parks*, 18 Ill. 460, 464;

See opinion of Lawrence, C. J., in *C. & A. R. Co.* v. *People*, 67 Ill. 11, 19-20; see note (23) to § 4.)

An agreement by a railroad company to carry goods for certain persons, at a cheaper rate than they will carry under the same conditions for others, is void as creating an illegal preference. (*Messenger* v. *Penn. R. Co.* 36 N. J. L. 407.)

The provision in the constitution of Colorado, that " all individuals, associations, and corporations shall have equal rights to have persons and property transported over any railroad in this state, and no undue or unreasonable discrimination shall be made in charges or facilities for transportation of freight or passengers within the state, and no railroad company, nor any lessee, manager, or employe thereof, shall give any preference to individuals, associations, or corporations, in furnishing cars or motive power," imposes no greater obligation on a railroad company than the common law would have imposed upon it. (*A. T. & S. F. R. Co.* v. *D. & N. O. R. Co.*, 110 U. S. 667; see, also, *Concord & P. R.* v. *Forsaith*, 59 N. H. 122.)

Telephone companies are common carriers of news and all persons are entitled to equal facilities in the enjoyment of the use of the telephone, and a refusal of such facilities without good reason, is an unjust discrimination. (*State* v. *Nebraska Telephone Co.*, 17 Neb. 126.) See (under statute) *State* v. *Telephone Co.*, 36 O. S. 296; *Chesapeake etc., Telephone Co.* v. *B. & O. Tel. Co.*, 35 Alb. L. J. 271.)

— **Express companies.** Railroad companies are not obliged either by the common law or by usage to do more as express carriers than to provide the public at large with reasonable express accommodation; and they need not in the absence of a statute furnish to all independent express companies equal facilities for doing an express business upon their passenger trains. (*Express cases*, 117 U. S. 1; 23 Am. & E. Ry. Cas. 545 and note; *Sargent* v. *B. & L. R.*, 115 Mass. 416.)

Railroad companies are bound to afford equal facilities to all; and they can not contract to give one person a preference over another. For instance, to give one express company exclusive or superior facilities. (Hutchinson on Carriers, § 207 et seq.; *New Eng. Exp. Co.* v. *Maine Cen. R. Co.*, 57 Me. 188; *McDuffie* v. *P. & R. R.*, 52 N. H. 430; *Sandford* v. *R. Co.*, 24 Pa. St. 378.)

English statutes and decisions. In England, prior to 1845, it had been customary to insert equality clauses in special acts incorporating railway companies, and which came to be known as "Lord Shaftesbury's Clauses," an instance of which is found in 7 and 8 Vict., c. 3, sec. 50 (*Railway Co.* v. *Sutton*, L. R. 4 Eng. and Ir. App. 238).

In 1845, the Railway Clauses Consolidation Act (8 and 9 Vict., c. 20) was passed, section 90 of which is as follows:

"And whereas, it is expedient that the company should be enabled to vary the tolls upon the railway so as to accommodate them to the circumstances of the traffic, but that such power of varying should not be used for the purpose of prejudicing or favoring particular parties, or for the purpose of collusively and unfairly creating a monopoly, either in the hands of the company or of particular parties; it shall be lawful, therefore, for the company, subject to the provisions and limitations herein and in the special act contained. from time to time to alter or vary the tolls by the special act authorized to be taken, either upon the whole or upon any particular portions of the railway, as they shall think fit; provided, that all such tolls be at all times charged equally to all persons, and after the same rate, whether per ton per mile, or otherwise, in respect of all passengers, and of all goods, or carriages of the same description, and conveyed or propelled by a like carriage or engine, passing only over the same portion of the line of railway under the same circumstances; and no reduction or advance in any such tolls shall be made either directly or indirectly in favor of or against any particular company or person traveling upon or using the railway." (Railway Clauses Consolidation Act, 1845, 8 and 9 Vict., c. 20, § 90.)

The Regulation of Railways Act, 1868, § 16 (see Appendix), provided that railway companies working steam vessels shall charge "all persons equally, and after the same rate in respect of passengers conveyed in a like vessel passing between the same places under like circumstances."

The English cases upon the question of equality of charges have chiefly, if not entirely, arisen upon the construction of these statutes, and of the equality clauses in the various private acts incorporating railway companies.

Section 90 of the 8 and 9 Vict., c. 20, Railways Clauses Act, 1845, requires equality of tolls for similar services rendered by railway companies to all persons; and section 2 of the 17 and 18 Vict., c. 31, Railway and Canal Traffic Act, 1854, forbids the giving of any undue or unreasonable preference or advantage to any particular person or company. A charge made by a railway company against A. for services rendered by that company to him, must not, therefore, be greater than the charge made by the same company against B. for rendering him services of like nature. (*London and North-western Railway Company* v. *Evershed*, 3 L. R. App. Cas. 1029; 39 L. T. (N. S.) 306—H. L.)

"According to the strict meaning of the acts of parliament, as interpreted by the decisions, from the very moment that the company charges A. a given sum, when B. and other persons (a mere stranger up to that time, if you will) comes to the company to have the same service rendered, under the same circumstances, he can not be charged one farthing more than has been charged to A.; he can only be charged precisely what the act authorizes the company to charge, namely, that which has been charged to others, and the moment the directors take to themselves to charge less to another person they must charge less to him. The charge must be the same to all for the same services performed in the same manner, for carrying goods for the same distance, and for similar services rendered in any other way." (Lord Hatherly in *Lond. & N. W. Ry. Co. v. Evershed*, L. R. 3 App. Cas. 1029, 1036 (1878).

A case may, by reason of a difference in circumstances, not amount to a violation of this section, and yet may create an undue preference under section 3, *post*. (Pollock, B., 4 Ry. & Can. Traf. Cas. 449.) All such cases are reserved for consideration under that head.

The Great Eastern Railway Company fixed certain package rates for the conveyance of fish from Yarmouth to London, as follows:

Under and not exceeding 18 lbs. 3*d*. per package.
" " 28 " 4*d*. " "
" " 42 " 6*d*. " "
" " 56 " 8*d*. " "

W., a trader at Yarmouth, sent a package of fish in baskets of 20 lbs. weight by the Great Eastern Railway to London, for which he was charged, under the above scale, at the rate of 4*d*. for 28 lbs. It was proved that he could not alter the size of his baskets without injury to his business, and that baskets 21 lbs. in weight did not cost the company more expense or labor than the baskets of 18 lbs. in weight.

Held, that the rate must be 21 lbs., and not 18 lbs., for 3*d*., so as to make it uniform, and after the same rate as and in due proportion with the charge for packages of greater weight. (*Woodger* v. *Great Eastern Ry. Co.*, 2 Nev. & Mac. 102.)

—**Foreign traffic.** The obligations created by statute as to equality of charges is confined to England. It does not cover a carriage from a foreign country. (*Branley* v. *S. E. Ry. Co.*, 12 C. B. (N. S.) 63.)

The obligations created by the Railway and Canal Traffic Act, 1854, do not apply to transportation in a foreign country. (*Zuns* v. *S. E. Ry. Co.*, 4 L. R., Q. B. 539; 38 L. J., Q. B. 209.)

— **Recovery of excessive rates paid.** "Money extorted by inequality of charge is to be recovered in exactly the same way as if it had been money extorted by making an unreasonable charge—that is to say, by an action for money had and received." (*Lond. & N. W. Ry.*

Co. v. *Evershed*, L. R. 3 App. Cas. 1029, 1039; *G. W. Ry. Co.* v. *Sutton*, L. R. 4 H. L. 226; *Lancashire R. Co.* v. *Gidlow*, L. R. 7 H. L. 517. See notes 41 and 42 to § 8.)

— **Evidence of violation of the statute.** In an action for money had and received to recover back charges alleged to have been improperly made on the plaintiff, evidence was tendered at the trial, and received, to show that mercantile houses were in the habit of dispatching to the railway packed parcels—that is, parcels containing numbers of different parcels of different kinds of goods, and sent from and to different persons; that these packed parcels were so packed by these mercantile houses for the accommodation of their own customers and friends, and that these facts were well known in the trade, and (inferentially) to the railway company, but that a lower charge was made for them than for parcels packed in the same manner by the plaintiff, who was a carrier, and who collected and packed parcels of the same sort in the way of his business. On exception that this evidence was insufficient without affirmatively showing that, as a fact, the defendants knew that these mercantile houses did so pack the parcels, and, so knowing, made a difference in the charge, it was held in the court below, and affirmed in this House, that the evidence was admissible, and warranted the judge in telling the jurors that " there was evidence that parcels were carried by the defendants for other persons containing goods of a like description, and under like circumstances, at a rate less than such goods were carried by them for the plaintiffs."

The agent and the traffic manager of the defendants had been present as parties at a reference where facts of this sort were proved in their hearing:

Held, that evidence of their having been so present was properly admissible as part of the proof that the defendants were informed and knew of the habits and practices of the mercantile houses, and knowingly charged the plaintiff a higher rate than was demanded of other persons for the carriage of like packed parcels of goods carried under the like circumstances. (*Great Western R. Co.* v. *Sutton*, L. R. 4 Eng. & Ir. App. 226.)

— **Interests of company.** The fair interests of the company are to be considered. (*Ransome* v. *Eastern Co.'s Ry. Co.*, 1 C. B. (N. S.) 437; 26 L. J. (C. P.) 91; 1 Nev. & Mac. 63; *Baxendale* v. *G. W. Ry. Co.*, 5 C. B. (N. S.) 336; 28 L. J. (C. P.) 81; *Nicholson* v. *G. W. Ry. Co.*, 5 C. B. (N. S.) 366; 28 L. J. (C. P.) 89; 1 Nev. & Mac. 121.)

— **A charter right** to charge such sum as the company might see fit to make, is not contravened by a statute requiring charges to all persons to be equal. (*Ry. Co.* v. *Sutton*, L. R. 4 Eng. & Ir. App. 226; *Baxendale* v. *G. W. Ry. Co.*, 14 C. B. (N. S.) 1; 16 *Id.* 137; *Crouch* v. *G. N. Ry. Co.*, 9 Exch. 557.)

Cash and ticket fares. A regulation of a railroad, that a passenger purchasing a ticket before entering the cars shall be entitled to a discount from the advertised rates, but if such ticket is not purchased, the full rate of fare shall be charged, is a reasonable regulation, and does not violate a rule prescribed by statute, that the rates of fare shall be the same for all persons between the same points. (*Swan* v. *Railroad*, 132 Mass. 116; *Indianapolis, etc., R. Co.* v. *Rinard*, 46 Ind. 293; *Hilliard* v. *Goold*, 34 N. H. 230.)

(12) LIKE KIND OF TRAFFIC.

"Goods of like description and quantity," and "goods of the same description," refer not to the contents of the parcels, but to the parcels themselves—that is, like or different for the purposes of carriage. (*Gt. West. Ry. Co.* v. *Sutton*, L. R. 4 Eng. & Ir. App. 226.)

A railway company carried coal to G. for shipment, from collieries situate on different branches of their line. On one branch, the company charged different rates per ton per mile for the carriage of different descriptions of coal—a gas-coal rate and a common coal rate. No such classification was made on the other branch.

Cannel coal (the only coal raised by the complainants) was the only coal charged at the gas-coal rate, splint coal being classed as common coal.

The gas produced from splint coal is inferior in quality and quantity to that produced from an equal amount of cannel coal, but both are used in different proportions for mixing with common coal in the manufacture of gas, for the purpose of increasing its illuminating power.

Found, as a matter of fact, that splint coal and cannel coal had enough in common of gas-producing quality to be competitive, and to make them commercially and substantially of the same description for the purpose for which they were used, and that the cost of conveyance to the railway company of splint and cannel coal was the same; and therefore,

Held, that the carriage of cannel coal and splint coal by the railroad company at unequal rates per ton per mile was an undue prejudice to the complainants. (*Nitshill, etc., Coal Co.* v. *Caledonian Ry. Co.*, 2 Nev. & Mac. 39.)

By agreement A. was to be charged "rates and charges for his traffic similar to those which may, for the time being, be charged to and paid by B. under schedules A. and P." of a certain agreement between the railway company and B., "and that in terms of the provisions of the said agreement, or of any amendment or alteration thereof." The agreement between the railway company and B. was that "B. shall, subject to exceptions and provisions hereinafter mentioned, pay" to the railway company the charges mentioned in schedules A. and B. It further provides that "notwithstanding what is before written that for and in respect of all limestone, calcined ironstone, hematite, sand, and fire-clay, passing along the railways formerly belonging to the Ardrossan Railway Company," to and from the B. works, B. should pay the charges specified in schedule D: Held, by Sir Frederick Peel, that A.'s traffic in hematite and limestone along the Ardrossan railway was not within schedules A and B. But held, by Mr. Commissioner Miller and Mr. Commissioner Price, that it was similar traffic to that mentioned in schedules A and B, and was chargeable at the rates of those schedules. (*Merry* v. *Glasgow, etc., Ry. Co.*, 4 Ry. and Can. Traf. Cas. 383.)

Pleading. To allege that the respective freights were one car load of ponies and one car load of horses, does not sufficiently show them to be "like quantities of freight of the same class" under Ills. statute. (*C. B. & Q. R. Co.* v. *People*, 77 Ills. 443; see *Paxson* v. *Ills. Cent. R. Co.*, 56 Iowa, 427; see, also, note (42) to § 8).

(13) SIMILAR CIRCUMSTANCES AND CONDITIONS.

The English cases upon the question of what constitutes a difference in "circumstances and conditions," have chiefly, if not entirely, arisen upon the construction of section 90 of the Railway Clauses Act, 1845, *supra*, p. 42, and of the equality clauses in the special acts incorporating way companies.

The differences in circumstances and conditions, are those "relating to the carriage of the goods," to the nature and character of the service rendered by the carrier, and not to the business motives either of the shipper or carrier. It does not refer to who the shipper may be, whether he is a competitor, or friendly or unfriendly to the interests of the railway company. (*Gr. Western Ry. Co.* v. *Sutton*, L. R. 4 Eng. & Ir. App. 226 (H. L. 1869); *Denaby, etc., Co.* v. *Manchester, etc., Ry. Co.*, L. R. 11 App. Cas. 97, 120 (H. L. 1885.) Nor is the fact that one shipper "can go by another route, and probably will do so if charged as much as the charge made to the complaining party, a circumstance justifying an unequal charge." (*Evershed's case*, L. R. 3 App. Cas. 1029 (H. L. 1878.)

"Neither is it a difference of circumstances justifying an inequality of charge that those whom the railroad company charges less are seeking to develop a new trade. (*Denaby, etc., Co.* v. *Manchester, etc., Co.*, L. R. 11 App. Cas. (H. L.) 97, 120.)

These cases are stronger from the fact that the language of section 90 is "under the *same* circumstances," whereas, in the present act the language is "under substantially similar circumstances and conditions."

Cost of service. A difference in the cost of the service of transportation is a proper ground for a difference in charge. In other words, it constitutes a real difference in "circumstances and conditions." (*C. & A. R. Co.* v. *People*, 67 Ill. 11, 24; *Denaby Main Colliery Co.* v. *Manchester, etc., Ry. Co.*, L. R. 11 App. Cas. 97 (H. L. 1885); *s. c.*, 26 Am. & E. R. Cas. 293; *Nicholson* v. *G. W. Ry.* (No. 1), 5 C. B. (N. S.) 366; *s. c.*, 1 Nev. & Mac. 121; *Ransome* v. *Eastern Co.'s Ry. Co.*, 1 Nev. & Mac. 63; 1 C. B. (N. S.) 437; 26 L. J. C. P. 91; *Foreman* v. *G. W. Ry. Co.*, 2 Nev. & Mac. 202; *Nitshill, etc., Coal Co.*, v. *Caledonian Ry. Co.*, 2 Nev. & Mac. 39.)

Such as the fact that return loads could not be had, and the cars had to be sent back empty. (*C. & A. R. Co.* v. *People*, 67 Ill. 24; *Girardot* v. *Midland Ry. Co.*, 4 Ry. & Can. Traf. Cas. 291.)

Expense of loading or unloading. (*C. & A. R. Co.* v. *People*, 67 Ill. 26.)

Owning private side tracks and returning cars more promptly. (*Denaby, etc., Co.* v. *Manchester, etc., Ry. Co.*, L. R. 11 App. Cas. 101–2.)

Furnishing freight in fully loaded trains at regular intervals. (*Nicholson* v. *G. W. Ry. Co.* (No. 1), *supra.*)

Steep grades. (*Bellsdyke Coal Co.* v. *North B. Ry. Co.*, 2 Nev. & Mac. 105; *Nitshill Coal Co.* v. *Caledonian Ry. Co.*, 2 Nev. & Mac. 39.)

A long distance proportionately lower than a shorter distance, as the expense of marshaling cars, starting train, etc., is the same without reference to distance. (*Ransome* v. *Eastern Co.'s Ry. Co.*, 1 Nev. & Mac. 117, 63, 155.)

Average weight of truck loads. (*Girardot* v. *Midland Ry. Co.*, 4 Ry. & Can. Traf. Cas. 291.)

Difference in bulk, as compressed and uncompressed cotton, will warrant difference in rates. (*Lotspeich* v. *Cent. R. Co.*, 73 Ala. 306; *s. c.*, 18 Am. and Eng. R. Cas. 490.)

As to the character of charges growing out of increased cost of service and the principles upon which they should be made, see *Bellsdyke Coal Co.* v. *N. B. Ry. Co.*, 2. Nev. & Mac. 105; *Bell* v. *London, etc., Ry. Co.*, 2 Nev. & Mac. 185. See note to § 3, Par. 1.

The railway company alleged that the applicants being obliged to use smaller wagons for their slates than those used by the favored quarry owner, and sending slates of a lighter description, occasioned the railway company greater cost for carriage. *Held*, that 1*d*. per ton would be a reasonable allowance for such increased cost. (*Holland, etc.*, v. *Festiniog Ry. Co.*, 2 Nev. & Mac., 278.) See note "Cost of Service" under section 3, Par. 1.

The difference in rates must bear some proportion to the difference in cost to the carrier (Cockburn, C. J., in *Harris* v. *Cockermouth, etc., Ry. Co.*, 1 Nev. & Mac. 97, 102; 3 C. B. (N. S.) 693; *Garton* v. *Bristol, etc., Ry. Co.* 1 Nev. & Mac., 227; 6 C. B. (N. S.) 639, 655, Willes, J.; note to *Nicholson* v. *G. W. Ry. Co.* (No. 1) 1 Nev. & Mac. 121, 143; *Bell* v. *London, etc., Ry. Co.*, 2 Nev. & Mac. 185.)

But if "the difference in charges actually made were so disproportioned to the difference in the cost as to be made undue and unreasonable, a case of undue preference would be made out." (*Denaby, etc., Co.* v. *Manchester, etc., Ry. Co.* L. R. 11 H. L. 122, Lord Blackburn; see, also, Cockburn, C. J., in *Baxendale* v. *Ry. Co.* (*Reading case*), 1 Nev. & Mac. 202, 211; *Bell* v. *London, etc., Ry. Co.* 2 Nev. & Mac. 185.)

Or, as put by the Earl of Selborne in the same case, if the difference were such as "properly to lead to the conclusion that what has really been done is a reduction 'in favor of or against' particular persons under the colorable pretense of different circumstances," it would amount to an undue preference. (L. R. 11 H. L., page 115; see, also, *Bellsdyke Coal Co.* v. *N. R. B. Co.*, 2 Nev. & Mac. 105.) Or, if the differences "were intentionally preferential arrangements favoring a particular trader," as was said by Lord Chancellor Halsbury, also in the *Denaby case* (L. R. 11 H. L., page 112).

The difference in charge based upon the difference in cost of transportation, will be valid if there was a *bona fide* difference for this purpose founded on the saving to the company and without any improper object. (*Denaby, etc., Co.* v. *Manchester, etc., Ry. Co.*, L. R. 11 H. L. 97.) In that case "a railway company which carried coals for the appellants and also for B. and J. 'over the same portion of their line of railway,' and made allowances and a rebate to B. and J., proved that they carried for B. and J. at a less cost to the company, but did not show that the allowances and rebate were adequately represented by the saving to the company.

"*Held*, affirming in this respect the decision of the Court of Appeal, that the difference in cost constituted a real difference in the "circumstances;" that there being nothing to show any want of good faith, the company were not bound to prove that the allowances and rebate were adequately represented by the saving; that there was no breach of section 90 of the railways clauses consolidation act, 1845; and that the appellants could not maintain an action for overcharges under that section." (*Denaby, etc., Co.* v. *Manchester, etc Ry. Co., supra.*)

The **burden of proof** does not, though, rest upon the company to show that the difference in charge is proportioned to the saving. The Earl of Selborne in the *Denaby case*, said: "But I am not satisfied that any precise measure of value could be applied *a priori* to such savings as these, which might vary in amount from time to time; and I do not find in the act that when there is a real difference of circumstances and nothing to show any want of good faith, the burden of justifying the exact difference of charge (or what is the same thing, the deduction of allowance) by showing a numerical or 'necessary relation' between it and the actual saving, is cast upon the company." (L. R. 11 H. L., page 115.)

Quantity of freight shipped. At first blush there may seem to be great contrariety in the decisions and opinions of judges as to whether the quantity of freight shipped constitutes a difference in circumstances as between shippers. It is believed that the cases are capable of being reconciled, and that the true rule is that there is a real difference between large and small shipments whenever they are shipped in such quantities or under such conditions as to affect the cost of transportation. "As, for instance, if a company were to lay down a rule that if a certain large quantity of goods were brought to be conveyed they would charge less for the conveyance of that large quantity than they would for the conveyance of a less quantity, regard being had to the cost of working the particular line; that would be a very fair ground to justify them in making a distinction between the case of a person who sent a ton of goods at a time, and the case of a person who sent only a hundred weight." (Cockburn, C. J., in *Harris* v. *Cockermouth, etc., R. Co.*, 1 Nev. & Mac. 97, 102–3; see *Ransome* v. *Eastern Counties Ry. Co.* (No. 1), 1 Nev. & Mac. 63, 69, note 3, Par. 1.)

"A wholesale charge compared with a retail charge and the like, which would be a difference of circumstances, has been decided to be an essential difference." (Lord Hatherly, in *Lond. & N. W. R. Co.* v. *Evershed*, L. R. 3 App. Cas. 1029, 1036.) "There may be a difference between wholesale and retail; a large quantity of goods may be carried cheaper than a smaller quantity of goods; that would be a difference of circumstance." Lord Blackburn, in *Ib.* 1037.

Such a difference has regard not only to the fair interests of the company. (*Ransome* v. *Eastern Counties Ry. Co.*, 1 C. B. (N. S.) 437, 1

Nev. & Mac., 63), but is in conformity with common experience in all departments of trade and business. Such I understand to be the basis of the cases of *Nicholson* v. *G. W. R. Co.* 5 C. B. (N. S.) 366; 1 Nev. & Mac., 121; and *Concord & P. R. Co.* v. *Forsaith*, 59 N. H. 122.

But there is a clear line of distinction, it seems to me, between such cases and those in which a difference in charge has been made, based solely on the amount of freight shipped, without reference to any conditions tending to decrease the cost of transportation; cases where the shipments for a year have been aggregated and rates made on the basis of quantities thus shown, without regard to the mode or times in which the shipments were actually made. Such I understand to be the cases of *Hays* v. *Penn. Co.*, 12 Fed. Rep. 309; *Scofield* v. *Ry. Co.*, 43 O. S. 571; s. c., 23 Am. & Eng. Cas. 612, cited and approved in *Mo. Pac. Ry. Co.* v. *T. & P. Ry. Co.*, 30 Fed. Rep. 2, 7, 10; *S. P. Girardot* v. *Midland Ry.*, 4 Ry. & Can. Traf. Cas. 291.

In other words, it is reasonable that a man shipping a car-load of freight should have a lower rate than a man shipping a hundred pounds; and that a man furnishing a train-load of freight at a time should have a cheaper rate than one furnishing a car-load. It would seem just as unreasonable, other things being equal, that the shipper sending fifty car-loads of freight in a year should have a lower rate than the man shipping five car-loads; or that the man shipping a thousand hundred weight of freight in a year, in quantities of one hundred weight at a time, should have a lower rate than a man shipping half that amount, under the same conditions.

The dangers incident to the rule adopted, even in the *Nicholson case*, are shown by the court, being evenly divided, when the case came before it a second time; Erle, C. J., who upheld the difference in charge complained of, being the judge who dissented in the *Sutton case*, and whose views were overruled by the House of Lords in that case. (*Nicholson* v. *G. W. Ry. Co.* (No. 2), 1 Nev. & Mac., 143; 7 C. B. (N. S.) 55; *Sutton* v. *G. W. Ry. Co.*, L. R. 4 H. L. 226, 230, 243–4.)

— **Cases stated—Under statutes.** It is competent for a railway company to enter into special agreements, whereby advantages may be secured to individuals in the carriage of goods upon the railway, where it is made clearly to appear that in entering into such agreements the company has only the interests of the proprietors and the legitimate increase of the profits of the railway in view, and the consideration given to the company in return for the advantages afforded by them is adequate, and the company is willing to afford the same facilities to all others upon the same terms. (*Nicholson* v. *Great Western Ry. Co.*, 5 C. B. (N. S.) 366; 4 Jur. (N. S.) 1187; 28 L. J. C. P. 89; 1 Nev. & Mac. 121.) The difference in charge must be proportionate to the difference in cost of service. (*Garton* v. *Bristol, etc. Ry. Co.*, 1 Nev. & Mac. 227, Willes, J.; see p. 49, *supra*.)

Where a coal company made a contract for a period of ten years, to ship as much coal for a distance of at least one hundred miles, over defendant's road, as would produce an annual gross revenue of forty thousand pounds to the railroad company, in fully loaded trains, at the rate of seven trains per week, and there was evidence that the cost of carrying coal in fully loaded trains, regularly furnished, at the rate of seven trains per week, was less per ton than coal carried in the usual way and at irregular intervals and quantities, was not an undue or unreasonable discrimination against the complainant, who shipped the coal in the usual way at irregular intervals and in unequal quantities. (*Nicholson* v. *G. W. R. Co.*, *supra*.)

The *Nicholson case* again came before the court upon a rule to show cause. The affidavit upon which the rule was obtained stating, in addition to the complainant's former case, that they verily believed that the low rates charged to the Ruabon Coal Company, taken in conjunction with the other advantages afforded to the said company by their agreement with the railway company, were not remunerative to the said railway company, or, if in any degree remunerative, not nearly as much so as the higher rates charged to the complainants and to other traders in Forest of Dean coal. This was contradicted by the defendant's affidavits.

The court were evenly divided as to whether the question should be referred under section 3 of the railway and canal traffic act, 1854. (*Nicholson* v. *Great Western Ry. Co.* (No. 2.), 1 Nev. & Mac. 143; 7 C. B. (N. S.) 755.)

Erle, C. J., said: "Railway companies have that power [of making contracts for commercial profit] as free as any merchants," subject to the duty to act impartially. "Large contracts may be beyond the means of small capitalists; contracts for long distances may be beyond the needs of those whose traffic is confined to a home district; but the power of the railway to contract is not restricted by these considerations." (*Nicholson* v. *Gt. Western Ry. Co.* (No. 2), 1 Nev. & Mac. 143, 149.) But the court (four judges) were evenly divided in this case, Willes, J., on the other hand, saying: "No difference of charge has ever been held justified in this court by the circumstance of its being part of a transaction in which the company has a commercial advantage, if, as is alleged here, they obtain it by an undue preference of the complainant's rivals, or by putting him to an unfair disadvantage." (1 Nev. & Mac. 154; 7 C. B. (N. S.) 755.) See, also, *Harris* v. *Cockermouth, etc., Ry. Co.*, 1 Nev. & Mac. 97, 102–3; *Ransome* v. *Eastern Co's Ry.*, 1 Nev. & Mac. 63; *Menacho* v. *Ward*, 27 Fed. Rep. 529; 23 Am. & E. R. Cas. 647; 34 Alb. L. J. 44.

The same advantage must be extended to all persons under like circumstances. (*Baxendale* v. *Ry. Co.* (*Reading case*), 1 Nev. & Mac., 202, 211.)

The S. E. Ry. Co. entered into a special agreement with Messrs. F., by which the latter guaranteed to send between Boulonge Quay and London by the S. E. Ry. Co.'s steamers and railway, 850 tons of goods each calendar month. In consideration of that agreement, the railway company allowed Messrs. F. a rebate of fifteen per cent off their tariff of station to station rates, exempted them from a landing charge at Folkestone of 4d. a package payable to the railway company on goods of particular descriptions, and charged them from 6d. to 1s. less than others on parcels exceeding fifty-six pounds in weight.

Held, that as there were circumstances which enhanced the value to the railway company of the guarantee of quantity, and compelled Messrs. F. to incur considerable expense and labor to earn the allowance, and as the railway company had always been ready to make a proportionate allowance for a smaller amount of traffic to any one giving a guarantee similar (except as to amount), no injunction should be granted.

The S. E. Ry. Co. carried goods at agreed through rates between London and Paris, as to which the railway companies undertook, for the fixed amount paid, every kind of service and charge incidental to the transit from point to point. The sum paid included clearing the goods in the custom-house, which was done only by the railway company's servants, or if done by custom-house agents no rebate was allowed by the railway company.

Held, that the plan of delivering goods between London and Paris at one fixed sum for the entire service, and free of any intermediate charges, was a great convenience to the public, and did not involve any infringement of the Railway and Canal Traffic Act, 1854.

Semble, if a trader is able and engages to supply traffic with regularity and in certain quantities for the accommodation of a railway company, so that a lower rate in his case is as remunerative to the railway company as a higher rate on similar traffic in the case of others, such an arrangement is not an inequality within the Railway and Canal

Traffic Act, 1854. (*Greenop, etc.,* v. *The S. E. Ry. Co.*, 2 Nev. & Mac. 319.

The New Hampshire statute requiring that " the rates shall be the same for all persons and for like descriptions of freight between the same points," and that all persons shall have reasonable and equal facilities, etc., for the transportation of persons and property, *held* to be a re-enactment of the common law against unreasonable and unjust discrimination, and does not require the same price per pound for transporting large and small quantities of coal between the same points. As the carrier's labor and expense of transporting a quantity of coal in many small parcels might be more than the labor and expense of transporting the same in one parcel, the owner of the latter might suffer from an unreasonable and unjust discrimination if the price per pound were the same for all quantities. (*Concord & P. R.* v. *Forsaith*, 59 N. H. 122 (1879); *s. c.*, 47 Am. Rep. 181.) See *McDuffee* v. *Railroad*, 52 N. H. 430, 457.

— **At common law.** Discriminations in the rates of freight charged by a railroad company to shippers, based solely on the amount of freight shipped, without reference to any conditions tending to decrease the cost of transportation, are discriminations in favor of capital, are contrary to sound public policy, violative of that equality of rights guaranteed to every citizen, and a wrong to the disfavored party (*Hays* v. *Penn. Co.*, 12 Fed. Rep. 309; *Scofield* v. *Railway Co.*, 43 O. S. 571; *s. c.*, 23 Am. & Eng. R. Cas. 612), for which he is entitled to recover from the railroad company the amount of freight paid by him in excess of the rates accorded by it to his most favored competitor, with interest on such sum (*Hays & Co.* v. *The Penn. Co., supra*), or, the court may intervene by injunction to prevent a multiplicity of suits, and it is not a prerequisite that the plaintiffs should have first established their rights by an action at law. (*Scofield* v. *Ry. Co., supra.*)

The plaintiffs were engaged in mining coal at Salineville, Ohio, for sale in the Cleveland market. They were wholly dependent on the defendant for transportation. The regular tariff between those points was $1.60 per ton, with a rebate of from thirty to seventy cents per ton to persons shipping over 5,000 tons during a year, the amount of rebate being graduated according to the quantity shipped. Under this schedule plaintiffs were required to pay higher rates on the coal shipped by them than were exacted from other and rival parties who shipped larger quantities. The defendant claimed that the discriminations were made in good faith, to stimulate production and increase its tonnage, and were within the discretion confided by law to every common carrier. In an action to recover back the excess of tariff paid by plaintiffs, *held*, that such discriminations were illegal, and that plaintiffs were entitled to recover the amount paid by them in excess of the rate accorded to their most favored competitor, with interest thereon. (*Hays & Co.* v. *The Penn. Co., supra.*)

A contract of the Lake Shore and Michigan Southern Railway Company with the Standard Oil Company, by which the former gave the latter a rebate in rates charged to the rest of the public, *held* illegal, and the railway enjoined from continuing the discrimination. (*Scofield* v. *Railway Co.*, 43 O. S. 571.) This case was said by Pardee, J., in a recent case, to contain the most satisfactory statement of the law to be found in any of the cases. (*Mo. Pac. Ry. Co.* v. *Tex. & P. Ry. Co.*, 30 Fed. Rep. 2, 10.)

Competition. The question of whether competition with other modes of conveyance is a difference in circumstances has been much litigated in England under section 90 of the act of 1845, above, and under section 2 of the traffic act of 1854. In *Evershed's case* the question was squarely presented whether a railroad company could, in order to compete with other lines that would naturally obtain the traffic of certain shippers, make a reduction in their rates to such shipper as compared with others. The Queen's Bench Division, the Court of Appeal, and finally the House of Lords, decided that the company could not do so—Lord Chancellor Cairns saying: "That is exactly one of those things which parliament has not left open to railroad companies to judge of—whether in that way they will equalize their capacity for competing with other lines or not." (*Lond., etc., Ry. Co.* v. *Evershed*, L. R. 3 App. Cas. 1029, 1035; L. R. 3 Q. B. Div. 134 (Court of Appeal); L. R. 2 Q. B. Div. 254.)

The same result was reached by the Exchequer Division in a case in which a lower charge was made for a longer haul in order to compete with communication by sea at the port from which the longer haul was made. (*Budd* v. *Lond., etc., Ry. Co.*, 36 L. T. (N. S.) 802; 4 Ry. & Canal Traffic Cas. 393.)

The same conclusion was reached in the well considered opinion of Lawrence, C. J., in *C. & A. R. Co.* v. *People*, 67 Ills. 11, 19, 222. And in an admirable discussion of the question by Mr. Adelbert Hamilton in the 16 Am. Law Review, page 833 et seq. (See, also, *Thompson* v. *London & N. W. Ry. Co.*, 2 Nev. & Mac. 115; *Greenop* v. *S. E. Ry. Co., Id.* 319.) See further notes to sections 3 and 4.

The contrary result seems to have been reached in some of the earlier English cases, but these must be considered as overruled by the *Evershed case;* and the same result in at least two American cases. (*Foreman* v. *G. W. Ry. Co.*, 2 Nev. & Mac. 202; Williams, J., in *Jones* v. *Eastern Cos.*

Ry. Co., 1 Nev. & Mac. 45, 46; Creswell, J., in *Ransome* v. *Eastern Cos. Ry. Co.*, *Id.* 63, 70; Cockburn, C. J., in *Harris* v. *Ry. Co.*, *Id.* 97, 103; *Ex parte Koehler*, 23 Fed. Rep. 529; *Munhall* v. *Penn. R. Co.*, 92 Pa. St. 150.)

E. was a brewer at the town of B., where three railways had their stations. With one of these railways, M., certain brewers in the town had direct communication by sidings, which enabled goods to be sent to the trains, and taken from the trains of railway M. with greater ease and less loss of time than by the way of ordinary cartage. M. charged them nothing for cartage, and made a rebate in the charge for station to station conveyance. These brewers had no such communications with railway N. W., but it was often convenient for them to send by that railway; and the directors of that railway, in order to compete with railway M., allowed these particular brewers the same advantages as to cartage and rebate as railway M. did. As to all others in the same trade (E. among the rest), the directors of railway N. W. made the ordinary charge for cartage, and allowed no rebate on the charge for conveyance on the line. *Held*, that this was an inequality and an undue preference within the meaning of the statutes. (*London & N. W., Ry. Co.* v. *Evershed*, L. R. 3 App. Cas. 1029 (1878); affirming *s. c., nom. Evershed* v. *London and North-western Railway Company*, 3 L. R. Q. B. Div. 134; 47 L. J. Q. B. Div. 284; 37 L. T. (N. S.) 623; 26 W. R. 863—C. A.; which affirmed 2 L. R. Q. B. Div. 254; 46 L. J. Q. B. Div. 289; 36 L. T. (N. S.) 12; 26 W. R. 102.)

Where a difference in rates was made by a railway company in order to compete with another railway company for carriage of goods between shippers, rebating to one the carting and loading charges and not to others, it was held not a sufficient ground for the discrimination, and that in order to justify a difference being made by the railway company in favor of one or more individual members of their general class of customers, there must be adequate consideration to the railway company lessening the cost to them of the services rendered to such individual members of the general class; and it is not sufficient that the railway company merely desires to attract traffic from another line to themselves, especially when the favor thus shown to the few is prejudicial to many others in the same trade as the same favored persons. (*Thompson* v. *London and North-western Railway Company*, 2 Nev. & Mac. 115.)

The Railway and Canal Traffic Act does not prevent a railway company from having special rates of charge to a terminus to which traffic can be carried by other modes of carriage with which theirs is in competition. Disproportion in rates by reason of **sea competition** was justified in this case. (*Foreman* v. *G. W. Ry. Co.*, 2 Nev. & Mac. 202.)

By canal act the company was entitled to demand a fixed sum for goods carried upon any part of the canal, and by another act might vary tolls: "Provided, that they are equal for goods conveyed in boats using the same portion of the canal under like circumstances." The company was permitted to take proportionately less per ton per mile for goods carried a given distance along any part of the canal than for goods carried less than that distance, and also that it was competent for the company to agree to carry at a lower rate for a particular individual in consideration of a large guaranteed minimum toll, in order to enable them to enter into a successful competition with a rival line of railway. (*Strict and others* v. *Swansea Canal Co.*, 16 C. B. (N. S.) 245.)

The fact that, at one point, there is **competition** by **water transportation**, constitutes a different circumstance or condition, as compared with another point where there is no such competition. (Under Oregon statute.) (*Ex parte Koehler*, 23 Fed. Rep. 529; 21 Am. & E. Ry. Cas. 52, 58; see note (23) to § 4.)

The Allegheny Valley railroad crosses the Pennsylvania railroad at Allegheny Junction. To **compete** more successfully with the **river transportation**, the Allegheny Valley railroad carried crude oil to the refineries at Pittsburgh, and the manufactured product back to Allegheny Judction, at a uniform rate, thus giving to the refiner at Pittsburgh as favorable terms as if located at Allegheny Junction, and thereby securing a uniform rate on oil from the oil regions to the seaboard. *Held*, that to deny the right to make such an arrangement would be an unwarranted interference with the management of the business of the road, and deprive the public of the benefit of the competition to which it is justly entitled. (At common law.) (*Munhall* v. *Pa. R. Co.*, 92 Pa. St. 150.)

Developing trade. The English decisions are uniform in holding that it does not constitute a difference in circumstances that goods are shipped to places to develop a new trade, or open up new markets. (*Denaby, etc., Co.* v. *Manchester, etc., Ry. Co.*, L. R. 11 App. Cas. 97; *Ransome* v. *Eastern Co.'s Ry. Co.* (No. 1), 1 Nev. & Mac. 63; *Oxlade* v. *N. E. Ry. Co.* (No. 1), *Id.* 72; 1 C. B. (N. S.) 454; *Harris* v. *Ry. Co.*, 1 Nev. & Mac. 97.)

Where goods are carried for different customers "over the same portion of the line of railway," the fact that the goods carried for one customer are to be shipped to certain ports to develop a new trade, or open up new markets, and so to increase the tonnage carried, does not constitute a difference in the "circumstances" so as to justify inequality of rates.

Therefore, where a railway company carried coals over the same portion of the line to G., both for the appellants and also for B., and allowed B. 8d. per ton in respect of all coal carried to G., and there shipped for the West Indian market; and, also, allowed B. 6d. per ton in respect of all coal carried to G., and there shipped by him to certain ports, in consideration of a *bona fide* undertaking by B. to develop the trade to those ports, to provide the vessels, and to run the risks incidental to the working of such a traffic:

Held, affirming in this respect the decision of the Court of Appeal, that the coals were carried 'under the same circumstances,' and that the allowances were breaches of section 90 of the Railways Clauses Consolidation Act, 1845.

Held, also, reversing in this respect the decision of the Court of Appeal, that the appellants were entitled to recover the overcharges by action against the company, the amount to be ascertained by finding what quantity of coal carried under the same circumstances and over the same portion only of the line was charged at the higher rate to the appellants at the time the lower rate was charged to B. (*Denaby Main Colliery Co. v. Manchester, etc., Ry. Co.*, L. R. 11 App. Cas. 97.)

At common law, a common carrier may discriminate in favor of persons living at a distance from the end of the route, where the object is to secure freight which would otherwise reach its destination by a different route, and other customers, not in like condition, will have no right of action because of the discrimination, if the charges made against them are reasonable. (*Ragan v. Aiken*, 9 B. J. Lea (Tenn.), 609 (1882.))

A threat of **building a rival line**, made by a shipper, is not a circumstance authorizing a lower rate to him. (*Harris v. Cockermouth, etc., Ry. Co.*, 1 Nev. & Mac. 97; 3 C. B. (N. S.) 693; *Diphwys, etc., Co. v. Festiniog Ry. Co.*, 2 Nev. & Mac. 73.)

Nor that the shipper **contracts to furnish all his freight** to the carrier favoring him. (*Scofield v. Railway Co.*, 43 O. S. 571; *Baxendale v. G. W. Ry. Co.*, 5 C. B. (N. S.) 309; *Diphwys, etc., Co. v. Festiniog Ry. Co.*, 2 Nev. & Mac. 73; *Bellsdyke Coal Co. v. N. B. Ry. Co.*, 2 Nev. & Mac. 105; see note to § 3, Par. 1, *ante*.)

Nor can a carrier discriminate against a shipper who refuses to patronize him exclusively. (*Menacho v. Ward*, 27 Fed. Rep. 529; *Diphwys, etc., Co. v. Festiniog Ry. Co.*, 2 Nev. & Mac. 73.)

Place of shipment or destination. A railroad company has no power to make any discrimination in its rates of freight, on the ground that certain goods are to be carried to their final destination, by another route, after reaching the terminus of the company's road. (*Twells* v. *Penn. R. Co.*, 3 Am. L. Reg. (N. S.) 728; *s. c.*, 21 Leg. Int. 189.)

Or, that certain goods have come by sea and others by rail. (*Ransome* v. *Eastern Co.'s Ry. Co.*, 1 Nev. & Mac. 63; 1 C. B. (N. S.) 437.)

Like conditions. Under Iowa statute (Laws 1874, ch. 68, § 10), providing that "no railroad company shall charge any person, company, or corporation, for the transportation of any property, a greater sum than it shall charge and collect from any other person, company, or corporation, for a like service from the same place, and upon like conditions, and all concessions of rates, drawbacks, and contracts for special rates, founded upon the demands of commerce and transportation, shall be open to all persons, companies, and corporations alike:" *Held*, that no recovery can be had from a railroad company, under this section, for discrimination in charges for cars between different shippers of stock, unless it is shown that the shipments were made under like conditions. (*Paxon* v. *Ill. Cent. R. Co.*, 56 Iowa, 427.)

Pleading. The petition in this case set out that plaintiff had shipped from Manchester to Chicago car loads of hogs, upon defendant's road, for which it had charged him $56 per car; that, during the same time, defendant allowed another shipper rebates and drawbacks of from $6 to $16 per car; and that defendant charged plaintiff $104 "over what the defendant charged the said Gannon for the same service during the same time:" but there was no allegation that the shipments of plaintiff and Gannon were made under "like conditions."

The court said: "Cases, we incline to think, may be supposed, when it would be competent for the carrier, under the statute, to charge one person more than another for a like service. For instance, suppose the cars loaded by one person were attached to express trains and those of another to ordinary freight trains." (*Paxon* v. *Ill. Cent. R. Co.*, *supra*, 430; see, also, note (42) to § 8.)

(14) OTHER ENGLISH DECISIONS.

Carriers—Express companies. A railway company is bound to treat carriers in the same manner as the rest of the public. (*Great Western Ry. Co.* v. *Sutton*, L. R. 4 Eng. & Ir. App. 226 (1869); *Parker* v. *Great Western Ry. Co.*, 3 Ry. Cas. 563 (Exch.); *Crouch* v. *Great Northern Ry. Co.*, 9 Exch. 556; 11 *Id.* 742.)

— Charter right of company to fix charge. A railway company was authorized by statute to enter into such arrangements as they might think fit with reference (*inter alia*) to the collection and delivery of goods, also to charge for small parcels, *i. e.* not exceeding five hundred pounds weight, any sum they liked. *Held*, that the company were still bound to charge equally, and could not lawfully demand for carriage of parcels from station to station a sum including the cost of collection and delivery, and so impose an unequal burden on those who do not require the performance of the service. (*Baxendale* v. *Great W. Ry. Co.*, 14 C. B. (N. S.) 1; affirmed by the Exchequer Chamber, 16 *Id.* 137; *Great Western Ry. Co.* v. *Sutton, supra.*)

The special act of the Great Northern Railway Company empowers the company to charge for the carriage of small parcels any sum which they may think fit. 8 and 9 Vict., c. 20, § 90, is incorporated with the special act. *Held*, that the company were compelled to charge all persons alike, and that they were not justified in charging a carrier more than the rest of the public. (*Crouch* v. *Great N. Ry. Co.*, 9 Exch. 557; *Gt. Western Ry. Co.* v. *Sutton, supra.*)

Authority to a railway company to fix such sum for the carriage of smaller parcels, not exceeding five hundred pounds weight, as they should see fit, did not extend to articles sent in large aggregate quantities, though made up of separate and distinct parties, but only to include parcels, in connection with parcels of a like nature, which might be sent upon the railway at the time. (*Edmonds* v. *The Great Western Ry. Co.*, 11 C. B. 588.)

The provision relied upon by the railway company in the last case has been held not to repeal the Equality clause, but only the clause limiting the maximum of tolls. (*Baxendale* v. *The Great Western Ry. Co.*, 16 C. B. (N. S.) 137–140.)

— **What amounts to inequality.** A railway company acted themselves as carriers, charging the public at the rates specified in their printed bills for carriage, including the collection, weighing, loading, unloading, and delivery of the goods. They also carried goods for other carriers, allowing them a certain deduction for the trouble of collection, etc., which was performed by the carriers. In their dealings with a particular carrier they refused to make such allowance, but were willing to perform for him all the things which formed the consideration for that allowance, and which, in fact, he performed by himself. *Held*, that the company were not justified in withholding the allowance from such carrier, and that, therefore, the charges to him were not equal or reasonable. (*Parker* v. *Great Western Ry. Co.*, 3 Ry. Ca. 563; and see *Parker* v. *The Same*, 6 E. & B. 77.)

The plaintiffs were common carriers trading under the name of "Pickford & Co.," and they were in the habit of collecting parcels in

London and forwarding them to customers in the country. Each parcel was addressed to the person to whom it was ultimately to be delivered, but it was labeled with the name of "Pickford & Co.," and that of the station to which it was to be sent, and all the parcels for the same station were delivered in one consignment consigned to the plaintiffs at that station. The defendants refused to charge the plaintiffs for the carriage of their parcels at a tonnage rate upon the gross weight, and charged for each parcel separately according to its individual weight. *Held*, that this created an inequality. (*Baxendale* v. *S. W. Ry. Co.*, 35 L. J. Exch. 108; and see *Baxendale* v. *Eastern Counties Ry. Co.*, 4 C. B. (N. S.) 63; 27 L. J. C. P. 137.)

The defendants, a railway company, advertised themselves to carry parcels, etc., from London to Glasgow (though their own line ended at Preston), and habitually received, booked, and carried parcels of all descriptions from London to Glasgow (receiving prepayment for the whole distance), having made arrangements with other companies, by which the defendants' vans, being locked in London, were carried through from Preston to Glasgow, under the management and by the locomotive power of the other companies. The defendants had issued written orders to their servants that "packed" parcels should be invoiced to termini of the defendants' line only. The plaintiff had received notice of this order, but it had never been enforced against any one but the plaintiff, and the defendants had knowingly carried packed parcels from London to Glasgow since the order was issued; but they refused to carry a packed parcel for the plaintiff further than Preston. *Held*, first, that by the 8 and 9 Vict., c. 20, ss. 86, 87, and 89, the defendants were in the position of common carriers, and that having held themselves out, and acted as common carriers from London to Glasgow, they were bound by the common law to receive and carry all goods tendered to them to be carried from London to Glasgow, although the latter place was out of England. Secondly, that being common carriers, and having carried packed parcels for some persons, they were bound to carry them for all. (*Crouch* v. *London, etc., Ry. Co.*, 7 Ry. Ca. 717.)

A railway company conveyed goods on the L. and B. line, and published a list of charges for their carriage from Manchester to London, among which "Manchester packs" were charged 65*s.* per ton. At foot of the list was a notice that "goods were brought to Camden Town Station without extra charge, and no charge was made for booking or delivering in London." The company made arrangements with Messrs. C. & H. that the latter should carry from Camden Town station and deliver in London all such goods, and receive 10*s.* per ton for so doing. *Held*, that a charge of 65*s*. per ton to other persons willing to receive their own goods at the station was unequal and unreasonable. (*Pickford* v. *Grand J. Ry. Co.*, 10 M. & W. 399; 3 Eng. Ry. Cas. 144.)

The Grand Junction Railway Company was required by act 3 Vict., ch. 49, sec. 26, to charge equally and after the same rate in respect to all passengers, goods, etc., conveyed or propelled by a like carriage or engine passing on the same portion of the line and under the same circumstances. The published list of carriages divided the merchandise carried into seven classes, of which the lowest was 16*s*. and the highest 60*s*. per ton, and for boxes, barrels, etc., when they contained parcels or other packages under 112 pounds in weight, consigned or intended for different persons, they embodied a charge of 1*d*. per pound weight, but it was held that this last charge was unreasonable in the case of a package above 500 pounds made up by a carrier and directed to one person, although containing a number of parcels under 112 pounds weight, each consigned or directed to different persons. (*Pickford* v. *Grand Junction Ry. Co.*, 10 Mees. & W. 399; 3 Eng. Ry. Cases, 144.)

— **Delivery—Services not rendered.** A railway company can not, in addition to the charges for the carriage of goods between the place where the goods are handed to them and the place where they are ordered to be delivered, charge for collection and delivery, where they have not in fact collected or delivered them. (*Garton* v. *Bristol & E. Ry. Co.*, 30 L. J. Q. B. 273; *Same* v. *Same*, 1 Nev. & Mac. 218; 6 C. B. (N. S.) 639.)

— **What does not constitute an inequality.** A railway company agreed to pay a carrier £1,000 a year to collect and deliver parcels for them in London, he relinquishing the charge for "booking." *Held*, that another carrier could not complain of this being an inequality of treatment toward him. (*Parker* v. *Great W. Ry. Co.*, 11 C. B. 545.)

The defendants carried goods from London to the Isle of Wight by their own railway from London to Southampton, and thence by tramway and steamer. The plaintiffs also were in the habit of carrying goods from London to the Isle of Wight, using the defendants line from London to Southampton, and thence conveying them by carts and steamer. The plaintiffs claimed to have their goods carried by the defendants from London to Southampton at a sum equivalent to the defendants' through charge from London to the Isle of Wight, less a fair charge for collection in London and for carrying from Southampton station to the Isle of Wight. *Held*, that they were not entitled to this, the delivery by the defendants beyond the limits of their line not being a delivery auxiliary or subsidiary to their business as carriers on their own line, but to their general business as common carriers, and therefore differing from a delivery in the immediate neighborhood of a station. (*Baxendale* v. *S. W. Ry. Co.*, 35 L. J. Exch. 108.)

Over the same portion of the line of railway. It is to be noted that section 2 of the present act does not limit it to the carriage of goods "passing only over the same portion of the line of railway under the same circumstances," as in section 90, *supra*, p. 43, of the Railway Clauses Act, 1845. The House of Lords in the case of *Denaby Main Colliery Co.* v. *Manchester, etc., R. Co.*, L. R. 11 App. Cas. 97, have held that the provision in section 90 of the Railways Clauses Consolidation Act, 1845 (8 & 9 Vict., c. 20), requiring equality of rates for carriage of goods "passing only over the same portion of the line of railway under the same circumstances," applies only to goods passing between the same points of departure and arrival, and passing over no other part of the line. And mere inequality in the rate of charge, when unequal distances are traversed, does not constitute a preference inconsistent with the concluding words of that section.

Therefore, where a railway company carried coals from a group of collieries situate at different points along their line, and charged all the collieries with one uniform set of rates in respect of such carriage, and the owners of the colliery lying nearest to the point of arrival brought an action for overcharges:

Held, affirming in this respect the decision of the court of appeal, that the railway company had not infringed the provisions of section 90 of the Railways Clauses Consolidation Act, 1845. (*Denaby, etc., Co.* v. *Manchester, etc., R. Co.*, L. R. 11 App. Cas. 97.)

To constitute an undue or unreasonable preference by reason of an inequality of charge, it must be an inequality in the charge for traveling over the same line, or the same portion of the line. (*Caterham Ry. Co.* v. *London, etc., Ry. Co.*, 1 C. B. (N. S.) 410; 26 L. J. C. P. 16; 1 Nev. & Mac. 32.)

This act did not apply to Scotland, but the Railways Clauses Consolidation (Scotland) Act, 1845, section 83, is in precisely the same words. In *Finnie* v. *Southwestern R. Co.*, the House of Lords, consisting of Lord Cranworth and Lord St. Leonards, were equally divided in opinion. In that case the G. Railway Company leased a branch line on which F., a coal dealer, resided, and they made two tables of rates for coals—one applicable to the main line and the other to the branch line, the latter being the higher of the two rates. When F. sent his coals along the branch line, he was charged at the branch rates, but when his coals got to the main line, then at the main rates; whereas, when coal owners living on the main line sent their coals from the main line on to the branch line, they were charged for the whole distance (*i. e.*, both on the branch and the main line) at the main line rates only. The special act applicable to the branch line (which also incorporated the Railways Clauses Act) provided that the rates should "be made equally to all persons in respect of goods passing over the same portion of and over the same distance along the railway, and under the like circumstances," etc. Lord Cranworth held that the rate charged upon F. was no violation of the equal rates clause; but Lord St. Leonards held that it was a gross violation of that clause. (*Finnie* v. *South-western Ry. Co.*, 2 Macq. 177; 26 L. T. 14.)

Lord Blackburn, in the *Denaby case*, says of the opinion of Lord Cranworth, in the *Finnie case*, that he "throws out some opinions which I think (since the subsequent decision of this house in the *Great Western R. Co.* v. *Sutton*, L. R. 4 Eng. & Ir. App. 226) can not be supported." (L. R. 11 App. Cas. 119.)

Subsequently the Court of Sessions of Scotland held that the act applied only to goods passing between the same points and over the same portion of the railway. (*Murray* v. *Glasgow, etc., Co.*, 11 Court Sess. Cas. (4 Ser.), 205; 4 Ry. & Can. Traf. Cas. 456.)

A railroad whose special act provided that charges for the carriage of passengers, etc., "shall be at all times charged equally and after the same rate per ton per mile, in respect to all passengers and goods of a like description, and conveyed or propelled by a like carriage or engine passing on the same portion of the line within and under the same circumstances," charged passengers conveyed by their carriages, from Derby to Hampton-in-Arden 8*s.*, while they charged other passengers from Derby to Hampton-in-Arden and thence to London only 2*s.* between Hampton-in-Arden and Derby. The lord chancellor held that the clause above set forth was only meant to prevent the exercise of a monopoly to the prejudice of one passenger or carrier and in favor of another, and that he would not interfere unless it was clear that the public interest required it, and that in this case it being admitted that the higher charge was not more than the act permitted, it did not appear that the public were prejudiced by that arrangement. (*Attorney-General* v. *Bingham, etc., Ry. Co.*, 2 Eng. Ry. Cas. 89.)

STATE STATUTES AND DECISIONS.

Massachusetts. "Every railroad corporation shall give to all persons or companies reasonable and equal terms, facilities, and accommodations for the transportation of themselves, their agents, and servants, and of any merchandise and other property, upon any railroad owned or operated by such corporation, and for the use of the depot and other build-

§ 3, PAR. 1.]   INTER-STATE COMMERCE ACT.   65

ings and grounds of such corporation; and at any other point where its railroad shall connect with any other railroad, reasonable and equal terms and facilities of interchange." (General R. R. Act, 1874, Mass. c. 372, § 138; also act 1867, c. 339.)

A., who was a student over twenty years of age, paid to a railroad corporation the regular price of a season ticket, entitling him to transportation over its road, between two stations, for three months. The directors of the corporation had authorized its president, upon special application, and in his discretion, to allow season tickets to be sold to students over twenty years of age, for the same term, between the same stations, for one-half the price A. paid, and such tickets had been sold. *Held*, in an action by A. to recover of the corporation one-half of the amount paid by him, that there was no violation of the above section; and that the action could not be maintained. (*Spofford* v. *Boston & M. R.*, 128 Mass. 326.)

The above statute does not render it unlawful for a railroad to carry on the **express business** itself and to refuse to allow similar privileges to another person. (*Sargent* v. *Boston & L. R.*, 115 Mass. 416.)

Pennsylvania. Under a charter requiring a railroad to transport all merchandise "so that equal and impartial justice shall be done to all owners of property" who pay or tender the toll due: *Held*, that **express companies** had as good a right to the benefits of the road as the owners of the packages which they conveyed personally had; but that a contract giving to one express company an exclusive right of transportation in the passenger trains was illegal and void. (*Sandford* v. *Railroad Co.*, 24 Pa. St. 378; see *Audenried* v. *P. & R. Co.*, 68 Pa. St. 370.)

Illinois. Where appellant charged appellees two cents more per 100 lbs. per car load for carrying grain from C. to B. than it did to others, *held* unjust discrimination within the statute. (*Railroad Co.* v. *Hill*, 14 Bradw. (Ill. App.) 579.

UNDUE PREFERENCES PROHIBITED.(15)

Sec. 3, Par. 1. That it shall be unlawful for any common carrier subject to the provisions of this act to make or give any undue or unreasonable preference or advantage to any particular person, company, firm, corporation, or locality, or any particular description of traffic, in any respect whatsoever, or to subject any particular person, company, firm, corporation, or locality, or any particular description of traffic, to any undue or unreasonable prejudice or disadvantage in any respect whatsoever.

(15) English Statutes and Decisions.

This paragraph was taken from the second section of the Railway and Canal Traffic Act of 1854, as will be apparent from the following cormparison of the two statutes:

Present Act.

"That it shall be unlawful for any common carrier subject to the provisions of this act to make or give any undue or unreasonable preference or advantage to any particular person, company, firm, corporation, or locality, or any particular description of traffic, in any respect whatsoever, or to subject any particular person, company, firm, corporation, or locality, or any particular description of traffic, to any undue or unreasonable prejudice or disadvantage in any respect whatsoever."

English Act.

"No such company shall make or give any undue or unreasonable preference or advantage to or in favor of any particular person or company, or any particular description of traffic, in any respect whatsoever, nor shall any such company subject any particular person or company, or any particular description of traffic, to any undue or unreasonable prejudice or disadvantage in any respect whatsoever." (See the entire act in Appendix.)

Attention is also called to the undue preference and prejudice features of the equality clause of the Railway Clauses Consolidation Act, 1845, in note to section 2, *supra*, p. 43, and of section 16 of the Regulation of Railways Act, 1868, in Appendix.

There would seem to be no difficulty in discovering the purpose of disconnecting this provision of the statute from section 2. Section 2 is a substantial embodiment, though less limited, of the equality clause of the English act of 1845. It was found that very many unjust discriminations did not fall within its terms, and accordingly the act of 1854 was passed. Section 2 of the present act of congress prescribes equality in compensation as to all services that are of a like nature in the transportation of a like kind of traffic, under substantially similar circumstances and conditions. As has been pointed out in the notes to section 2, and will be more apparent in the notes to the present section, there are cases in which, by reason of a dissimilarity of circumstances, the second section will not apply, and yet the charge will amount to an undue preference. (*Denaby, etc., Co.* v. *Manchester, etc., R. Co.* L. R. 11 H. L. 112, 115, 122; *Bell* v. *Lond., etc., R. Co.*, 2 Nev. & Mac. 185; *Baxendale* v. *Railway Co.* (*Reading case*), 1 Nev. & Mac. 202, 211; Pollock, B., in note, 4 Ry. & Can. Traf. Cas. 449.)

In come cases, also, the same rates for different distances may amount

§ 3, PAR 1.] INTER-STATE COMMERCE ACT. 67

to an undue preference, as in the case of "group rates." Section 4 prohibits the charging of a greater compensation in the aggregate for transportation for a shorter than for a longer distance, but expressly provides that this "shall not be construed as authorizing any common carrier within the terms of this act to charge and receive as great compensation for a shorter as for a longer distance." A number of English cases hold that making the same charge for a shorter as for a longer distance, amounts to an undue preference. (*Denaby Main Colliery Co.* v. *Manchester, etc., Ry. Co.*, 3 Nev. & Mac. 426; *Ib.* 433; *Ib.* 438–41; *Ib.*, 4 Ry. & Can. Traf. Cas. 23; *Ib.*, 28.)

These are given merely as illustrations. Many others will be apparent from a perusal of the succeeding notes. It therefore seems apparent that the operation of this paragraph extends to charges and compensation as well as to facilities for transportation and in receiving, delivering, storing, and handling property, and can not be confined, as has been suggested, "to preferences and disadvantages arising from the giving or withholding of facilities," excluding all matters of charge. (Mr. Easley, Railway Age, March 25, 1887.) Such is the construction of the English statute. (*London, etc., R. Co.* v. *Evershed*, L. R. 3 App. Cas. 1029 (H. L. 1878); *Denaby, etc., Co.* v. *Manchester, etc., Ry. Co.*, L. R. 11 App. Cas. 97 (H. L. 1885.)

Weight of English decisions. In view of the fact that this paragraph is copied almost literally from the English act of 1854, it may be well to again mention the rule that the settled construction of the statute by the English courts is either considered as silently incorporated into the present statute, or will be received with all the weight of authority. (*McDonald* v. *Hovey*, 110 U. S. 619, and cases cited *supra*, p. 29.)

What amounts to an undue preference is a question of fact and not of law. (*Diphwys, etc., Co.* v. *Festiniog Ry. Co.*, 2 Nev. & Mac. 73; *Watkinson* v. *Wrexham, etc., R. Co.*, 3 Nev. & Mac. Ry. Cas. 5; *Denaby Main Colliery Co.* v. *Manchester, etc., Co.*, 3 Nev. & Mac. 441.)

As was said by Lord Chancellor Selborne, in *Denaby, etc., Co.* v. *Manchester, etc., R. Co.*: "Unless you could point to some other law which defines what shall be held to be reasonable or unreasonable, it must be and is a mere question, not of law, but of fact." (3 Nev. & Mac. 441.)

Interests of company. In determining whether a regulation of a railway company operates as an undue preference or advantage, the fair interests of the company are to be taken into account. (*Ransome* v. *Eastern Co.'s Ry. Co.* (No. 1), 1 C. B. (N. S.) 437; 26 L. J. C. P.

91; 1 Nev. & Mac. 63; *Nicholson* v. *Gt. Western Ry. Co.*, 1 Nev. & Mac. 121; *s. c.*, 5 C. B. (N. S.) 366.)

Rates as well as facilities. The provisions of section 2 of the Railway and Canal Traffic Act, 1854, as to undue preferences and advantages, are held to apply to rates or charges, as well as to facilities. (*Denaby, etc., Co.* v. *Manchester, etc., Ry. Co.*, L. R. 11 App. Cas. 97; *London & N. W. Ry. Co.* v. *Evershed*, L. R. 3 App. Cas. 1029; *Macfarlane* v. *Ry. Co.* (No. 2), 4 Ry. & Can. Traf. Cas. 269.)

A railway company, if it makes illegal or excessive charges for the conveyance of traffic, subjects such traffic to undue prejudice within the meaning of section 2 Railway and Canal Traffic Act, 1854. (*Aberdeen Co.* v. *Gt. North, etc., Ry. Co.*, 3 Nev. & Mac. Ry. Cas. 205 (Court of Session of Scotland.)

"**Group rates**"—**The Denaby Main Colliery Company cases.** Among all the cases that have arisen under the English statutes, the case of the *Denaby Main Colliery Co.* v. *The Manchester, Sheffield and Lincolnshire Ry. Co.*, in its various phases, is one of the most instructive. The case in its several stages presented the question of the legality of "group-rates," which were similar to what is known in our practice as Missouri river rates, Ohio river rates, etc., making the rates from or to a group of cities from or to a common point the same, without reference to the actual distance between them; the question of difference in circumstances growing out of a difference in cost to the carrier, and also an effort to develop a new trade; what amounts to an undue preference. etc.

The case first arose in July, 1880, upon an application under section 2 of the Railway and Canal Traffic Act, 1854, to the railway commissioners, and was directed against the "group rates," or a uniform rate for an entire coal district or coal field, some of the collieries in which were some twenty miles apart. The railway commissioners found that the "group rates" operated as an undue prejudice to the Denaby Company, and enjoined the railroad company from their continuance. The syllabus is as follows:

As a general rule, charges on traffic using the same railway under the same circumstances ought to be after the same rate per ton per mile, but the rule is not so rigid that any scale that is not in conformity with it is illegal, nor are charges that are unequal, or cause prejudice or disadvantage, prohibited by section 2 of the Railway and Canal Traffic Act, 1854, unless they act in that way unduly and unreasonably.

A railway company charged a uniform rate for traffic from an entire district or coal-field; the collieries were grouped because they all worked the same bed of coal, and the grouping applied compulsorily to a coal-field extending 20 miles, and covering an area in which some of the collieries were that distance apart. Collieries in one part of such district paid no higher rate than collieries in another for their coal traffic to any particular station, all alike paying one uniform rate, irrespective of any difference in their actual distances from such station.

Upon complaint by a colliery company in the district that the effect of the uniform rate was to subject their coal to a higher charge per ton per mile than coal from other collieries, and to deprive them of the advantage of their greater proximity to places to which the coal was sent, it was proved that the applicants were charged the same rate for conveyance of their coal to a particular station as was charged for coal sent from other collieries in the same district, although the addittonal distance to be run was ten or fifteen miles. *Held*, that the grouping system, as it affected the applicants, subjected them to an undue and unreasonable prejudice and disadvantage, and that the railway company ought to carry the applicants' coal at a rate per ton per mile not exceeding that charged to other coal owners of the district; in ascertaining the mileage rate an allowance of 1s. per ton in all cases being first made for fixed expenses. (*Denaby, etc., Co.* v. *Manchester, etc., Ry. Co.*, 3 Nev. & Mac. 426.)

The commissioners subsequently declined to state a case for the opinion of a superior court, holding that the question as to whether the rates constituted an undue prejudice was a question of fact and not of law, and therefore, under the statutes, was vested exclusively in them for determination. (*Ib.*, page 435.) Afterward, the counsel for the railway company applied to the Queen's Bench Division for a rule for prohibition to the railway commissioners to prohibit them from proceeding further on the order made by them, or for a mandamus to compel the commissioners to state a case for the opinion of a superior court. The court (Field and Manisty, JJ.) denied both applications, also holding that the question was one of fact and not of law. (*Ib.*, pages 438–440.) An appeal was then taken to the Court of Appeal, and the appeal upon both branches was refused, the court consisting of Lord Chancellor Selborne and Lord Justices Baggallay and Brett. Prohibition being refused on the ground that it was clear that the parties and subject-matter were within the jurisdiction of the railway commissioners. As to the mandamus, "the sole ground alleged must be that on some matter of law a question has arisen before the railway commissioners upon which the railway company has a right to have a case stated," but the question in the case, he continued, is "altogether a question of fact. It is admitted that if the preference is constituted by a railway company carrying for certain colliery proprietors on more favorable terms than for others, *prima facie* that fact was proved, because beyond question, they did carry upon the same terms as a charge for the collieries for which they performed more than the same services. They gave a decided, distinct, and great advantage, as it appears to me, to the distant collieries. That may be due or undue, reasonable or unreasonable, but under those circumstances is not the reasonableness a question of fact? . . . Unless you can point to some other law which defines what shall be held to be reasonable or unreasonable, it must be, and is, a mere question, not of law but of fact." (Lord Chancellor Selborne, 3 Nev. & Mac. Ry. Ca. 441.)

In July, 1881, an application was made to the railway commissioners to review their decision, nominally presented in behalf of the railway company, but really in behalf of the colliery proprietors, in whose interest the group rates were made, showing the injury that the decision of the commissioners had wrought to their business, but the railway commissioners re-affirmed their former decision. (4 Ry. & Can. Traf. Cas. 23.)

In November, 1881, the case again came before the railway commissioners as to the rates over certain canals owned by the railway company, and in which they had made a difference of $\frac{1}{2}d.$ per ton per mile. The railway commissioners found that this difference in charge was wholly disproportioned to the difference in the distance, and therefore an undue prejudice to the Denaby Company, and granted an injunction as follows:

Upon complaint by the D. Colliery Company that the toll charged for coal sent from their colliery by canal to K. was greater in proportion to the distance than the toll charged upon coal similarly sent by other colliery proprietors whose collieries were also situated in or near the same canal, but at a distance from K. exceeding by several miles the distance therefrom of the D. colliery, it appeared that the toll charged on coal to K. from the D. colliery was 13$d.$, and from the other collieries 13$\frac{1}{2}d.$, and that the coal traffic on the canal between the D. colliery and K. was worked with less expense and trouble to the canal owners than the traffic between the other collieries and K.; *Held*, that the D. Colliery Company were subjected to an undue and unreasonable prejudice and disadvantage by being charged a toll only one-half penny less in amount than the toll charged to the other colliery proprietors. (*Denaby, etc., Co. v. Manchester, etc., Ry. Co.*, 4 Ry. & Can. Traf. Cas. 28.)

The other case arose in this wise: The railroad company brought an action against the Denaby Colliery Company for a balance of carriage account, to which the defendant interposed a counter-claim for overcharges. This counter-claim for overcharges included other matters than those which had been before the railway commissioners. In the Queen's Bench Division the court held that an action for damages did not lie for the breach of the Railway and Canal Traffic Act, 1854, § 2, but held that there had been a breach of the Railway Clauses Consolidation Act, 1845, § 90, for which an action could be maintained. (4 Ry. & Can. Traf. Cas. 437.) Upon appeal by both plaintiff and defendant, the Court of Appeal affirmed the judgment of the Queen's Bench Division as to the Act of 1854, and reversed it as to the Act of 1845, holding that the facts of the case did not constitute a breach of section 90 of that Act. (*Manchester, etc., Ry. Co.* v. *Denaby, etc., Co.*, 4 Ry. & Can. Traf. Cas. 450.)

Upon appeal to the House of Lords, the decision of the Court of Appeal was affirmed in part and reversed in part (*Denaby, etc., Co.* v. *Manchester, etc., Ry. Co.*, L. R. 11 App. Cas. 97), the official syllabus stating:

"*Held*, also, that in this case an action did not lie for breach of section 2 of the Railway and Canal Traffic Act, 1854 (17 and 18 Vict., c. 31), undue or unreasonable preference or prejudice not having been made out.

"*Quaere*, whether under any circumstances an action lies for breach of that section."

The opinions show, though, that Lords Blackburn and Fitzgerald and the Earl of Selborne held that no action for damages could be maintained in any case for a violation of section 2 of the Railway and Canal Traffic Act, 1854, the only remedy being by injunction (L. R. 11 App. Cas. 113, 121, and the Act in Appendix, *post*), while Lord Chancellor Halsbury reserved his opinion upon the question. (*Ib.*, p. 112.) Intimations are given of doubts as to the correctness of the decisions of the Railway Commissioners upon the "group rates" (*Ib.*, p. 114), but a careful examination of each opinion has failed to reveal any explicit disapproval of their holding; and, in view of the fact that the question came before them only upon a counter-claim for damages, and the majority ruling that no action for damages could be maintained even for an acknowledged breach of the statute, it is not seen how the question of the legality of the "group rates" could properly be considered in the case.

It is to be noted with reference to the "group rates" of which the Denaby Company complained that they applied only one way—as to points to which it was nearest—while in the other direction, from which they would have been benefited, the "group rates" did not prevail.

A difference in the distance the traffic is carried is not of itself a valid answer to a complaint of undue preference under section 2 of the Railway and Canal Traffic Act, 1854, and no conclusive inference is to be drawn either on the one hand from a railway company not carrying at an equal mileage rate, or not making an equal profit per mile, or, on the other hand, from the rate for the longer distance, though less per mile amounting to more for the whole distance, or leaving a larger sum as profit after payment of expenses; and in determining the question whether the lower mileage rate is or is not an undue advantage, it is necessary to consider whether either traffic is able to be carried at a less cost to the railway company than the other, or whether either traffic is under different conditions as regards competition of routes or other special circumstances. (*Broughton, etc. Coal Co.* v. *G. W. Ry. Co.*, 4 Ry. & Can. Traf. Cas. 191.)

A railway company carried coal to B. from the N. W. collieries, an average distance of thirty miles, at an average rate of 2*s*. 2*d*. per ton, and from the S. W. collieries, an average distance of 156 miles, at a uniform rate of 6*s*. per ton. Upon a complaint by the N. W. colliery owners that the rates charged for their coal to B. were an undue prejudice to that traffic by reason of the lower rate at which S. W. coal was carried: Found, as a matter of fact, that the cost of conveyance to the railway company of coal from S. W. was not proportionately less than from N. W., and that a competition existed between such coal at B. sufficient to lay the foundation for a charge of undue prejudice, provided damage had accrued to the complainants as a consequence of the relative rates complained of; but that there was no evidence of such damage, the complainants not having shown that their output of coal was in excess of the demand, nor that they could not find a market for all their coal at existing rates:—*Held*, that the carriage of such N. W. and S. W. coal to B. by the railway company at unequal rates per ton per mile was not an undue prejudice to the complainants. (*Ib.*)

This case is distinguished from the *Denaby case* (3 Nev. & Mac. 426) by the fact that no special damage is shown; while in the *Denaby case* there was, it appearing that the output was in excess of the demand for their coal. (4 Ry. & Can. Traf. Cas. 203.)

Upon complaint by a trader that he was subjected to an undue prejudice, within the meaning of section 2 of the Railway and Canal Traffic Act, 1854, because he was charged the same through rates to certain places, for traffic from his siding, as was charged for traffic from a siding situated two or three miles further from them. Both sidings were situated in the same district, and had been grouped together by the railway company for through rate purposes.

Held, that as a through rate was a gross sum of a small amount for conveyance over a long route, it was enough if places that were practically in the same district had the same rate, and that no undue prejudice was caused to the applicant by the same rate being applicable to both sidings. (*Lloyd* v. *Northampton, etc., R. Co.*, 3 Nev. & Mac. 259.)

A railway company established a system of carrying coals according to assigned districts, comprising certain places on their lines and branches, carrying them within those several districts at certain lower rates for quantities not less than a train load of 200 tons. The complainants, who were coal dealers at Ipswich, also carried on that business at N. S., E. T., and B., also at M. and D., which are on another branch line communicating with that first mentioned, and also at H., which is in another district branch. These districts are so adjusted that the places where the complainants dealt were distributed into three of them, so that in order to take advantage of the reduced rates the complainants would have to send from Ipswich three full train loads, which was a larger quantity than they could profitably send to those districts, and thus they sustained great injury; whereas, the rival dealers at Peterborough, by reason of one of the assigned districts embracing seven of those places at which the complainants dealt, were enabled to send their coals in such quantities as to avail themselves of the reduction. It being sworn on the part of the company that these districts were adjusted, not with a view to give an undue preference to the one set of dealers over the other, but solely with regard to their own convenience and the wants of the neighborhood: *Held*, that the complaint was not sustained. (*Ransome* v. *Eastern Counties Ry. Co.*, 4 C. B. (N. S.) 135; 4 Jur. (N. S.) 282; 27 L. J., C. P. 166; 1 Nev. & Mac. 109; but see note 7 on page 115 of 1 Nev. & Mac., and Williams, J., in *Ransome case* No. 4 (1 Nev. & Mac. 160–1), where it is suggested that this decision proceeded on mistaken grounds.)

And where it appeared that the railway company was in the habit of carrying coals along the line, belonging to various owners, who competed to supply the population along the line, and by the tariff of charges published by the company, and approved by the Court of Common Pleas, lower rates were charged for the carriage of all coal consigned to places along the line, which were distributed into districts, in quantities of 200 tons at a time, and such population was supplied with inland coal from Peterborough, and with seaborne coal from Ipswich, situated in No. 8 district:—*Held*, that it was no undue preference to the Peterborough owners, and no undue disadvantage to the Ipswich owners, if the company, starting from S. with coal trains of 200 tons each, should habitually break off portions of those trains at C., in their progress to the No. 8 district, leaving such portions of trains at C., whilst the residue went on to its original destination, the parts left at C. being always sent on by detachments of fewer than 200 tons each, and the lower rates being charged for such detachments; the tariff being valid it was immaterial how the company carried the coals most conveniently to themselves, provided the tariff was not infringed. (*Ransome* v. *Eastern Co.'s Ry. Co.* (No. 4) 8 C. B. (N. S.) 709; 7 Jur. (N. S.) 99; 29 L. J., C. P. 329; 8 W. R. 527; 2 L. T., (N. S.) 376; 1 Nev. & Mac. 155.)

A railway company classified the coal on one branch at a gas coal rate and a common coal rate. No such classification was made on the other branch. Canal coal was the only coal shipped by the complainants, and was the only coal charged at the "gas coal rate," "splint coal" being classed as common coal. Gas is produced from splint coal, but from inferior quality and quantity as compared with canal coal, but both are used in different proportions for mixing with common coal in the manufacture of gas. The commissioners found that they were commercially and substantially of the same description so as to be competitive, and that the classification was an undue prejudice to the complainant. (*Nitshill, etc., Coal Co.* v. *Caledonian Ry. Co.*, 2 Nev. & Mac. 39.)

Natural advantages—Company can not destroy. Every one has a right to the natural advantages which have been acquired by the proximity of his land to a railway, and a railway company is not justified in depriving him of it, by allowing to another not so favorably situated the expense which the latter has incurred in connecting his place with the railway, in the reduced charge at which they carry his goods on their railway. (*Harris* v. *Cockermouth & Workington Railway Company*, 3 C. B. (N. S.) 693; 4 Jur. (N. S.) 239; 27 L. J., C. P. 162; 1 Nev & Mac. 97.)

The company made a scale of charges for the carriage of coals from Peterborough and Ipswich respectively, to various places, the effect of which was to diminish the natural advantages which the Ipswich dealers possessed over those of Peterborough, from their greater proximity to those places, by annihilating (in point of expense of carriage), in favor of the latter, a certain portion of the distance between Peterborough and those places: *Held*, an undue preference of the Peterborough dealers over those of Ipswich. (*Ransome* v. *Eastern Co.'s Ry.*

Co. (No. 2), 4 C. B. (N. S.) 135; 4 Jur. (N. S.) 282; 27 L. J. C. P. 166; 1 Nev. & Mac. 109.)

The court refused to grant an attachment against a railroad company for disobedience to a writ of injunction under the Railway and Canal Traffic Act, 1854, enjoining them to desist from giving an undue preference, in the respect of the carriage of coals, to persons carrying coals from P. or other places, to or toward certain places mentioned in the rules—the affidavits on the part of the company showing a *bona fide* endeavor on their part to conform to the order of the court—although it appeared that the reformed scale of charges still operated in some other respects injuriously to the interests of the complainants, and advantageously to the other parties. (*Ransome* v. *Eastern Co.'s Ry. Co.* (No. 3) 4 C. B. (N. S.) 159; 1 Nev. & Mac. 116; but see *Ransome* v. *Same Co.* (No. 4), 1 Nev. & Mac. 155, 160, Williams, J.)

Competition with other lines. In order to compete with rival railway companies, the defendants gratuitously carted certain goods of A., B. and C., and also allowed them a rebate which the rival companies allowed in consequence of A., B. and C. having sidings in connection with the lines of their railways. *Held*, in an action brought by D., a person in the same trade, who was charged for cartage and allowed no rebate, to be an undue preference. (*London & N. W. Ry. Co.* v. *Evershed*, L. R. 3 App. Cas. 1029.)

A manufactory of plaintiff was situate twelve miles from the seaport of Swansea, and on the defendant's railway from that seaport to Liverpool. The defendants charged the plaintiff 12*s.* 6*d.* per ton for the carriage of iron and tin plates over their line from his manufactory to Liverpool, while other manufacturers of iron and tin plates whose works were situate within a radius of six miles of the seaport of Swansea, and further, therefore, from Liverpool than the plaintiff's works, were charged by the defendants for the carriage of their plates from Swansea to Liverpool 11*s.* 4*d.* per ton only. There is a communication by sea between Swansea and Liverpool, and the rate of 11*s.* 4*d.* was fixed by the defendants as the charge for the carriage of the goods of these manufacturers within the six mile radius in order to enable the defendants to **compete** with the **sea carriage**; and by reason of the lesser charge, those manufacturers who were thus favored were enabled to sell their plates at a lower price per ton, delivered at Liverpool, than the plaintiff. *Held*, that the charging of a lower rate to the manufacturers within the six mile radius, for the carriage of their goods a longer distance than the plaintiff's, was an undue and unreasonable preference and advantage granted to them by the defendants, and was in contravention of section 2 of the Railway and Canal Traffic

Act, 1854, and the plaintiff was entitled to recover the amounts paid by him to the defendants in excess of the 11*s*. 4*d*. rate. (*Budd* v. *London & N. W. Ry.*, 36 L. T. (N. S.) 802; 25 W. R. 752; 4 Ry. & Can. Traf. Cas. 393.)

A company made an agreement with A. to carry for him coals during three years, from Petersborough to various places on their line of railway, at certain rates. B., a coal merchant at Ipswich, sent coals (which had been brought to that port by sea) to various places on the same lines of railway, and the company charged him a much larger sum per ton in proportion to the distance over which his coals were carried than the company charged to A.; the professed object of the difference being to enable A. (whose coal came to Peterborough by railway) to compete in the coal trade of the district with B., who had the advantage of having his coals brought to Ipswich by sea. *Held*, that this was giving an undue preference to A., and the company was required to carry coal for B. on equal terms with A., due regard being had to any circumstances rendering the cost of carrying for one less than for the other. (*Ransome* v. *Eastern Co.'s Ry. Co.*, 1 C. B. (N. S.) 437; 3 Jur. (N. S.) 217; 26 L. J. C. P. 91; 1 Nev. & Mac. 63.)

The N. W. Railway Company carried goods by their railway for the complainants, who were brewers at B. They charged the complainants, and the public generally, 1*s*. per ton for the cartage of goods to and from their B. station, and 9*d*. per ton for terminal services there.

T. & Co. and C. & Co., who were also brewers at B., had breweries connected with the M. Railway Company's station at that place by continuous railway communication; the goods which they sent or received by the M. line were loaded and unloaded on their own premises by their servants, and they were consequently not charged by the M. Railway Company any rate for cartage or terminal services.

The N. W. Railway Company, in order to compete with the M. Railway Company for the carriage of the goods of T. & Co. and C. & Co., exempted them from the above mentioned rates of 1*s*. 9*d*. respectively, carting and loading their goods gratuitously. There being nothing to show that there was a saving of cost to the company by reason of the quantity of goods carried for T. & Co. and C. & Co., to compensate for the loss of 1*s*. 9*d*. per ton, and T. & Co. and C. & Co. being the only firms to whom the reduced rates were applicable.

Held, that there was not a sufficient ground for the arrangements made in their favor, and that an injunction should issue against the N. W. Railway Company, under the 3d section of the Railway and Canal Traffic Act, 1854.

In order to justify a difference being made by a railway company in favor of one or more individual members of their general class of customers, there must be an adequate consideration to the railroad company lessening the cost to them of the services rendered to such individual members of the general class, and it is not sufficient that the railway company merely desire to attract the traffic from another line to themselves, especially where the favor thus shown to a few is prejudicial to many others in the same trade as the favored persons.

The railway company having acted *bona fide* in the matter, and with no intention of prejudicing the complainants as rivals in trade with others, the injunction was granted without costs. (*Thompson et al.* v. *The London, etc., Ry. Co.*, 2 Nev. & Mac. 115; see notes to § 2, p. 56 *et seq., ante.*) For a further discussion of the subject of competition, see notes to § 2, *ante*, p. 55 *et seq.*, and § 4, *infra*, p. 127.

Developing business. The North-eastern Railway Company, from a desire to introduce the northern coke into Staffordshire, made special agreements with certain merchants for the carriage of coal and coke at a lower rate than their ordinary charge; there being nothing to show that the pecuniary interests of the company were affected: *Held*, that the lowering of the rate for this traffic was giving it an undue prefference. (*Oxlade* v. *North-eastern Ry. Co.* (No. 1), 1 C. B. (N. S.) 454; 3 Jur. (N. S.) 637; 26 L. J. C. P. 129; 1 Nev. & Mac. 72.)

Carrying coals from a colliery along a railway at a lower rate of charges than coals from other coal-pits situate in the same locality, in consequence of a threat from the owner of the colliery to construct another railway, by which the traffic would have been diverted if the railway company had not consented to carry at such lower rate, is an undue preference by the railway company. (*Harris* v. *Cockermouth & Workington Ry. Co.*, 3 C. B. (N. S.) 693; 4 Jur. (N. S.) 239; 27 L. J. C. P. 162; 1 Nev. & Mac. 97; *Diphwys* v. *Festiniog Ry. Co.*, 2 Nev. & Mac. 73.)

Contract to furnish shipper's entire freight. A railway company, with the object of discouraging the construction of a competing line, carried slate for certain quarry owners, who agreed to send all their slate over the railway company's line for a fixed number of years at a less rate than they charged for the same service to the complainant quarry owners who were offered, but refused to bind themselves by such an agreement.

Held, that this was an undue preference within the meaning of the Railway and Canal Traffic Act, 1854, § 2. (*Diphwys, etc., Co.* v. *Fes-*

tiniog Ry. Co., 2 Nev. & Mac. 73; *Scofield* v. *Ry. Co.*, 43 Ohio St. 571; *Baxendale* v. *G. W. Ry. Co.*, 5 C. B. (N. S.) 309; *Menacho* v. *Ward*, 27 Fed. Rep. 529.)

A railway company agreed with certain quarry owners, for a term of fourteen years, to carry slates for them over the railway at rates varying from 3*s*. 3*d*. to 2*s*. 6*d*. per ton, according to the total quantity of slates carried by the railway company in each year, the quarry owners on their part agreeing to send their slates by no other mode of transit during that term; subsequently a fresh agreement was entered into with one of the quarry owners for a term of thirty years, reducing the rate to 2*s*. 1½*d*.

Upon an application for an injunction by quarry owners, parties to the original agreement, *held*, that there was nothing in the consideration as to the exclusive use of the railway, being in the one case for thirty years, and in the other for fourteen years, which would justify the difference between 2*s*. 6*d*. and 2*s*. 1½*d*. as charges for railway transit, and that such difference was an undue preference and prejudice within the meaning of the Railway and Canal Traffic Act, 1854. (*Holland* v. *Festiniog Ry. Co.*, 2 Nev. & Mac. 278.)

A preference with respect to a reduced rate of carriage of certain goods given by a railway company to certain individuals, in consideration of their contracting to have all such goods consigned to them through the railway, and not by water or other means, is an undue preference within the Railway and Canal Traffic Act, 1854, unless it be clearly shown that it is done in order to prevent a competition with the railway, or that there is secured thereby to the company such an amount of traffic as to compensate for making the reduced rate. (*Garton* v. *Bristol, etc., Ry. Co.*, 1 Nev. & Mac. 218; 6 C. B. (N. S.) 639; 28 L. J., C. P. 306.)

Employment of other lines. It is not a legitimate ground for giving a preference to one customer of a railway company that he engages to employ other lines of the company for the carriage of traffic distinct from and unconnected with the goods in question, and it is undue and unreasonable to charge more or less for the same service according as the customer of the railway thinks proper or not, to bind himself to employ the company in other and totally distinct business, the advantage of carrying goods to other points not affecting the cost of carriage between the particular points. (*Baxendale* v. *G. W. Ry. Co.* (*Bristol case*), 5 C. B. (N. S.) *309; 1 Nev. & Mac. 191; 28 L. J. C. P. 69; 4 Jur. (N. S.) 1241; see *Scofield* v. *Railway Co.*, 43 O. S. 571; *Twells* v. *Railroad Co.*, 3 Am. Law Reg. (N. S.) 728.)

It is not a valid consideration for a reduced rate that the party favored is a customer also of the same railway company in goods of a quite different kind. (*Bellsdyke Coal Co.* v. *North British Ry. Co.*, 2 Nev. & Mac. 105.)

A railway or canal company can not charge a higher wharfage rate on goods about to be conveyed by the railway of another company than on goods about to be conveyed on their own railway. (*Toomer* v. *London, etc., R. Co.*, 3 Nev. & Mac. 79.)

Cost of service. The general rate of charge for the carriage of goods from Bristol to Bridgewater, and *vice versa*, was 6s. 8d. per ton for first class; 8s. 4d. for second class; 12s. 6d. per ton for third class; and 16s. 8d. per ton for fourth class goods. The company had special contracts with certain grocers and ironmongers at Bridgewater, under which they agreed to carry all their grocery and ironmongery goods at a uniform rate of 6s. per ton, including delivery. *Held*, an undue preference, it not appearing that this diminished charge was justified by any special circumstances of advantage to the company, or to meet competition by another railway or any other mode of carriage. (*Garton* v. *Bristol and Exeter Railway Company*, 6 C. B. (N. S.) 639; 5 Jur (N. S.) 1313; 28 L. J., C. P. 306; 1 Nev. & Mac. 218.)

A railway company is justified in carrying goods for one person at a less rate than that at which the company carries the same description of goods for another, if there are circumstances which render the cost to the company of carrying for the former less than the cost of carrying for the latter. (*Oxlade* v. *North-eastern Ry. Co.* (No. 1), 1 C. B. (N. S.) 454; 3 Jur. (N. S.) 637; 26 L. J., C. P. 129; 1 Nev. & Mac. 72.)

A railway company entered into an agreement with a firm of colliery owners to carry their coal at certain rates lower than those charged to other colliery owners, with whom they had no agreement. The railway company attempted to justify the preference on the ground that the traffic not covered by the agreement was more costly to carry in consequence of a steep descending incline from the collieries to the main line. The higher rate was imposed whichever direction the coal traffic took, while it passed down the incline in going in one direction only.

Held, that a charge purporting to be in respect of a special service— such as in respect of the incline—should not have its incidence extended to traffic for which that service was not performed, and that payment in respect of such incline should, under the circumstances, take the form of a fixed reasonable toll payable only for the traffic using the incline.

A railway company pays no more than a due regard to its own interests if it charges for its services in proportion to their necessary cost, and has only such a variation in its rates as there is in the circumstances of its customers affecting the cost and labor of conveyance. (*Bellsdyke Coal Co.* v. *N. B. Ry. Co.*, 2 Nev. & Mac. 105.)

If by reason of the gradients or otherwise the cost of conveyance of the coal to the railway company on the one branch was different from the cost on the other, a proportionate difference might be made by the railway company in the mileage rate. (*Nitshill, etc., Coal Co.* v. *Caledonian Ry. Co.*, 2 Nev. & Mac. 39.) See, further, notes to § 2, *supra*, p. 48 *et seq.*)

Quantity of freight shipped. The 17 and 18 Vict., c. 31, s. 2, is not contravened by a railway company carrying at a lower rate, in consideration of a guaranty of large quantities and full train loads at regular periods, provided the real object of the company is to obtain thereby a greater remunerative profit by the diminished cost of carriage, although the effect may be to exclude from the lower rate those persons who can not give such a guaranty. (*Nicholson* v. *Great Western Railway Company*, 5 C. B. (N. S.) 366; 4 Jur. (N. S.) 1187; 28 L. J., C. P. 89; 1 Nev. & Mac. 121; but see *s. c.*, 1 Nev. & Mac. 143; 7 C. B. (N. S.) 755.) See this subject fully considered in note to § 2, *supra*, p. 50 *et seq.*)

Diversion of traffic. There were two routes between C. & C. A., the N. W. route and G. W. route. The G. W. Co. having in their own hands at the outset traffic consigned by the N. W. route to and from C. & C. A., sometimes diverted such traffic, and carried it by their own route, and at other times caused undue delay in the delivery thereof at C.: *Held*, ground of complaint and injunction granted. (*Cent. Wales, etc., Ry. Co.* v. *G. W. Ry. Co.*, 2 Nev. & Mac. 191.)

Through rates. The granting of through rates to steamboat owners at other ports, and the refusal of such rates to a steamboat owner at a particular port, is not an undue preference of which either the steamboat owner or the harbor board at the latter port can complain under section 2 of the Railway and Canal Traffic Act, 1854. A harbor board can not apply for through rates under section 11 of the Regulation of Railways Act, 1873.

Semble, a railway company can not make a distinction in its rates for the same railway journey, according as the traffic is booked no further than it goes by railway, or is booked to a destination beyond the limits within which the traffic act is applicable, *e. g.*, to places across the sea where section 2 of the act has not been extended to the carriage by water. (*Ayr Harbour Trustees, etc.*, v. *Glasgow Ry. Co.*, 4 Ry. & Can. Traf. Cas. 81.)

§ 3, PAR. 1.]　　　INTER-STATE COMMERCE ACT.　　　81

— **Two lines.** Steamers were provided and worked for the conveyance of mails and passengers between Holyhead and Kingston by D. Steamboat Company, under statutory powers and agreements obtained and made between that company and N. W. Railway Company. It was agreed that the charges for the conveyance of passenger traffic by such route (called the mail route) between Kingstown and London, etc., should be fixed as regards the through rates by N. W. Railway Company. The N. W. Railway Company subsequently established a service of steamers for passengers between Holyhead and the North Wall in Dublin (called the North Wall route).

The effect of the statutory agreement between the two companies was to give N. W. Railway Company as complete control over the fares of both routes, as if they were sole owners of both, and therefore the provisions of the Railway and Canal Traffic Act, 1854 (which were made expressly applicable to both those lines of steamers) applied to both routes as if they had been parts of the same system.

The N. W. Railway Company's service of steamers was almost equal to the mail service in point of speed and accommodation, and its fares were much lower. The first and second class passengers, who were charged 60s. and 45s. respectively between Euston and Dublin by the mail route, being only charged 47s. 6d. and 36s. 6d. by the North Wall route, a difference of 12s. 6d. and 8s. 6d. respectively. The service over the distance between Holyhead and Dublin were substantially the same; the mileages (adding the railway from Kingstown to Dublin) were nearly equal; the accommodation by the North Wall route was practically as good as that by the mail route, and the vessels of the two companies were worked at about the same cost. The mail through fares were divided by mileage and the N. W. Railway Company received for their land portion of the through service 46s. 10d. out of the first class fare, and 35s. 3d. out of the second class.

In both cases they carried the passengers the same distance by railway, but the passengers to and from North Wall traveled in addition by the railway company's steamboat.

Their boat fare was 8s. first or second class, and they received, therefore, in respect of the North Wall passengers, 39s. 6d. first class, and 28s. 6d. second class for railway fare from London to Holyhead, as against 46s. 10d. and 35s. 3d. for the same railway journey, with only the difference in the class of trains, in respect of the mail route passengers: *Held,* that the amounts by which the fares by the mail route were thus more than those by North Wall route (whether in regard to the fares charged for the entire service to Dublin or the portions due to the land journey only) were excessive and an undue prejudice to the traffic by the former route, and that the circumstances did not justify an excess in the total fares to Dublin by the mail route of more than, at the outside, ten per cent. (*Dublin Steam Pack. Co.* v. *London, etc., Ry. Co.*, 4 Ry. & Can. Traf. Cas. 10.)

The rates charged by railway companies for traffic to ports, where such traffic is to be carried from such ports to others, must be relatively to the service equal. (*Ayr Harbour Trustees* v. *Glasgow Ry. Co., etc.*, 4 Ry. & Can. Traf. Cas. 90.)

Through tickets. The S. Steamboat Company and the R. Steamboat Company respectively owned passenger steamboats plying between S. and R., and the B. and S. W. railway companies carried passengers by their own lines to S.; and having entered into a traffic arrangement with the R. Steamboat Company that their vessels should run between S. and R. in connection with the lines of railway companies, issued through tickets to passengers from places on their lines to R., available by the boats of the R. Steamboat Company, to the exclusion of the boats of the S. Steamboat Company.

Held, that, under the circumstances, this arrangement did not amount to an undue preference of the R. Steamboat Company. (*Southsea, etc., Ferry Co.* v. *London, etc., Ry. Co.*, 2 Nev. & Mac. 341.)

Held, that section 2 of the Railway and Canal Traffic Act, which prohibits undue and unreasonable preferences, or advantages, being given by railways and canal companies to particular persons, did not apply to the case of arrangements made by a railway company, whose line terminates at the sea, with a steamboat owner for carrying across the sea goods and passengers, brought by the railway, and the railway company is not bound to extend to other steamboats the same facilities as to through rates, etc., as it extends to the steamboat it selects to transact its business. (*Napier* v. *Glasgow, etc., Ry. Co., etc.*, 1 Nev. & Mac. 292; 4 Sess. Ca. 87 (3 Ser.))

Two lines—Through service, etc. Under a working agreement by which the working company is to work the railway of the worked company as part of their system of railways, and " convey traffic thereon in a proper and convenient manner, and so as fairly to develop the traffic of the district :"

1. The trains on the worked line must be timed, so as to correspond with the trains on the lines of the working company rather than with the trains of another company with which they might be made to connect.

2. The working company must as fully advertise a competitive

route over the line of the worked company as they do the route on their own line which competes with it.

3. The working company must give equal facilities as to through booking via the worked line, as via their own, must not prefer their own route in the matter of rates, and must not fix the rates on the worked line too high in proportion to the rates on their own line. In failing to do any of these things the working company would subject the traffic of traders desirous of using the worked line to an undue and unreasonable prejudice. (*Clonmel Traders* v. *Waterford Ry. Co.*, 4 Ry. and Can. Traf. Cas. 92.)

Facilities and rates to carriers and other shippers—Delivering goods on general orders. Where a railway company employed an agent to receive goods arriving at the Cirencester station and deliver them to the consignees in the town, and refused to deliver at the station to carriers who had general written orders from persons in the town, authorizing delivery of all goods arriving for them, but required written orders specifying the goods, the court held that there was an undue preference of the company's agent, and enjoined the company to act on the general orders. (*Parkinson* v. *Great Western Ry. Co.*, 40 L. J. C. P. 222; 6 L. R. C. P. 554; 24 L. T. (N. S.) 830; 19 W. R. 1063; 1 Nev. & Mac. 280.)

F. &. Co., carriers, delivered to a railway company at their station goods for conveyance addressed to the consignees. With such goods a consignment note was handed to the railway company containing in addition to the names and address of the consignees the words "To the care of F. & Co."

The railway company refused to recognize the latter words, and delivered the goods to the consignees by their own agents or other carriers.

Held, that the words "To the care of F. & Co." imported that the goods on their arrival at the terminal stations were to be given to F. & Co. or their agents for delivery to the consignees; that as between the railway company and F. & Co., the latter were the consignors, and that the railway company accepted the goods upon the terms stated in the consignment note; and that the railway company were precluded by the consignment note from being at liberty to employ their own or other carriers to deliver the goods from their railway to the consignees, and should have delivered the same to F. & Co. or their agents. (*Fishbourne etc.*, v. *Great S. & W. Ry. Co.*, 2 Nev. & Mac. 224.)

Where customers had left orders with a railway company to deliver to W., a carrier, all goods addressed or consigned to them, and also where goods had come addressed to consignees of W. in his care, and in both cases the company refused to deliver the goods to W., but delivered them to others, who acted as the agent of the company: *Held*, that such conduct was not a violation of any right of W. either at common law or under Railway and Canal Traffic Act, 1854. (*Wannan* v. *Scottish Cent. Ry. Co.*, 2 Sess. Cas. 1373 (3d. Ser.); 1 Nev. & Mac. 237; but see *Parkinson* v. *G. W. Ry. Co.*, *supra*.)

A railway company which employed agents for delivering in a large town goods brought by the railway to the parties to whom they were addressed, arranged within the station the goods to be delivered by these agents, and afforded to them other facilities in the use of the station: *Held*, that the company, in refusing to give the same advantages to carriers to whom goods were consigned, were not guilty of a contravention of the provisions of the Railway and Canal Traffic Act.

A railway company receiving from another railway company goods addressed by the sender to A. B., Argyle street, Glasgow, is not bound to regard markings by the latter company in the way-bill or invoice as to the carriers to be employed in the delivery. (*Pickford* v. *Caledonian Ry. Co.*, etc., 1 Nev. & Mac. 252; 4 Sess. Cas. 755 (3d Ser.); but see *Parkinson* v. *G. W. Ry. Co.*, *supra*.)

— **Receiving and delivering goods, etc.** A railway company, with a view to compete with other carriers in the collection and carriage of goods, established receiving-offices in various parts of London, from which goods were brought in vans to the railway station. The gates of the station were closed against the vans of the complainant and other carriers at 6:30 P. M., but the company's own vans were admitted at a much later hour, and the goods brought by them were forwarded by the same night's trains: *Held*, that this was giving an undue and unreasonable preference to the company's own traffic, to the prejudice of the complainant, and a rule for an injunction was made absolute, with costs. (*Palmer* v. *London, etc., Ry. Co.*, 1 Nev. & Mac. 271; 6 L. R. C. P. 194; 40 L. J. C. P. 133; 24 L. T. (N. S.) 135; 19 W. R. 627; see *Palmer* v. *London, etc., Ry. Co.*, 1 Nev. & Mac. 243; 1 L. R. C. P. 588; 12 Jur. (N. S.) 926; 25 L. J. C. P. 289; 15 W. R. 11; 15 L. T. (N. S.) 159, where court was evenly divided; see also note, 1 Nev. & Mac. 279.)

A railway company closed its goods station at B. at 5:15 P. M., against all persons except its agent, W., who had a receiving house about a mile distant from the station, and from whom the company received goods up to 8 P. M. For the conveyance of goods from the receiving house to the station, W. charged 1*s*. 8*d*. per ton on all goods above 3 *cwt*. and 3*d*. for each package below that weight: *Held*, upon the complaint of a rival carrier, that the refusal to receive goods sent by him to the station after 5:15, unless sent through the receiving house of W., was imposing upon him an undue prejudice, although it appeared that the goods so brought to the station by W. came there properly classified, weighed and prepared for loading. (*Garton* v. *Bristol, etc. Ry. Co.*, 6 C. B. (N. S.) 639; 5 Jur. (N. S.) 1313; 28 L. J. C. P. 306; 1 Nev. & Mac. 218.)

An injunction may be granted against a railway company to restrain them from requiring other carriers to bring their goods to the railway station at an earlier hour than they received their goods delivered at their own receiving offices. (*Baxendale* v. *London & Southwestern Ry. Co.*, 12 C. B. (N. S.) 758; 1 Nev. & Mac. 231; see *Garton* v. *Bristol, etc., Co. supra.*)

A railway company has no right to impose a charge for the conveyance of goods to or from their station, where the customer does not require such service to be performed by them. (*Garton* v. *Bristol, etc., Ry. Co.*, 1 Nev. & Mac. 218; 6 C. B. (N. S.) 639; 28 L. J. C. P. 306; 5 Jur. (N. S.) 1313.)

A railway company formerly charged a uniform rate of 3*s.* 6*d.* per ton on all goods conveyed on their line between R. and P. The goods were collected and delivered both by the company and B. at a charge of 4*s.* 10*d.* per ton. The company, who had power under their acts to impose their own rates of charge for carrying, but no power to impose tolls for collecting and delivering, raised the charge for carrying to 8*s.* 4*d.*, being the aggregate of the above two charges, with an intimation to the public that they would collect and deliver goods free from all charge. The real purpose of this arrangement was to compel persons delivering to have their goods conveyed by the railway, to employ the company to collect and deliver such goods, and thus to secure this business, and the profits upon it, to the company, as well as to exclude B. from competing with them in this department of business: *Held*, that this arrangement was an undue preference to the company in their separate capacity of carriers, other than on the line of railway; and also an undue prejudice to B. (*Baxendale* v. *Great Western Ry. Co.* (*Reading case*), 5 C. B. (N. S.) 336; 28 L. J. C. P. 81; 4 Jur. (N. S.) 1279; 1 Nev. & Mac. 202; see *s. c.*, on rehearing, 5 C. B. (N. S.) 356.)

A railway company had been in the habit of carrying goods between the termini of their line, according to a tariff of rates, from which they made deductions to persons who brought or took away their goods to or from the termini, discontinued these deductions, with a view to exclude other carriers from competing with them as carriers: *Held*, an undue prejudice to all such customers as did not desire to have their goods collected and delivered for them by the company. (*Garton* v. *Great Western Ry. Co.*, 5 C. B. (N. S.) 669; 5 Jur. (N. S.) 685; 28 L. J. C. P. 158; 1 Nev. & Mac. 214.)

A railway company had been in the habit of unloading goods coming by railway from the Southampton docks, consigned to carriers in London, out of their trucks, and of placing them (by their servants) in or conveniently near to the wagons of the consignees, without extra charge. This practice they discontinued, refusing to allow their servants to unload the trucks without an extra charge for such service, except in the case of Pickford & Co., whose goods they continued to unload as before, the smallness of their quantity and the fact of their being carried intermixed with the company's own traffic rendering it (as the company alleged) more convenient to themselves to do so. C., however, another carrier, was denied the aid of the company's servants in the unloading of his goods of the same description, and coming from the same place, the company alleging that the same reason did not apply to his goods as to Pickford & Co.'s, inasmuch as the former came in large quantities and in separate trucks. The court refused to make absolute a rule enjoining the company to unload the trucks containing C.'s goods, and to deliver such goods to C., by placing the same in or adjacent to his wagons, holding the demand to be too large; but the court intimated that if C.'s complaint had been confined to the company's giving an advantage to Pickford & Co. in the unloading of their goods, which they withheld from him, and that the company had refused to remove such ground of complaint, C. might have been entitled to relief. (*Cooper* v. *South-western Ry. Co.*, 4 C. B. 738; 27 L. J. C. P. 324; 1 Nev. & Mac. 185.)

A railway company had two scales of charges for the carriage of parcels by their line. One of the scales was much lower than the other, but was only applicable when the parcels to be carried by it fulfilled certain conditions as to size and value, and were prepaid by having adhesive stamps affixed to them. Both the scales included delivery from the railway company's receiving offices to their railway terminus. The railway company allowed their agents for carting parcels from their receiving offices to the railway terminus 1*d.* on every unstamped parcel.

Upon complaint by a carrier, who collected and carted stamped and unstamped parcels to the railway company's terminus, that although the trouble and expense was the same to him whether parcels were stamped or unstamped, yet the railway company allowed him nothing in respect of the former.

Held, that the railway company had not given an undue preference either to themselves or the person they employed as their carting agent, because they charged the public nothing for collection, and the collection of stamped parcels cost them nothing, the carting agent consenting to carry stamped parcels gratis in consideration of being paid 1*d*. for every unstamped parcel.

Semble, such an arrangement would be an undue preference over a carrier who only carted stamped parcels. (*Robertson* v. *Midland, etc., Ry. Co.*, 2 Nev. & Mac. 409.)

The N. W. Railway Company had a station at B., connected by branch lines of their own with the premises of certain traders there. The company charged the same station to station rates between other places and any part of B. to which their line extended. The traders at B. hauled the trucks containing their own goods between the company's station and their own premises, loading and unloading them upon the latter. The company allowed them a rebate on the station to station rates of 4½*d*. per ton in respect of haulage, and 9*d*. per ton in respect of loading and unloading deals and staves. Upon the application of a trader at B., dealing in deals and staves, whose premises were not connected with the company's lines, and who complained that these allowances were excessive, and amounted to an undue preference of the first-mentioned traders:—

Held, that this allowance of 4½*d*. could not be justified if it related simply to haulage, but was not excessive if the convenience of having the trucks loaded and unloaded off the company's lines and premises was taken into consideration, and that the allowance of 9*d*. for loading and unloading deals and staves was excessive and must be reduced to 4½*d*. (*Bell* v. *London, etc., Ry. Co.*, 2 Nev. & Mac. 185.)

— **Conditions of shipment.** A railway company permitted a carrier (who also acted as superintendent of their goods traffic) to hold himself out as their agent for the receipt of goods to be carried on their line, and his office as the receiving office of the company; and the goods were received by him at that place without requiring the senders to sign conditions which the company required all other carriers who brought goods to their station to sign. *Held,* an undue preference. (*Baxendale* v. *Bristol, etc., Ry. Co.*, 11 C. B. (N. S.) 787; 1 Nev. & Mac. 229.)

A company, possessed of a line from B. to C., advertised to convey goods from A. to C. (in conjunction with another company), at the rate of 50*s*. per ton, provided they were consigned to their own agents at those respective places; but if consigned through any one else they charged 2*s*. 6*d*. per ton more. *Held,* ground for injunction. (*Baxen-*

dale v. *North Devon Ry. Co.*, 3 C. B. (N. S.) 324; 1 Nev. & Mac. 180.)

The rule was made absolute with costs, although it prayed a writ enjoining the company to charge an equal rate for the carriage from A. to C.; and the writ was granted as from B. to C. only. *Semble*, that both companies ought to have been brought before the court. (*Baxendale* v. *North Devon Ry. Co.*, 3 C. B. (N. S.) 324; 1 Nev. & Mac. 180.)

Omnibus facilities. A railway company made arrangements at one of their stations with A., the proprietor of an omnibus running between the station and K., to provide omnibus accommodation for all passengers by any of their trains to and from K., and allowed A. the exclusive privilege of driving his vehicle into the station yard for the purpose of taking up and setting down passengers at the door of the booking office. *Held*, that in the absence of special circumstances showing it to be reasonable, the granting of such exclusive privilege to one proprietor, and refusing to grant the like facilities to another, who also brought passengers from K. as well as from other places beyond, was a breach of the prohibition against the granting of undue and unreasonable preferences. (*Marriott* v. *London, etc., Ry. Co.*, 1 C. B., (N. S.) 499; 3 Jur. (N. S.) 493; 26 L. J., C. P. 154; 1 Nev. & Mac. 47.) This "decision rests expressly upon the inconvenience inflicted upon the public, not upon the particular grievance to the applicant." (Williams, J., 1 Nev. & Mac. 57.)

— A railway company made arrangements with a cab proprietor whereby the company gave him the exclusive right of plying for hire within their station. Injunction refused at the instance of another cab proprietor, who had been refused leave for his cabs to stand and ply at the station, on the ground that no inconvenience to the public was made out. (*Beadell* v. *Eastern Counties Ry. Co.*, 26 L. J., C. P. 250; 2 C. B. (N. S.) 509; 1 Nev. & Mac. 56.)

— A railway company granted exclusive right to a limited number of fly-proprietors to ply for hire within their station. The court refused to grant a writ of injunction against the company, at the instance of a fly-proprietor who was excluded from participation in this advantage, although it was sworn by the complainant, and by several other fly-proprietors who were likewise excluded, that occasional delay and inconvenience resulted to the public from the course pursued. (*Painter* v. *London, etc., Ry. Co.*, 2 C. B. (N. S.) 702; 1 Nev. & Mac. 58; *Ilfracombe, etc., Co.* v. *London, etc., Co.*, 1 Nev. & Mac. 61.) It is necessary that the company make reasonable regulations to prevent confusion and obstruction. (1 Nev. & Mac. 62.)

Preferences to localities. To furnish facilities to one town to ship goods to market and deprive another competing town thereof, would be an unjust preference. (*Hozier* v. *Caledonian Ry. Co.*, 17 Sess. Cas. 302; 1 Nev. & Mac. 27, 30.)

The court refused to grant a rule for an injunction against the Eastern Counties Railway Company to compel them to issue season tickets between Colchester and London, on the same terms as they issued them between Harwich and London, upon a mere suggestion that the granting the latter (the distance being considerably greater) at a much lower rate than the former was an undue and unreasonable preference of the inhabitants of Harwich over those of Colchester. (*Jones* v. *Eastern Counties Ry. Co.*, 3 C. B. (N. S.) 718; 1 Nev. & Mac. 45.)

To a complaint under section 2 of the Railway and Canal Traffic Act, 1854, of an inequality of charge, it is no answer that the traffic favored and the traffic prejudiced are not in the same locality or district; and, assuming that there is a competition of interests, and that circumstances in other respects are not dissimilar, the traffic of two localities, both on the same system of railways, although at a distance from each other, is as much within the Act as the traffic of two or more individuals in the same locality. *Nicholson* v. *Great Western Ry. Co.*, 5 C. B. (N. S.) 366, followed. (*Richardson* v. *Midland Ry. Co.*, 4 Ry. & Can. Traf. Cas. 1.)

A railway company carried beer from B. at lower rates than from N., which was forty miles distant from B. Upon complaint by brewers at N. that their traffic was unduly prejudiced by not being carried on as favorable terms as the traffic of brewers from B., competitors in trade with the applicants, it appeared that the railway company charged all brewers at B. a uniform rate of $1\frac{1}{2}d.$ per ton per mile, station to station, with a minimum of 5s., including loading and unloading, and an abatement off the quoted rates of 9d. per ton for loading or unloading, and $4\frac{1}{2}d.$ per ton for haulage when the brewers did those services themselves instead of employing the railway company to do them, and that the railway company's charges for brewers traffic from N. exceeded the charges from B. to the extent of twenty-five to thirty per cent. *Held*, that the lower charges for carrying beer from B. were justified by the special advantages the railway company received in dealing with such traffic as compared with the applicants' traffic. (*Ibid.*)

The railway company carried beer in consignments not exceeding 500 pounds in weight for brewers at B. at the same rate per hundred-weight as corresponded to the tonnage rate which they charged such brewers for the carriage of consignments of over 500 pounds in weight, whereas at N. they had one tariff for consignments over 500 pounds, and another for consignments of 500 pounds or under in weight; the latter tariff, known as the "small package rates," being on a higher scale than the tonnage rate the railway company charged at N., and also than their tonnage rates at B. *Held*, that such rates gave an undue and unreasonable preference or advantage to the brewers at B. over the brewers at N., and that the railway company must frame their scale of charges for the carriage of consignments of beer not exceeding 500 pounds in weight upon the same principle at both places as regards the relation of such charges to the tonnage rates obtaining at such places respectively. (*Ibid.*)

Where the railway company carried beer sent from B. in cask by their railway to any place thereon where B. brewers had an agency, and such beer was there bottled and afterward consigned in bottle from such last-mentioned place to any station on their railway, it was carried at the B. special rate, which was lower than that charged by the railway company for the carriage in bottle of beer not brewed at B., between the same places, and also lower than that charged for the carriage of beer in bottle from N. *Held*, that the brewers at B., or their agents, were duly and unreasonably preferred over the brewers at N., and that the railway company must carry beer in bottle from N. for brewers there, on equal terms with the terms on which they carried B. brewers' beer in bottle from places other than B. for such brewers or their agents. (*Ibid.*)

The railway company carried to B. from other places on their lines of railway for brewers and maltsters at B., malt, hops, and barley, at lower rates and on more favorable terms than they carried similar traffic to N. for brewers there. *Held*, that the railway company must carry malt, hops, and barley to N. for the brewers there on equal terms with the terms on which similar traffic was carried to B. for brewers at that place, having due regard to the circumstances, if any (whether consisting in the routes differing, or in portions of the line passed over being more costly to work, or having been more costly to construct in the one case than in the other), which may render the cost to the railway company of carrying such traffic for the applicants greater than the cost of carrying similar traffic for brewers at B. (*Ibid.*)

A railway company carried to B. from various places on their lines of railway for brewers and maltsters at B. barley and malt at lower rates and on more favorable terms than they carried similar traffic to D. for maltsters there. Upon complaint by maltsters at D. that their traffic was unduly prejudiced by not being carried on as favorable terms as the traffic of brewers and maltsters at B., competitors in trade with the complainants, it appeared that the charge for barley from stations from which barley was sent to both places averaged to D. 6s. 11d. per ton, and to B. 5s. or 1s. 11d. per ton less. The railroad company sought to justify this inequality in the rates for the inwards grain traffic of the two places on the following grounds, viz: (1) That the traffic of the two places differed greatly in amount, the total traffic of B. being 600,000 tons per annum, of which 55,000 tons were barley, and that of D. 220,000 tons, of which 6,900 tons were barley. (2) That the truck loads conveyed to D. did not weigh as much per truck as to B. The average extra weight of the truck load to B. was from 8 to 10 cwt., and the earnings on the extra weight were claimed to be all clear profit, on the ground that half a ton more of paying load did not increase the cost of hauling the truck. (3) That about seventeen per cent of the trucks received loaded with barley at D. could not be reloaded there with any other traffic, and came away empty on the outward journey, whereas loaded wagons into B. were practically certain of a back load. (4) That the cost of the goods station staff was 5d. more per ton at D. than at B. *Held* (1) That a difference of charge could not be sustained on the general ground that the aggregate traffic of the one town exceeded that of the other, it having been proved that the B. rates were charged not only to the large brewers and maltsters, but to all inhabitants of the place, however small might be the quantity of their traffic, and that there was nothing exceptional in the natural position of B. to affect the rate at which goods could be carried. (2) That some differences in the rates of competitive traffic to B. and D. might be allowed in respect of the average weight of truck loads, and that assuming traffic to D. to pay the same rate per mile as traffic to B., there ought to be an addition made to the D. rate, as for 8 or 10 cwt. more per truck, to equalize matters with B. as regard mileage receipts per truck. (3) That some difference in such rates might be allowed in respect of the certainty of back loads from B., and that as it was proved that one-fifth part of the loaded wagons to D. were in excess of its requirements for outward journeys, a fourth or fifth part of 4d. a ton should be added to the D. rate, assuming traffic to D. to pay the same rate per mile as traffic to B. (4) That as barley was not a part of the merchandise handled in the goods station either at B. or at D., the cost of the goods staff was no part of the working charges in carrying it, and that the alleged greater amount of such cost in proportion at D. did not furnish a ground for a higher rate on barley carried to that place, and only using a siding in the goods yard for the same purposes and to the like extent as the like traffic at B. used the deposit sidings there. *Held*, therefore, that the railway company must carry barley and malt to D. for maltsters there on terms equally favorable to such maltsters with those on which similar traffic was carried to B. for maltsters at that place, having due regard to the differences which had been proved to exist in the traffic to the two places respectively in respect of the average weight of truck loads, and of certainty of back loads, and to such other circumstances (if any), as might render the cost to the railway company of carrying such traffic to maltsters at D. greater than the cost of carrying similar traffic for maltsters at B. (*Girardot* v. *Midland Ry.*, 4 Ry. & Can. Traf. Cas. 291; see *Richardson* v. *Midland Ry.*, 4 Ry. & Can. Traf. Cas. 1.)

Particular description of traffic—Terminal services. A railway company, in order to prevent the obstruction of their railway, which would be caused by an unlimited coal traffic, ascertained the probable consumption of coal in the neighborhood of each of their stations, and the sort required, and made arrangements with the collieries supplying the particular sort of coal for the requisite supply; they appointed depot agents to manage the sale of the coal, who, from time to time, ordered the quantity wanted from the collieries, and caused the wagons wanted for the carriage to be sent up. All the depots were in the hands of these agents, who accounted to the collieries for the proceeds of the sale. No coal merchant was dealt with in this way, but only coal owners; but each dealer was treated alike and as one of the public. On a motion by a coal merchant to enjoin the company to afford him the same facilities for receiving and forwarding his coals as to those who consigned their coals to the company: *Held*, that the arrangements of the company were proper, and not such as gave or caused any unreasonable preference or disadvantage, the company not being common carriers of coal, and only being bound to carry according to their profession. (*Oxlade* v. *North-eastern Ry. Co.* (No. 1), 1 C. B. (N. S.) 454; 3 Jur. (N. S.) 637; 26 L. J., C. P. 129; 1 Nev. & Mac. 72; *s. c.* (No. 2), 1 Nev. & Mac. 162; 15 C. B. (N. S.) 680.)

In determining whether a preference shown by a railway company to one of its customers is undue or unreasonable, within the meaning of the second section of the Railway and Canal Traffic Act, 1854, regard should be had to the benefit and convenience of the public, and also to the convenience of the railway company with reference to its general traffic.

Therefore, when a railway company was compelled, by the increase of its business, to separate its mineral from its goods traffic at O. station, and transferred the former to another station, retaining only at

O. station the mineral traffic, in favor of the corporation of M., who lighted M. and its suburbs, and whose gas-works were close to O. station, communicating therewith by a siding, so that such traffic could be removed at once from the O. station without impeding the goods traffic.

The Commission found as facts, that it was a matter of public benefit and convenience that the corporation should be supplied with coal at the O. station, and that the nature and magnitude of their supplies enabled the railway company to make such special arrangements for passing them through and out of O. station with less inconvenience to the general and ordinary business thereof than would be caused by carrying for the applicants, and therefore:—*Held*, that the preference to the corporation was neither undue nor unreasonable. (*Lees* v. *Lancashire, etc., Ry. Co.*, 1 Nev. & Mac. 352.)

The N. E. Railway Company carried coals to certain stations on their line for colliery owners only, and at such stations there were cells for the receipt and sale of the coal let to colliery owners for their separate use, at rents averaging less than 3*d.* per ton on the coal sold, and also unappropriated cells for the receipt of coal sent by colliery owners not renting cells. The latter were charged a higher rate of carriage than the colliery owners renting cells, and in addition a charge of 3*d.* per ton in lieu of rent. The rent and charge respectively covered all terminal services, but the services rendered the colliery owners renting cells exceeded those rendered at the unappropriated cells:—*Held*, that the extra charge for carriage, and the charge of 3*d.* per ton in lieu of rent, occasioned an undue prejudice to the colliery owners not renting cells. (*Locke* v. *N. E. Ry. Co.*, 3 Nev. & Mac. 44.)

The railway company charged the complainants 1*d.* per ton for shunting goods on to a siding, connecting their quarry with the railway, which was the property of the complainants; while no charge was made to other quarry owners for shunting on sidings (the property of the company) connecting their quarries with the railway.

The Commissioners found as a fact that the service rendered to the complainants was not more onerous to the railway company than the working of the other sidings for which no charge was made, and therefore:—*Held*, that the extra charge was an undue preference under the second section of the said act. (*Diphwys, etc. Co.* v *Festiniog Ry. Co.*, 2 Nev. & Mac. 73.)

Practice—Injunction. Upon a complaint by a trader that a railway company had made excessive charges for the conveyance of his traffic, and unduly preferred the traffic of another trader, the company admitted that they had done so, but contended that, as such causes of complaint had been removed before the application was filed, it was not necessary that an injunction should issue: *Held*, that the applicant was entitled to be fortified for the future with such security as the Railway Commissioners had power to give him, if it was not unreasonable for him not to be content without it, and that an injunction must issue. (*Macfarlane* v. *N. B. Ry. Co.* (No. 2), 4 Ry. & Can. Traf. Cas. 269.)

Damage. Upon an application to the Railway Commissioners for an order restraining an infringement of the provisions of section 2 of the Railway and Canal Traffic Act, 1854, it was not necessary to prove actual damage, if damage can be inferred from the circumstances. (*Denaby, etc., Co.* v. *Manchester, etc., Ry. Co.*, 3 Nev. & Mac. 426.)

At common law. The provision in the constitution of Colorado that "no undue or unreasonable discrimination shall be made in charges or facilities for transportation of freight and passengers within the state; and no railroad company, nor any lessee, manager, or employe thereof, shall give any preference to individuals, associations, or corporations in furnishing cars or motive power," imposes no greater obligation on a railroad company than the common law would have imposed upon it. (*A. T. & S. F. R. Co.* v. *D. & N. O. R. Co.*, 110 U. S. 667.)

— **Unjust discriminations—Delivery.** When the company has fixed its rates for the transportation of grain from any given station on the line of its road to Chicago, it can not charge different rates for delivery to different **warehouses** in Chicago on the line of its track. (*Vincent* v. *Chicago & A. R. Co.*, 49 Ill. 33.)

A railroad company can not bind itself to deliver to a particular **stock yard** all live stock coming over its line to a certain point, but it is bound to transport over its road and deliver to all stock yards, at such point reached by its tracks or connections, all live stock consigned or which the shippers desire to consign to them, upon the same terms and in the same manner as under like conditions it transports and delivers to their competitors; and the performance of this duty may be compelled by injunction at the suit of the proprietor of the stock yards discriminated against. (*McCoy* v. *C. I. St. L. & C. R. Co.*, 13 Fed. Rep. 3, Baxter, J.; *Cincinnati Stock Yards Co.* v. *United R., etc., Co.*, 7 Cincinnati Weekly Law Bulletin, 295, Minshall, J. (now of Supreme Court, Ohio); *Coe* v. *L. & N. R. Co.*, 3 Fed. Rep. 775.)

— **Station facilities.** A railroad passing through a town of 1,500 inhabitants unjustly discriminates against such town (if it is necessary to have a station therein) by placing its depot a mile and a half distant at its junction with another road, and a court may determine whether such station in the town is necessary, and enforce its erection by mandamus. (*State* v. *Republican V. R. Co.*, 17 Neb. 647; affirmed on rehearing, 18 Neb. 512; see *State* v. *Chicago, etc., R. Co.*, 19 Neb. 476.)

Shipment of goods in order of receipt. An honest effort to aid the public in the prosecution of business, by furnishing such facilities as are best calculated for that purpose, is required of railroad companies; but if they shall, in good faith, from a pressing cause, take grain from wagons or boats, while grain remained for shipment in private warehouses, they will not thereby incur liability. (*Galena & Chicago Union R. R. Co.* v. *Rae*, 18 Ill. 488 (1857).)

A carrier may have regard to the character and condition of the goods in sending them forward, and is not bound to do so in the order of their receipt without reference to such facts. (*Peet* v. *Chicago R. Co.*, 20 Wis. 594.)

A common carrier can not delay the transportation of goods already delivered to it and awaiting shipment, in order to receive and forward other goods. (*Great Western R. Co.* v. *Burns*, 60 Ill. 284.)

Shipper's contract to furnish entire freight. It is not a legitimate ground of discrimination that the shipper contracts to furnish all his freight to the carrier favoring him. (*Scofield* v. *Railway Co., supra*; *Baxendale* v. *G. W. Ry. Co.*, 5 C. B. (N. S.) *309; *Diphwys, etc., Co.* v. *Festiniog Ry. Co.*, 2 Nev. & Mac. 73.)

Nor can a carrier discriminate against a shipper who refuses to patronize him exclusively. (*Menacho* v. *Ward*, 27 Fed. Rep. 529; *Diphwys, etc., Co.* v. *Festiniog Ry. Co.*, 2 Nev. & Mac. 73.)

Express facilities. It is not an unjust discrimination for a railroad company to refuse to furnish to other express companies the same facilities which it accords to the company with which it has contracted to do the business. (*Express Cases*, 117 U. S. 1; 23 Am. & E. Ry. Cas. 545, and note; *Sargent* v. *Boston & L. R.*, 115 Mass. 416.)

Statute requiring all railroads to give all expressmen "reasonable and equal terms, facilities, and accommodations for transportation," is violated by giving one express company exclusive express facilities; and *semble*, that an action would lie at common law. (*N. E. Exp. Co.* v. *Me. Cent. R. Co.*, 57 Me. 188; *Sandford* v. *Railroad Co.*, 24 Pa. St. 378.)

Discriminations in favor domestic traffic justifiable. (*Shipper* v. *Pa. Ry. Co.*, 47 Pa. St. 338, 341.)

"Ownership may not be a reasonable ground for a distinction [discrimination], but weight, bulk, value, place of production, and many others may be." (*Shipper* v. *Pa. R. Co.*, 47 Pa. St. 338, 341; see this case criticised 16 Am. Law Review, 832.)

REASONABLE AND EQUAL FACILITIES FOR THE INTERCHANGE OF TRAFFIC MUST BE GIVEN, AND DISCRIMINATIONS BETWEEN CONNECTING LINES FORBIDDEN. (16)

Sec. 3, Par. 2. Every common carrier subject to the provisvisions of this act shall, according to their respective powers(16*a*), afford all reasonable, proper, and equal facilities(16*b*) for the interchange of traffic between their respective lines, and for the receiving, forwarding, and delivering of passengers and property to and from their several lines, and those connecting therewith, and shall not discriminate in their rates and charges between such connecting lines(17), but this shall not be construed as requiring any such common carrier to give the use of its tracks(18) or terminal facilities to another carrier engaged in like business(19).

(16) ENGLISH STATUTES AND DECISIONS.

There are two clauses of section 2 of the Railway and Canal Traffic Act, 1854 (which act will be found in full in the Appendix), from which the above paragraph was evidently drawn. The first clause is as follows:

"Every railway company, canal company, and railway and canal company shall, according to their respective powers, afford all reasonable facilities for the receiving and forwarding and delivering of traffic upon and from the several railways and canals belonging to or worked by such companies, and for the return of carriages, trucks, boats, and other vehicles." Or, to put the matter in another form, quoting the English statute and inserting in brackets the changes made in the above paragraph, as follows: "Every railway company, canal company, and railway and canal company [every common carrier subject to the provisions of this act] shall, according to their respective powers, afford all reasonable [proper and equal] facilities for the [interchange of traffic between their respective lines and for the] receiving and ["and" dropped out], forwarding and delivering of [English statute: "Traffic upon and from the several railways and canals belonging to and worked by such companies respectively;" present statute: "Passengers and property to and from their several lines and those connecting therewith."]

The second clause is: "And every railway company and canal company, and railway and canal company, having or working railways or canals which form part of a continuous line of railway or canal, or railway and canal communication, or which have the terminus, station, or wharf of the one near the terminus, station, or wharf of the other, shall afford all due and reasonable facilities for receiving and forwarding all the traffic arriving by one of such railways or canals by the other without any unreasonable delay, and without any such preference," etc. (See these provisions quoted and commented on by Supreme Court in the *Atchison case*, 110 U. S. 667, 685 ; see, also, note (37) to section 7, *post.*)

In this connection I refer to the rule recognized by the Supreme Court of the United States, that where English statutes have been adopted into our own legislation, the known and settled construction of those statutes by courts of law has been considered as silently incorporated into the acts, or has been received with all the weight of authority. (*McDonald* v. *Hovey*, 110 U. S. 619; *Cathcart* v. *Robinson*, 5 Pet. 265; *Pennock* v. *Dialogue*, 2 Pet. 1 ; *McCool* v. *Smith*, 1 Black, 459 ; The Abbotsford, 98 U. S. 440.)

Section 2 of the Railway and Canal Traffic Act, 1854, was enlarged and extended as to the duties of connecting lines, by section 11 of the Regulation of Railways Act, 1873, in full in Appendix.

Railroad companies were compelled by the English courts to afford " facilities" under the Railway and Canal Traffic Act, 1854, section 2, before the passage of the Regulation of Railways Act, 1873. (*Caterham Ry. Co.* v. *London, etc., Ry. Co.*, 1 C. B. (N. S.) 410; 1 Nev. & Mac. 32 ; *Barret* v. *Gt. North. Ry. Co.*, 1 Nev. & Mac. 38.)

Section 11 of the latter act merely enlarged and extended the provisions of the act of 1854, as to " through traffic."

Facilities for receiving, forwarding, and delivering of traffic—What they are. One of the most important cases upon the subject is that arising out of the complaint of the Hastings Town Council against the South Eastern Ry. Co. Upon complaint to the railway commissioners that two **stations of a railway company** were not adequate to the requirements of the traffic, the commissioners held that the railway company had not, under the circumstances, afforded reasonable facilities for the receiving, forwarding, and delivery of traffic upon its railway, and ordered that the platforms should be extended, and that a substantial part of such platforms should be so arranged as that carriages might set down and take up passengers under cover; that more waiting rooms should be provided and a part of the station reserved for refreshment purposes; that the booking offices should have more than one window for the issuing of tickets ; that cattle-pens into which the stock could be unloaded should be erected; and that a bridge which connected the up and down platforms, and by which persons at the station were required to cross the line, should be covered over. (*Hastings. Town Council* v. *S. E. Ry. Co.*, 3 Nev. & Mac. Ry. Cas. 179.)

Subsequently a proceeding in prohibition was begun in the Queen's Bench Division. A demurrer to a declaration in prohibition raising the question of the jurisdiction of the railway commissioners to entertain the application, was overruled and judgment rendered for plaintiffs in prohibition. The judges (Manisty, Lush, and Cockburn, C. J.) delivered elaborate opinions, Lush, J., dissenting from the decision of the majority, he holding that the commissioners had jurisdiction to make all the orders except the one to provide a refreshment room. The railway commissioners appealed. The Court of Appeal, reversing the judgment of the Queen's Bench Division, held that the subject-matter of the complaint and application was not beyond the scope of the jurisdiction of the commissioners, but that the commissioners had no power peremptorily to order particular works to be executed according to a specific plan.

That the orders with respect to the platforms and goods yards at H., and the approach road at L., were in excess of jurisdiction; that the orders as to refreshment accommodation, and the covering over of platforms, carriage yard and bridge, were not "facilities" within the statute; but that the orders as to booking office, waiting room, and cattle accommodation were such facilities. (Per Lord Chancellor Selborne and Lord Coleridge, C. J.)

That all orders except those relating to the cattle accommodation and the delivery of tickets at the booking office were in excess of jurisdiction. (Per Brett, L. J.) (*S. E. Ry. Co.* v. *Ry. Commissioners*, 6 Q. B. D. 586; 50 L. J. Q. B. D. 201; 3 Nev. & Mac. 464.)

The opinion of Lord Chancellor Selborne, in this case, is such a clear statement of the purpose and scope of the law, and as it met with the entire concurrence of Chief Justice Coleridge, whose judgments stand so deservedly high in this country, that a copious extract is made from the same.

"The first observation which arises upon this enactment, is that it does not enable the commissioners to impose upon a railway company any **new duties or obligations** depending upon any mere exercise of the commissioners' own judgment. Their authority is only to inquire into and prevent violations or contraventions of the statute. For this purpose alone they may issue a writ of injunction, the form of which (according to the 5th rule made under the Act by the Court of Common Pleas) was to be prohibitory, if the statute were contravened by any positive act, and mandatory, if it were contravened by any mere omission or nonfeasance. In both cases alike, the obligation to be enforced by the writ must have been already created by the statute. The question into which the court was to inquire was not one of expediency, but of fact. Such an authority was in harmony with the general functions of a court of law, although its exercise might require special powers (such as those to conduct inquiries by engineers or otherwise); and although it was given in a very peremptory form, all appeal (in the proper sense of that word), even from the decision of a single judge, being excluded. A discretionary power to dictate to a company what structural works it should or should not execute for the purpose of its undertaking, would have been evidently much more suitable to a practicable and scientific than to a legal tribunal.

"What, then, are the obligations imposed upon railway companies by this statute? They are contained in the second section, and are (substantially) three in number: First, a positive obligation to ' afford, according to their respective powers, **all reasonable facilities for the receiving and forwarding and delivering of traffic,** upon and from the several railways and canals belonging to or worked by such companies respectively, and for the return of carriages, trucks, boats, and other vehicles.' 'Traffic' (according to the interpretation clause, section 1) includes ' passengers and their luggage and goods, animals, and other things conveyed by any railway company.' 'Railway' includes ' every station of or belonging to such railway company, and used for the purpose of such traffic.' The second obligation is to give no undue preferences; the third, to do whatever may be necessary to enable the company's own line, and any other line connected with or having a terminus near it, to be used by the public as continuous lines of communication.

" It is unnecessary to state more particularly the terms in which the second and third obligations are created; the first alone being material to the present question. I notice, only to set it aside, the argument of the respondents, that this has no reference to any traffic of which a company is itself the original carrier upon its own line. There is nothing either in the words or in the reason of the thing to warrant any such restricted construction. A company may carry, or not, upon its own line as it thinks fit, and if it does so, may undertake that business under various conditions and limitations. But, if and so far as it does undertake so to carry either passengers or goods traffic, it comes (in my opinion) under the obligation to afford for the purposes of that traffic the facilities required by the first branch of the second section of the Act.

" With respect to **stations,** there is no obligation to establish them at any particular places or place unless the company thinks fit to do so. The 'railway,' as interpreted by the Act, only includes existing stations 'used for the purposes of public traffic.' But when the company has, in fact, opened a station at a particular place, and actually uses it for the purposes of public traffic, and invites the public to resort to it for the purpose of being received and delivered as passengers to or from trains announced as starting from or stopping at that station, or of having their goods received there for carriage or delivered there after carriage, it is, in my opinion, bound by the Act to afford at that station (to the extent of its powers) all reasonable facilities for 'receiving, forwarding, and delivering' such passengers and goods. It may not, in all cases, be a very easy thing to determine whether that obligation has been fulfilled or not. Nothing less than reasonable proof that it has not been fulfilled, can authorize the commissioners to interfere with the **discretion of the company** as to the arrangements or management of any of its stations; and, even then, the Act does not appear to contemplate an order for the execution of any particular works, if it can be obeyed without them. But I can not assent to the argument that, according to the true construction of this second section, the obligation to 'afford all reasonable facilities,' etc., is circumscribed by the precise extent, capacity, and structural arrangement of the buildings, booking-offices, and platforms, etc., *de facto*, provided at the time of complaint by the company, if these are insufficient for the ordinary traffic of the station, and if, by alterations or other improvements which the company has adequate power to make, all necessary facilities might be afforded. The words '**according to their respective powers**,' as well as the general scope of the enactment, seem to me to be very much opposed to so limited a construction. I am, therefore, of opinion that a company does not violate and contravene the Act, if, having sufficient powers, it keeps its platforms, booking-offices, and other structures at any station in such a condition, as to space and other arrangements, as to cause dangerous or obstructive confusion, delay, or other impediment to the proper reception, transmission, or delivery of the ordinary traffic of that station, whether consisting of passengers or of goods.

"Being of that opinion, I am unable to hold, upon the terms of the complaint itself, that the matter of it (which I regard as summed up in the 7th and 14th paragraphs) was beyond the scope of the commissioners' jurisdiction. The prayer, with which that complaint concluded, may have been improper either in form or in substance, but if the matter itself was within the jurisdiction of the commissioners, I conceive there is so far no ground for a prohibition. The matter, indeed, does not now remain exactly in that state. The commissioners proceeded to deliver what is called their judgment, and although no writ of injunction was issued (indeed I find it difficult to collect from the judgment in what precise form the commissioners intended it to issue), still it is plain to me, from the points noted for argument before the Queen's Bench Division on the part of the commissioners, that all parties thought it convenient practically to treat that judgment as embodying the substance of an order which, if not prohibited, they would have made. It is proper, therefore, if not necessary, that we should explain the view we take of the several matters and things which, for this purpose, appear to have been treated as if they had been ordered, as the effect of our decision might otherwise be misunderstood.

"One of these matters is an extension of the platform accommodation at the Hastings station, acccording to a plan prepared by the chief engineer, and approved by the directors of the company. The insufficiency of the platform accommodation appears to have been admitted by the company, and it may be that, if the plan prepared had been altogether within its powers, and had been at the company's instance, or by its consent, embodied in an order of the commissioners, it would not have been open to the same objection as if it had been dictated by the commissioners to the company. But this plan appears, by the judgment, to be dependent for its practicability upon the enlargement of a certain bridge, which the company at the time of the complaint had not power so to enlarge, and although it has since entered into an agreement with the owners of the land requisite for that purpose, the performance of that agreement involves (among other things) a money contribution by those owners toward the intended works. It appears to me to be impossible to hold that any particular improvements dependent upon the execution of such a plan could have been obligatory under the statute, the statutory obligations being limited by the company's powers. The company, therefore, had not in this respect 'violated' or 'contravened' the Act, and the commissioners could not order it to execute these particular works.

"An objection, similar in principal, applies to the suggestion (if meant to be imperative), contained in the judgment on two other subjects, the goods yard at Hastings and the approaches to the St. Leonards station. It is, therefore, superfluous to inquire (though on this point I certainly do not differ from Lord Justice Brett) whether, if the works contemplated by those particular suggestions had been within the company's powers, they could have been regarded as necessary to afford reasonable facilities for the purposes specified in the Act.

"That question, however, arises as to some other things which the commissioners have also proposed to order, and which, so far as appears, the company might have power to do. Of these, the reservation of part of the **station buildings** at Hastings f(r **refreshment purposes**, and the covering over of certain parts of the platforms, etc., at both stations, on account of the exposure of the site, and the resort of invalids to St. Leonards and Hastings, seem to me to be clearly not necessary as 'facilities for the receiving, forwarding, or delivering traffic upon the railway,' however desirable they may be for the comfort or convenience of passengers.

"The enlargement in some reasonable way (whether by platform or by waiting-room accommodation) of a space sufficient for the proper reception of ordinary passenger traffic, and some proper provision for the delivery of cattle from the company's wagons, without those risks which seem now to attend their passage through the station yard, are things which approach more nearly to my conception of facilities which the commissioners, in the due exercise of their jurisdiction, might hold to be necessary and required by the Act. I am by no means prepared to say that there is no form of mandatory injunction which they can properly issue for these purposes. It does not, however, follow that they can order a certain number of waiting-rooms to be provided, or dictate their classification, position, or dimensions, or enjoin the company to make cattle-pens upon a particular piece of ground now used for other purposes. It may well be, that by the execution of such works as these, or some of them, the obligation imposed upon the company by the statute might be fulfilled, nor should I be disposed to impute any excess of their jurisdiction to the commissioners, if they were merely to indicate, for the consideration of the company, these or any other convenient means by which, in their opinion, that obligation may be fulfilled. But between any such reasonable suggestions, and a peremptory order for the execution of these particular works, there is a wide difference. I can find no warrant in the statute for the assumption by the commissioners of a general control in matters of this kind over the discretion of the company as to the best means (when there is a choice of means), of fulfilling their statutory obligations.

"There remains the point as to **booking office accommodation** at both stations. The commissioners proposed to order that this should be increased in a manner as to which I consider them to have had jurisdiction to make such an order as I conceive them to have intended.

[The judgment of the commissioners was as follows: "There is but one window for the issue of tickets, and as the issue from one window of three classes of tickets for each of two companies, the Brighton and South-eastern, can not but cause an inconvenient crush at times, we are of opinion that the South-eastern Company should have a separate window for its tickets."]

"The result is, that the commissioners had, in my opinion, jurisdiction over the general matter of the complaint as summed up in paragraphs 7 and 14, and had also jurisdiction to order some, at least, of the things contemplated by their judgment, provided they did so in a proper manner and form; but that as to other things which they (apparently) intended to order, they had no jurisdiction, partly because those things were beyond the company's powers, partly because they were not facilities reasonably necessary for the particular purposes mentioned in the Act, and partly because they would have required particular structural works to be executed which are not prescribed by the Act, and which can not be supposed to be the only possible means of affording the facilities which the Act does require." (3 Nev. & Mac. 505–511.)

(16a) POWERS OF COMPANY.

"**According to their respective powers,**" has reference to the power possessed by the company to do that which is required. Such power may be derived from its charter or other statutory grant. (*Tharsis* v. *London, etc., Ry. Co.*, 3 Nev. & Mac. 455; *Watkinson* v. *Wrexham, etc., Ry. Co.*, 3 Nev. & Mac. 164;) or by contract or arrangement (*London, etc., Ry. Co.*, v. *Staines, etc., Ry. Co.*, 3 Nev. & Mac. 48.)

The Railway and Canal Traffic Act, 1854, section 2, requires facilities to be given according to the powers of railway companies, and as special Railway Acts make the powers of some companies larger than those of others, so they also extend or limit the facilities they give to the public, and thus the general enactment as to affording facilities has to be read and considered with reference to the language of any special clauses regarding them.

A railway was transferred to a railway company under a special Act, section 15 of which provided that the railway company, when requested so to do by any persons occupying works or manufactories adjacent to and having sidings connected with the railway transferred, was at all reasonable times and with all due diligence to **provide wagons** proper and sufficient for the conveyance of all traffic passing exclusively on the lines of railway transferred.

Upon complaint by persons occupying works or manufactories adjacent to the railway that the railway company did not supply sufficient wagons for the traffic on the railway: *Held*, that although the duty cast upon the railway company by the special Act was limited to cases where there was a request for wagons by members of a particular class, and where also only particular lines of railway were required to be used, yet where the duty did arise, it determined what was a reasonable facility within the meaning of section 2 of the Railway and Canal Traffic Act, 1854, as effectively as if it were a duty of a more general kind or one which applied under any circumstances; and the railway company was enjoined to afford all reasonable facilities for the receiving, forwarding, and delivery of the applicants' ore passing exclusively over the lines transferred having regard to the above section. (*Tharsis, etc., Co.* v. *London, etc., R. Co.*, 3 Nev. & Mac. 455; see *Watkinson* v. *Wrexham, etc., R. Co.*, 3. Nev. & Mac. 164.)

The S. W. Railway Company were the lessees of the S. railway under a lease, whereby it was provided that the lessors should execute all such additional works, if any, and in connection with the thereby demised railways, and for land-owners and others, as might from time to time be required in pursuance of the acts from time to time in force with respect to the management, working, user, and maintenance of the railways, and the works thereof, and the traffic thereon; nevertheless, that the lessees should maintain and repair such works when executed:

Held, that this provision extended to works necessary to afford due facilities for traffic under the Railway and Canal Traffic Act, 1854, including therein works which it is incumbent on a railway company to provide, if it would avoid contingencies for which it would incur a liability, such as new signals provided for putting the **block system** in operation.

Semble, that section 2 of the Railway and Canal Traffic Act, 1854, entitles the public, at stations where there are many passengers, to have the convenience of a **waiting room,** and to have platforms which are not long enough for the traffic extended, and to have also such siding accommodation as that goods can be received and delivered without delay. (*London, etc., Ry. Co.* v. *Staines, etc., Ry. Co.*, 3 Nev. & Mac. 48.)

The commissioners can not order accommodation to be provided which entails the acquirement by the company of additional land which they have no immediate power to take. (*Harris, etc.,* v. *London, etc., R. Co.*, 3 Nev. & Mac. 331.)

A railway company is under the same obligation as a common carrier undertaking to carry in accordance with the provisions of the Railway and Canal Traffic Act, 1854; therefore questions as to how far a sender of goods may require delivery at any station he may appoint, or as to how far a railway company is liable to carry goods of every kind, or for all persons alike, are to be determined in each case, not with reference to what a railway company may choose to do, or may ordinarily do, but with reference to what may be within its powers, and at the same time a reasonable requirement. (*Thomas* v. *N. Staff. Ry. Co.*, 3 Nev. & Mac. 1.)

Can not compel two companies to act jointly. Upon a complaint that two railway companies had not established a proper through service, via a junction, for traffic requiring to pass over a portion of each company's railway, and had not availed themselves of the junction for the interchange of passenger and goods traffic, and had not afforded all due and reasonable facilities for the through transmission of all descriptions of traffic between the two companies:—

Held, under the circumstances of the case, taken in connection with the powers and duties of the companies under their private acts, that (1) the companies must afford to the public as reasonable facilities a **train service** of eight trains daily each way, to connect the two railways as a continuous line; (2) **through booking** between the stations on the two railways; (3) but that through carriages need not be provided as long as passengers could exchange from one train to another at the same station; (4) that the companies must interchange goods at the junction.

Held, by the Exchequer Division of the High Court of Justice, upon an application by the Chatham Company for a prohibition restraining the railway commissioners from enforcing their order on the defendant railway companies in this case by penalties, that the commissioners have no power to make an order on two railway companies to act jointly in doing what neither company has power to do separately, and that where such an order has been made, a prohibition may issue from the High Court of Justice against the commissioners. (*Toomer, etc.* v. *London, etc., R. Co.*, 3 Nev. & Mac. 79.)

(16 *b*) FACILITIES FOR RECEIVING, FORWARDING, AND DELIVERING TRAFFIC.

Sufficient locomotive power—Return of cars, etc. Upon complaint by traders whose collieries and brickworks were connected by sidings with the respondents' railway that the respondents did not duly and properly work and manage their railway, and did not provide sufficient locomotive power for that purpose, and that they improperly and unnecessarily detained empty wagons destined for the collieries and works of the applicants, and failed to haul away with regularity and dispatch from the sidings connecting the said works and collieries with the railway, loaded wagons placed ready for the removal. The commissioners held that the respondents did not, according to their powers, afford all reasonable facilities for the receiving and forwarding and delivering of traffic upon and from their railway, and for the return of carriages and trucks; and the commissioners ordered the respondents to work and manage their railway duly and properly, and to provide sufficient locomotive power and labor for that purpose, and to desist from unduly detaining empty or unloaded wagons destined for the collieries and works of the applicants, and to haul away with regularity and dispatch from the sidings communicating with their railway loaded wagons properly placed ready for removal. (*Watkinson, etc.*, v. *Wrexham, etc., R. Co.*, 3 Nev. & Mac. 446.)

Quaere: Whether, if a railway company is bound by its special act to weigh coal at the point of discharge, such weighing is a facility for delivery under the Railway and Canal Traffic Act, 1854, section 2. (*Ibid.*)

Sufficient cars for traffic. The A. Railway Company exclusively worked and managed the B. railway as lessees of the line, under a special act, which provided that the A. Company "shall provide and employ all such locomotive powers, engines, carriages, wagons, and other rolling stock, plant, stores, materials, and labor, as shall be proper and sufficient for the working and user of the demised undertaking, and the reception, accommodation, conveyance, and delivery by the A. Company of the traffic thereof, and the B. Company shall not be bound to provide any such thing."

Upon refusal by the A. Company to provide wagons for the traders' traffic on the B. railway:—

Held, by the Common Pleas Division of the High Court of Justice (affirming the judgment of the railway commissioners), that the special act imposed an obligation on the A. Company to provide wagons proper and sufficient for the working and user of the B. railway, and that any one interested in procuring that accommodation had a ground of complaint under section 2 of the Railway and Canal Traffic Act, 1854, against the A. Company if they refused to provide it. (*Watkinson, etc., Copper Co.* v. *Wrexham, etc., R. Co.*, 3 Nev. & Mac. 164.)

Additional cars were required to be provided, also, in *Tharsis, etc.*, v. *London, etc., Ry. Co.*, 3 Nev. & Mac. 455.

Number and times of trains. To induce the court to interfere on a complaint by the proprietors of a branch line, that a sufficient number of trains of the main line does not stop at the junction, or stop at convenient times, it must be distinctly shown that sufficient accommodation is not afforded to meet the fair requirements of the public. (*Caterham Ry. Co.* v. *London, etc., Ry. Co.*, 1 C. B. (N. S.) 410; 26 L. J., C. P. 16; 1 Nev. & Mac. 32.)

Semble, if there were two competing companies having lines from A. to B., and one of them had a continuation from B. to C., and the company having such continuation arranged the departures from B. so as to interfere seriously with the other line, and put the public to inconvenience thereby, and force the traffic to B. over a greater extent of line at a sacrifice of time or cost, the court would interfere. (*Barret* v. *Great North. Ry. Co.*, 1 Nev. & Mac. 38; see *Toomer* v. *London, etc., Ry. Co.*, 3 Nev. & Mac. 79, where a train service of eight trains daily was prescribed as a reasonable facility.)

Additional trains—Facilities off line of railway. Upon complaint by an owning company that the working company did not use and work the railway, and all traffic arising from extensions of the railway efficiently, and so as fairly to develop, protect, and maintain the traffic fairly belonging thereto, as provided in the working agreement, the commissioners ordered the working company to run an additional third passenger train each way daily on week days at certain times; such trains to be worked in good connection for through traffic, and the time for stoppages at stations on the owning company's railway not to exceed an allowance at the rate of four minutes for each station stopped at; and further ordered the working company to run not less than two passenger trains each way daily on week days on the branch line of the owning company, timed for convenient connection and correspondence at the junction with the main line with trains arriving at and departing from such junction.

A railway company is not bound to provide booking offices for traffic at places off their railway, nor to arrange for the conveyance by road of goods between such places to the nearest station on their railway. (*Dublin, etc., R. Co.* v. *Midland, etc., R. Co.*, 3 Nev. & Mac. 379.)

The railway company charged the complainant quarry owners 9*d*. per ton for the use of their wagons off the line, and demurrage if they detained them more than twenty hours, while the quarry owners who had entered into the above-mentioned agreement were charged nothing for the use of wagons off the line, and were not charged for demurrage until after the expiration of thirty hours.

Held, that this service off the line was incidental to the receiving, forwarding, and delivering of the slate, and that the circumstance of the favor shown being in respect of something done off the line did not take the case out of the Railway and Canal Traffic Act, 1854, s. 2. (*Diphwys, etc., Co.* v. *Festiniog Ry. Co.*, 2 Nev. & Mac. 73.)

Continuous line—Through booking and facilities. Two railway companies ran trains to T. W., and each had a station there. The stations were a mile apart from each other, but were connected by a line of railway, which was used for the transit of goods only. The two railway systems were intended by the legislature to join at T. W. Upon complaint of the inhabitants of the district that no passengers were conveyed on the railway between the two stations, although there was a continuous line of railway:—

Held, that the case came within section 2 of the Railway and Canal Traffic Act, 1854, and accordingly an order was made enjoining both the companies to afford a continuous communication for passengers as well as for goods by means of their continuous lines.

A railway company received goods for conveyance from places on their own railway to places on the railway of another company. There was through communication between such places by a continuous line of railway. The sending company refused to book such goods through to their destination, and only invoiced them locally to the end of their railway, where they were rebooked to the stations on the forwarding company's line, to which they were directed to be delivered.

Held, that the sending company must allow through booking from their stations to stations on the forwarding company's line; that through booking was a facility which railway companies may reasonably be required to afford, and, as exhibiting the total charge made for conveyance from end to end, was especially of use where doubts existed whether companies were making unequal or excessive charges. (*Local Board, etc.*, v. *London, etc., Ry. Co. and S. E. Ry. Co.*, 2 Nev. & Mac. 214; see *Toomer* v. *London, etc., Ry. Co.*, 3 Nev. & Mac. 79.)

The obligation imposed upon every railway company to afford all due and reasonable facilities for receiving and forwarding by its railway traffic coming by another, which forms with it a continuous line of communication, is not limited to the cases in which a railway company has accommodation to take over such traffic at the point of junction.

Upon complaint by the lessees of a colliery, situated on the N. & B. Railway, at a short distance from its junction with the M. Railway to S., that they were prevented sending the traffic of their colliery to S. by the railways of the two companies, which formed a direct route, and in consequence had to send it by a circuitous route, it was proved that the two railways formed a continuous line of communication, and that, physically, there was no difficulty in the traffic of the colliery being carried to S. by the direct route.

Held, that the applicants were entitled, under section 2 of the Railway and Canal Traffic Act, 1854, to have their traffic conveyed by any route they pleased, and to use the two railways as if they were one continuous line. (*Victoria, etc., Co.* v. *Neath, etc., Ry. Co.'s*, 3 Nev. & Mac. 37.)

Two railway companies ran trains to C., and each had a station there. The stations were fifty-five chains apart, but were connected by a line of railway belonging to one of such companies. Upon complaint by the inhabitants of the district that no passengers were conveyed on the railway between the two stations, although there was a continuous line of railway, the commissioners made an order enjoining both the companies to afford a continuous communication for passengers by means of their continuous lines, and to afford due and reasonable facilities for forwarding through passenger traffic arriving by one of the lines at C. by the other. (*James, etc.*, v. *Taff Vale, etc., R. Co.*, 3 Nev. & Mac. 540.)

Two lines—Longer and shorter—Through rates. A route for which through rates are proposed, that would be a reasonable and serviceable route if worked throughout by one railway company, does not lose its serviceableness because two or more companies are concerned in working it; for the Railway and Canal Traffic Act, 1854, section 2, is intended to secure that, in the case of a continuous line formed out of the railways of different companies, the companies should co-operate for the transit of through traffic, and send it forward to its destination as though it were their own proper traffic. The S. & M. Railway formed an alternative route between certain stations on the G. W. Railway and other stations on the S. W. Railway. Upon an application by the S. & M. Railway Company for through rates between such stations via their railway, the rates to be the same as the existing rates between such stations by the alternative route, which were agreed through rates, it was proved that the route proposed by the S. & M. Railway would effect a great saving in time and distance, and that the transfers at junctions were the same by either route. The commissioners allowed the through rates and route as proposed, on the ground that the interests of the public were, under the circumstances, in favor of the existence of an alternative railway route at equal rates. The commissioners held that rates that excluded traffic from the shorter of these two through routes, and confined it to the longer, could not but be at the expense of public policy; and, though the quantity of traffic might be insignificant, and equal rates might not have much effect in developing through traffic by the route in question, it was a principle of importance to the public that a route between places offering the best opportunities for railway carriage, as far as distance was concerned, should not be placed at a disadvantage merely because portions of the route belonged to companies which had an alternative route and made lower charges in favor of the latter. It would be an undue preference if a company, as to traffic of the same description going between the same places, worked it at through rates if the traffic passed off their line at one point, and refused that facility if it passed off their line at another point. (*Swindon, etc., Ry.* v. *Great Western Ry.*, 4 Nev. & Mac. 349.)

Through car facilities—Pullman cars. The C. Company were bound to afford to Scottish east-coast traffic of the N. B. Company using their railway all usual facilities, including, so far as might reasonably be required, through carriages, and also any greater facilities which they might grant to any other company in respect to such traffic, or of any traffic competitive with it. The C. Company ran for the convenience of traffic competitive with the Scottish east-coast traffic of the N. B. Company—in one case a saloon sleeping-carriage, weighing three tons, and fitted to carry twelve persons; and in another a composite carriage, of which one compartment had sleeping berths for three persons: *Held*, that a Pullman car weighing twenty-one tons, and to hold twenty-two persons, was so dissimilar in character, both to the saloon and composite carriages, that the N. B. Company were not entitled, under the above provisions, to insist on the forwarding of it by the C. Company as a similar facility, nor as a reasonable requirement, unless the N. B. Company guaranteed to the C. Company a mileage proportion on eight fares. (*Caledonian Ry. Co.* v. *North British Ry. Co.*, 3 Nev. & Mac. 56.)

Third-class tickets. A railway company issued third-class return tickets to stations a certain distance only down their line. The court refused to enjoin them to issue such tickets to stations beyond that distance. (*Caterham Ry. Co.* v. *Ry. Co.*, 1 Nev. & Mac. 32; 1 C. B. (N. S.) 410.)

Station facilities. *Semble*, it is a good ground of complaint that there is no place of shelter provided at the junction of two roads for passengers waiting for the arrival of trains; the public being entitled, in this respect, to reasonable accommodation. (*Caterham Ry. Co.* v. *London, etc., Ry. Co.*, 1 C. B. (N. S.) 410; 26 L. J., C. P. 16; 1 Nev. & Mac. 32; see *Hastings Town Council* v. *S. E. Ry. Co.*, and the opinion of Lord Chancellor Selborne construing the English act, *supra*, p. 98 *et seq.*; see, also, *London, etc., Ry. Co.* v. *Staines, etc. Ry. Co.*, 3 Nev. & Mac. 48.)

A railway company, having land adjoinging one of their stations, let the whole of it to P., a coal merchant, for the purpose of storing coal brought by their line. P. did not require or actually use the whole of the land for this purpose. W., another coal merchant, applied to the company to provide him on similar terms with land for storing coal, or to let to him the part of the land not actually used by P. The company refused to do so. W. applied to the court for an order compelling the company to desist from allowing P. to store coals on the land, or to give similar facilities to him: *Held*, by Bovill, C. J., and Keating, J., that a means of storing coal at the station to which it is sent being a necessary facility for the proper carrying on of the coal trade, the company had no right to grant greater facilities to P. than to W., and that they ought to be restrained from doing so; but by Montague, Smith, and Brett, JJ., that the Railway and Canal Traffic Act only relates to facilities in the receiving, forwarding, and delivering traffic, and that the court had no jurisdiction to interfere with matters not relating to these, and that facilities for storing coal after it had been delivered to the consignee do not relate to the receiving, forwarding, or delivering of traffic, and are not therefore under the control of the court. (*West* v. *London & North-western Ry. Co.*, L. R., 5 C. P. 622; 39 L. J., C. P. 282; 23 L. T. (N. S.) 371; 18 W. R. 1028; 1 Nev. & Mac. 166.)

A railway company delivered minerals at T. station, but refused to deliver there damageable traffic consigned to the applicant, and delivered such traffic at L., one mile and a half from T., which was their general goods station for T.

The accommodation at T. station being insufficient to receive all the T. goods traffic, and the railway company having no power to enlarge it: *Held*, that the applicant was not entitled to have damageable goods delivered at that station.

Semble, if the accommodation at T. station had been sufficient to receive all traffic similarly sent, the company would have been ordered to deliver damageable goods to the applicant at T. station. (*Thomas* v. *North Staffordshire Ry. Co.*, 3 Nev. & Mac. 1.)

The Railway and Canal Traffic Act, 1854, § 2, does not compel a railway company to find reasonable accommodation for the public further than as it is in the interests of railway traffic that it should be found.

An application to the commissioners, under that section, to order a railway company to construct a foot-bridge over their railway in their station at H. for the more convenient ingress and egress of foot-passengers from and to the town refused, on the ground that such a bridge was not a due and reasonable facility under the circumstances.

(*Holyhead Local Board* v. *London Ry. Co.*, 4 Ry. and Can. Traf. Cas. 37; see *Hastings Town Council* v. *S. E. Ry. Co.*, 3 Nev & Mac. 179.)

— **Establishing new station—Principles governing.** The obligation imposed upon railway companies, by section 2 of the Railway and Canal Traffic Act, 1854, to afford to the public facilities for using a railway as regards the receipt and delivery of traffic is not confined to the granting of such facilities at existing stations only.

A railway commits an infringement of the above-mentioned section, if, not having the excuse of inability, it refuses to receive and deliver traffic of a particular district except at places on its railway which are unreasonably remote, and if, also, the convenience that the opening of a station within easy reach would be to traffic that would use it, measured by quantity and other considerations, has a clear preponderance over the inconvenience from expense and trouble which it would cause the railway company to give that accommodation.

Upon complaint of the inhabitants of the district of N., which was intersected by a line of railway, of there being no station in the district, it was proved that there was no station nearer than at A. on the one side, and the terminal station of H. on the other, the distance from A. to H. being about four and a half miles; that the railway company possessed surplus and unoccupied lands in such district, upon part of which they had placed a siding for the delivery of coal, and that there would be no physical or engineering difficulty in using part of such land for the establishment of a station at which traffic of every description could be dealt with: *Held*, that the railway company had not contravened the provisions of section 2 of the Railway and Canal Traffic Act, 1854, by omitting to provide a passenger station in the district, because it appeared that the number of passengers that would use such a station would be so limited that the saving to so few persons of the inconvenience of going an extra distance by road between their houses and the H. station was not a prospective gain from the point of view of public interest sufficient in degree to justify the commissioners in requiring the railway company to open a passenger station in the district of N., but that the railway company ought to provide siding accommodation reasonably sufficient for the receipt and delivery in N. of the station to station traffic of the district, and to give such a service for the delivery of inward traffic in the district, and the removal therefrom of outward traffic, as was given under corresponding circumstances to other places. (*Local Board, etc.,* v. *North Eastern R. Co.*, 3 Nev. & Mac. 306.)

The commissioners have jurisdiction to entertain an application, under section 2 of the Railway and Canal Traffic Act, 1854. for an order compelling a railway company to provide a station, on the ground that there are no stations in use where the traffic of a particular district traversed by the railway can come or go without public inconvenience. (*Harris* v. *London, etc., R. Co.*, 3 Nev. & Mac. 331.)

The **block signal system** is a "facility" within the statute. (*London, etc., Ry. Co.* v. *Staines, etc., Ry. Co.*, 3 Nev. & Mac. 48.)

See further notes to § 7, p. 148.

(17) DISCRIMINATIONS IN CHARGES BETWEEN CONNECTING LINES.

The clause "and shall not discriminate in their rates and charges between such connecting lines," was probably added because of the contrariety of opinion among the English judges as to whether "facilities" included charges.

The mere fact that railway companies make charges for the conveyance of passengers in excess of those authorized by their special acts, but without any undue preference, is not a breach of their obligation under 17 and 18 Vict., c. 31, s. 2, to "afford according to their respective powers all reasonable facilities for the receiving and forwarding and delivering of traffic upon and from the several railways and canals belonging to or worked by such companies respectively, and for the return of carriages, trucks, boats, and other vehicles." And the railway commissioners have no jurisdiction to grant an injunction to restrain the making of such excessive charges. (*Great Western Ry. Co.* v. *Railway Commissioners; In re Brown*, 7 L. R. Q. B. Div. 182; 50 L. J. Q. B. Div. 483; 45 L. T. (N. S.) 206; 29 W. R. 901—C. A.; affirming 45 L. T. (N. S.) 65—D.; see 3 Nev. & Mac. Ry. Cas. 523 for action of commissioners.) The commissioners had previously held in two other cases *contra*, that making illegal or excessive charges was a failure to afford all reasonable facilities. (*Aberdeen Co.* v. *Gt. North. Ry. Co.*, 3 Nev. & Mac. Ry. Cas. 205; *Chatterly Iron Co.* v. *North. S. Ry. Co., Ibid.* 238.)

Semble, that if the overcharges were of such an amount and of such a nature that they had the effect, or it could be presumed that they were made with the intention, of preventing the use by passengers of particular trains and stations, the commissioners might have jurisdiction to entertain a complaint in respect of them as being a refusal of "facilities" within the meaning of 17 and 18 Vict., c. 31, s. 2. (Per Brett, L. J., and Cotton, L. J., *Great Western Ry. Co.* v. *Railway Commissioners; In re Brown, supra*.)

Charges which a railway company have no statutory power to make, and which are intended or calculated to prevent, and do in fact prevent, the conveyance of traffic on the railway, are a violation of section 2 of the Railway and Canal Traffic Act, 1854. (*Young* v. *Gwendraeth Valley Railway*, 4 Ry. & Can. Traf. Cas. 247—Com'rs.)

The words in section 2 of the Railway and Canal Traffic Act, "every railway company shall afford all due and reasonable facilities for the receiving and forwarding of traffic," do not refer to the fares charged for passenger traffic. (Per Bramwell, L. J., *Great Western Ry. Co.* v. *Railway Commissioners*; *In re Brown, supra.*)

Charter of Texas and Pacific Railroad. "That all railroads constructed, or that may be hereafter constructed, to intersect said Texas and Pacific Railroad, shall have a right to connect with that line; that **no discrimination** as regards **charges for freight or passengers**, or in any other matter, shall be made by said Texas and Pacific Railroad Company against any of the said **connecting roads**; but that the same charges per mile as to passengers, and per ton per mile as to freight, passing from said Texas and Pacific Railroad over any of said connecting roads, or passing from any of said connecting roads over any part of said Texas and Pacific Railroad, shall be made by said company as they make for freight and passengers over their own road; provided, also, that said connecting roads shall reciprocate said right of connection and equality of charges with said Texas and Pacific Railroad; and provided, further, that the rates charged for carrying passengers and freight per mile shall not exceed the prices that may be fixed by congress for carrying passengers and freight on the Union Pacific and Central Pacific railroads." (Charter Texas and Pacific Ry. Co., 16 U. S. Statutes at Large, page 578, section 15.)

The act of congress approved May 2, 1872, 17 Statutes at Large, page 59, changing the name of the company to the Texas and Pacific Railway Company, provided: "That all railroads terminating at Shreveport shall have the right to make the same running connections, and shall be entitled to the same privileges for the transaction of business in connection with the Texas and Pacific Railway as are granted to roads intersecting therewith." These statutes commented on and construed by Pardee, J., in *Mo. Pac. Ry. Co.* v. *T. & P. Ry. Co.*, 30 Fed. Rep. 2.

(18) Drawing Cars of Other Roads.

It is held in several cases that a railway company, engaged in the transportation of freight for hire as a common carrier, is bound, as a common-law duty, to transport or haul upon its road the cars of any other railroad company when requested so to do. (*Vermont etc., R.* v. *Fitchburg R.*, 14 Allen (Mass.) 462, 469; *Mackin* v. *Boston & A.*

R., 135 Mass. 201, 206; *Peoria, etc., R. Co.* v. *Chicago, etc., R. Co.*, 109 Ill. 135; s. c., 19 Central L. J. 111, and see elaborate note thereto, s. c. 18 Am. & Eng. R. Cas 506, and note; see *McCoy* v. *C., I., St. L. & C. R. Co.*, 13 Fed Rep. 3.)

See collection of decisions and statutes as to duty of connecting roads as to transportation of cars of other roads, in notes, 19 Central L. J. 113.

See, further, note—"Continuous shipment in same cars"—to § 7, *post.*

(19) AT COMMON LAW AND UNDER STATE STATUTES.

"At common law a railroad common carrier is not bound to carry beyond its own lines" (*A. T. & S. F. R. Co.* v. *D. & N. O. R. Co.*, 110 U. S. 667, 680; *Rome R. Co.* v. *Sullivan*, 25 Ga. 228; *Atchison, etc., R. Co.* v. *Roach*, 35 Kans. 740); "and if it contracts to carry beyond it, it may, in the absence of statutory regulations, determine for itself what agencies it will employ." (*A. T. & S. F. R. Co.* v. *D. & N. O. R. Co., supra*; *Napier* v. *Glasgow, etc., Ry. Co.*, 4 Sess. Ca. (3d Ser.) 87; 1 Nev. & Mac. 292.)

The provisions in the constitution of Colorado that "every railroad company shall have the right with its road to intersect, connect with, or cross any other railroad," only implies a mechanical union of the tracks of the road, so as to admit of the convenient passage of cars from one to the other, and does not of itself imply the right of **connecting business with business**. There is nothing in the constitution of Colorado which takes away the common-law right of the company to select the agencies it will employ beyond its own line. (*A. T. & S. F. R. Co.* v. *D. & N. O. R. Co.*, 110 U. S. 667.)

A railroad company has authority to establish its own stations for receiving and putting down passengers and merchandise, and may regulate the time and manner in which it will carry them; and in the absence of statutory obligations it is not required in Colorado to **establish stations** for those purposes at a point where another railroad company has made a mechanical union with its road. (*Ibid.*)

A provision in a state constitution which prohibits a railroad company from **discriminations in charges** and **facilities** does not, in the absence of legislation, require a company which has made provisions with a connecting road for the transaction of joint business, at an established union junction station, to make similar provisions with a rival connecting line at another near point on its line at which the second line has made a mechanical union with its road. (*Ibid.*) Nor to make the same arrangements with a carrier connecting at the same place. (*Napier* v. *Glasgow, etc., Ry. Co.*, 4 Sess. Cas. 87 (3d Ser.); 1 Nev. & Mac. 292.)

A provision in a state constitution which forbids a railroad company to make discrimination in rates is not violated by refusing to give to a connecting road the same arrangement as to through rates which are given to another connecting line, unless the conditions as to the service are substantially alike in both cases. (*A. T. & S. F. R. Co.* v. *D. & N. O. R. Co., supra.*)

"Every railroad company shall have the right with its road to intersect, connect with, or cross any other railroad; and shall receive and transport each other's passengers, tonnage, and cars, loaded or empty, without delay or discrimination." (Const. Pennsylvania, Art. 17, § 1.)

Held, not to change previous policy of the state as to railroad intersections (which was to prevent railroad crossings at grade). (*Northern C. Ry. Co.'s Appeal*, 103 Pa. St. 621, 628.)

Railroad tracks laid on streets of a city, connected with existing railroads, and extending to public warehouses, malt-houses, or manufacturing establishments, or to public wharves and landings, are in their nature public and for the public good, and all railroad companies are required by law to permit such connections to be made with their tracks. (*Chicago Dock Co.* v. *Garrity*, 115 Ill. 155.)

Georgia statute—Connecting roads: "All railroad companies in this state shall, at the terminus, or any intermediate point, be required to switch off and deliver to the connecting roads having the same gauge in the yard of the latter all cars passing over their lines, or any portion of the same, containing goods or freight consigned, without rebate or deception, by any route, at the option of the shipper, according to customary or published rates, to any point over or beyond such connecting roads; and any failure to do so, with reasonable diligence, according to the route by which said goods or freight are consigned, shall be deemed and taken as a conversion in law of such goods or freight, and shall give a right of action to the owner or consignee for the value of the same with interest." (Act Feby. 14, 1874, Ga., § 1.)

Section 2 authorizes roads to connect, and section 4 provides how connection may be compelled.

"No railroad company shall discriminate in its rates, or traffic of freights, in favor of any line or route connected with it, as against any other line or route; nor, when a part of its own line is sought to be run in connection with any other route, shall such company discriminate against such connecting line, or in favor of the balance of its own line, but shall have the same rates for all, and shall afford the like usual and customary facilities for interchange of freights to each and all routes or lines alike. Any refusal of the same shall give a like right of action as mentioned in the first section of this act." (*Ib.*, § 3.)

In an action by a shipper, under the above statute, where the Central Railroad Company, whose road runs from Savannah to Macon, and thence, by itself and its branches, or roads controlled by it, to other points, passed a rule that, "on and after date, no shipment of salt or other merchandise from Brunswick, in competition with Savannah, will be received for local stations on this line, or passing over the South-western Railroad division for points beyond, unless charges are prepaid and shipments delivered at warehouses by drays, as local business, when regular local tariff rates from Macon will be assessed on same": *Held*, that such rule was contrary to said act, and that for damages resulting from its enforcement, as to salt shipped from Brunswick by the East Tennessee, Virginia and Georgia Railroad to Macon, and to be carried beyond that point by the Central Railroad, a right of action accrued. While the competing railroad company might sue for damages to its general business, the shipper, who is damaged by the wrongful requirement of unshipping, draying, and reshipping, and the consequent waste, delay, and injury, has a right of action against the railroad company causing the same. (*Logan* v. *Central Railroad*, 74 Ga. 684 (1885.)

A connecting line, in the sense of said act, is where any railroad, at its terminus, or any intermediate point along its line, joins another, or where two railroads have the same terminus; and where a railroad is adjacent to another, and capable of being joined to it by a switch, either at its terminus or anywhere along its line where they meet or converge, the right is given to make such connection, whether it be voluntarily granted or not. (*Ibid.*)

The statutes of Michigan require railroads to receive and draw the cars of other roads. (General Laws 1873, p. 99.)

Through rates. The defendants, owning a short railway, from New Orleans to Lake Pontchartrain, and one Morgan, owning a line of steamers plying from the lake terminus to Mobile, and the plaintiffs and other parties owning two other steamers in the same trade, an arrangement was made by defendant with Morgan and temporarily with the proprietors of the other steamers, respectively, to share *pro rata* the through freight from New Orleans to Mobile. It appeared that this arrangement was unprofitable to the defendant, for the lines of steamers, by competing and lowering the rates of freight, greatly reduced the share coming to the railway. The defendant, therefore, entered into an agreement with Morgan, by which the latter loaned it $250,000, and the former agreed to prorate with him the through freight from New Orleans to Mobile, and to charge all other steamers the rates paid by the public generally. The plaintiffs immediately laid up their steamer and sued for damages, on the ground that this prorating with Morgan and refusing to further prorate with plaintiffs was an illegal combination with Morgan to confer on him an unlawful monopoly and preference. *Held*, that the acts of defendant were not in contravention of any statute of Louisiana or of any principle of her jurisprudence; that they might agree or refuse to prorate through freight with any body. (*Eclipse Towboat Co.* v. *Pontchartrain R. R. Co.*, 24 La. An. 1, 1872.)

The right of connecting roads to make contracts for through rates is incident to their powers unless prohibited by their charter. Where such contracts are not unjust, unconscionable, or in restraint of trade they will not be interfered with. (*Munhall* v. *Pa. R. Co.*, 92 Pa. St. 150.)

Station facilities. Railroads may be required to afford proper station facilities and prevented from abandoning stations already established. (*Connecticut* v. *New Haven, etc., Co.*, 37 Conn. 153, 163; *State* v. *New Haven, etc., Co.*, 42 Conn. 56; *Railroad Co.* v. *Hammersley*, 104 U. S. 1; *R. Com'rs* v. *Portland, etc., R. Co.*, 63 Me. 269; *Commonwealth* v. *Eastern R. Co.*, 103 Mass. 254; *State* v. *Chicago, etc., R. Co.*, 19 Neb. 476.)

Receivers of a road which had established a stock depot at one stock yards, and contracted to deliver all stock there, were ordered to build a side track to a new stock yards and deliver all stock consigned to it upon same terms as at the old stock depot. (*Cin'ti Stock Yards Co.* v. *U. R. Stock Yards Co.*, 7 Cincinnati Weekly Law Bulletin, 295, Minshall, J.; see, further, notes to § 7.)

GREATER CHARGE IN THE AGGREGATE FOR SHORTER THAN FOR LONGER HAUL FORBIDDEN—COMMISSION AUTHORIZED TO RELIEVE CARRIERS IN SPECIAL CASES FROM OPERATION OF THIS SECTION.(20)

Sec. 4. That it shall be unlawful for any common carrier subject to the provisions of this act to charge or receive any greater compensation in the aggregate(21) for the transportation of passengers or of like kind of property,(22) under substantially similar circumstances and conditions,(23) for a shorter than for a longer distance over the same line,(24) in the same direction,(25) the shorter being included within the longer distance; but this shall not be construed as authorizing any common carrier within the terms of this act to charge and receive as great compensation for a shorter as for a longer distance :(26) *Provided, however*, That upon application to the Commission appointed under the provisions of this act, such common carrier may, in special cases, after investigation by the Commission, be authorized to charge less for longer than for shorter distances for the transportation of passengers or property; and the Commission may from time to time prescribe the extent to which such designated common carrier may be relieved from the operation of this section of this act.(27)

(20) INTRODUCTORY NOTE.

It has been claimed that section 4 is merely designed to fix a rule of evidence to be applied in determining questions arising under the preceding sections of the statute against unreasonable or discriminating rates, and establishes the rule that a greater charge for a less distance is *prima facie* an unreasonable or discriminative rate prohibited by the statute; and that the proviso authorizing the commissioners to limit or suspend the operation of the section confers upon them a power only of shifting the burden of proof. Under this construction of the section it does not make, by its general rule, the carrier liable for charging the greater rate, nor does its proviso exempt him from liability if he should charge the greater rate, but leaves the liability of the carrier in either case to be determined finally by the judgment of the jury and court as to whether the charge made is unreasonable or discriminative within the prohibitions of the statute. We find nothing either in the language of the section or in the circumstances leading to its adoption that will warrant this construction. The language of the act is absolute and prohibits the charges described without condition, and the proviso attached thereto is also absolute, exempting the carrier from liability as to the limitations of the general section permitted by the commissioners.

The complaints giving rise to this section are well known. It has been since the origin of railroads a source of trouble with local communities and of controversies with the railroads that a very great discrimination was made against such communities and in favor of competing points in the proportional rates for transportation charged. In connection with this discrimination a wide-spread feeling has prevailed among the local communities that they were compelled to make good the deficiencies in earnings over operative expenses in the carriage of freight between competing points by large additions to the reasonable charges for services rendered to themselves. Section 4 was designed to impose a limitation upon this discrimination that, without requiring proportional rates, the railroads should be prohibited from charging in any case a greater rate for the short distance than for the longer one. In terms, and certainly in intent, it imposes an absolute limit upon the right of the carrier to discriminate, in this respect, in charges between different points. It seems to me an unwarrantable qualification of the plain language of the section to give it the construction claimed.

There is no counterpart of this section in English legislation upon the regulation of railway traffic, although the construction placed upon the "undue preference" clause of section 2 of the Railway and Canal Traffic Act, 1854, by the courts and Railway Commissioners, has substantially accomplished the object of this section. Statutes of similar character are to be found in Illinois (Act of May 2, 1873, § 3; R. S. Ill., 1883. p. 884, § 125; Starr and Curtiss' Annotated Stat. Ill., 1885. § 147); Massachusetts (General Railroad Act, 1874, c. 372, § 140); and Oregon, (Act of Feb. 20, 1885, § 4; Laws 1885, p. 38.)

English decisions. A larger charge for a shorter haul is held to amount to an undue preference under the English statutes. (*Budd* v. *London & N. W. Ry. Co.*, 4 Ry. & Can. Traf. Cas. 393; 36 L. T. (N. S.) 302.)

And even the same charge for a shorter haul as for a longer haul has been held to be an undue preference. (*Denaby, etc., Co.* v. *Manchester, etc., Ry. Co.*, 3 Nev. & Mac. 426; see note to Par. 1, § 3, *ante*, p. 68 *et seq.*)

Quaere: Congress having specially legislated upon the subject of a larger charge for a shorter haul, are not such cases excluded from the general terms of Par. 1, § 3, of the act?

And yet, what is the meaning of the clause in section 4 providing "but this shall not be construed as authorizing any common carrier within the terms of this act to charge and receive as great compensation for a shorter as for a longer distance"? Does it not mean that the same charge for a shorter as for a longer haul may amount to an undue preference under § 3, Par. 1, as the English courts have decided? It is to be observed, also, that section 3 is broader in terms than the English statute, having added the word "locality" in its enumeration of the classes against which undue prejudice must not be made, although the construction put upon the English statute reached that end.

Reductions in fare in favor of longer distances have been recognized as proper under the English acts. (*Hozier* v. *Caledonia Ry. Co.*, 17 Sess. Ca. 302; 24 Law Times, 339; 1 Nev. & Mac. 27; *Jones* v. *Eastern Cos Ry. Co.*, 3 C. B. (N. S.) 718; 1 Nev. & Mac. 45; *Ransome* v. *Same Co.*, 1 Nev. & Mac. 117.)

— **Local and through traffic—Pro-rating**. Whether each company collects its own quota of a through toll, or one collects for all, the character of a through toll is the same; and, if made compulsory under the Regulation of Railways Act, 1873, is not subject to the equality clause of the special acts of the railway companies, so as to render it necessary to regulate the local tolls thereby.

The eleventh section authorizes the commissioners to allot to a company, out of a through rate, an amount less than its maximum charges, but not less per mile "than the mileage rates which such company may, for the time being, legally be charging for like traffic carried by a like mode of transit on any other line of communication between the same points, being the points of departure and arrival of the through route."

Held, that the "mileage rates" must be mileage rates for a line having the same termini as the through route and must be charged in respect of goods carried over it for its whole length. (*Warwick, etc., Canal Co.* v. *Birmingham, etc., Canal Co.*, 3 Nev. & Mac. Ry. Cas. 113.)

— **Competition of interest**. A railway company having fixed the rates for passengers traveling between the termini of the line much lower proportionately than between intermediate stations: *Held*, that passengers between intermediate stations had no right to complain, there being no competition of interest between the termini and such intermediate stations. (*Hozier* v. *Caledonia Ry. Co.*, 17 Sess. Ca. 302; 24 Law Times, 339; 1 Nev. & Mac. 27.)

A railway company (whose act contained an equality clause) charged a smaller fare to passengers who traveled from D. to H. intending to proceed from H. to London by another railway, than they charged passengers from D. to H. who had no such intention.

Held, by Lord Chancellor Cottenham, on motion for an injunction, that the equality clause was meant only to prevent the exercise of a monopoly to the prejudice of one passenger or carrier and in favor of another, and that, even if he had jurisdiction to interfere, he would not do so unless it was clear that the public interest required it; and in this case, it being admitted that the higher charge was not more than the act authorized, it did not appear that the public were prejudiced by the arrangement. (*Att.-Gen.* v. *The Birmingham, etc., Ry. Co.*, 2 Ry. Ca. 124.)

Statutes and decisions in the United States—Federal courts. The service rendered by a railway company in transporting a local passenger from one point on its line is not identical with the service rendered in transporting a through passenger over the same rails. (*Union Pacific Ry. Co.* v. *U. S.*, 117 U. S. 355.)

In this case the rate for local passengers between Council Bluffs and Ogden was $78.50. The proportion which the company received upon through tickets from sea-board to sea-board, for transportation between said cities, was $54. The court of claims having found the higher rate to be reasonable the supreme court (Matthews, J.) said: "No question of law arises upon it [the finding of these facts] unless it be one whether the service rendered in transporting a local passenger between the two points is in law identical with that rendered in transporting a through passenger between the same points as part of the transit over the distance of the whole line. This we can not affirm." (p. 363.)

The provision in section 15 of the Texas and Pacific Railway Company charter, that "the same charges per mile as to passengers, and per ton per mile as to freight, . . . shall be made by said company as they make for freight and passengers over their own road," was before Judge Pardee in the case of the *Missouri Pacific Ry. Co.* v. *Texas and Pacific Ry. Co.*, 30 Fed. Rep. 2, in which he said, instructing the receivers of the road, that "a proper construction of said section 15 does not permit that connecting roads should be charged less or more per ton per mile as to freight, or less or more per mile as to passengers, than the rates charged on or over the Texas and Pacific lines, but the same. In other words, section 15 is in the interest of and for the protection of shippers local to the Texas and Pacific Railway as well as in the interest of and for the protection of connecting lines. If the respondents are, as they seem to say, charging the petitioners' lines less per ton per mile than the charges made on respondents' lines to other shippers under the same conditions as to distance and shipping points, then respondents are discriminating (and probably against shippers that are forced to use their lines); which ought not to be permitted under any circumstances, and particularly on a railroad to the construction of which the general government and the State of Texas contributed so large a portion of the public lands." (p. 10.)

— **Illinois.** A larger charge for a shorter haul is an unjust discrimination against communities. (Lawrence, C. J., in *C. & A. R. Co.* v. *People*, 67 Ill. 11, 19, 20; see quotation in note on p. 127, *post*.)

If a lower rate is habitually charged for a longer distance in the same direction than for a shorter distance, it is not permissible to show that the higher rate for the shorter distance is reasonable; the lower charge for the longer distance makes it unreasonable. (*C. & A. R. Co.*, 67 Ill. 11, 20, 22; see Act of 1873, § 3; Starr & Curtiss' Ann. Stat. Ill. 1885, § 147; note on p. 128, *post*.)

Where the railroad commissioners had fixed the rates between points, the fact that a railroad company greatly reduced the rate for the longer distance did not amount to unjust discrimination, if the rate for the shorter distance did not exceed the rate fixed by the commissioners although it did exceed that charged for the longer distance. (*Railroad Co.* v. *Hill*, 14 Bradw. (Ill. App.) 579.)

— **Massachusetts.** "No railroad corporation shall charge or receive for the transportation of freight to any station on its road a greater sum than is at the time charged or received for the transportation of the like class and quantity of freight from the same original point of departure to a station at a greater distance on its road in the same direction. Two or more railroad corporations, whose roads connect, shall not charge or receive for the transportation of freight to any station on the road of either of them a greater sum than is at the time charged or received for the transportation of the like class and quantity of freight from the same original point of departure to a station at a greater distance on the road of either of them in the same direction. In the construction of this section the sum charged or received for the transportation of freight shall include all terminal charges; and the road of a corporation shall include all the road in use by such corporation, whether owned or operated under a contract or lease." (Gen'l R. R. Act, 1874, c. 372, § 140.)

Where flour was shipped from Terre Haute, Ind., to Nashua, N. H., at a lower rate than from Terre Haute, Ind., to Pepperell, a less distance from said Terre Haute, and in the same direction as Nashua, both Nashua and Pepperell being stations on defendant's road, the transportation having been over defendant's road only from Worcester, Mass., the transportation to Worcester being by other railroads: *Held*, that section 140, above, applies to the transportation of freight by such a corporation as a common carrier over its own road, and not over other roads, for which it charges and receives nothing, except as collecting agent of the corporations owning such other roads; and that the action was not maintainable. (*Commonwealth* v. *W. & N. R. Co.*, 124 Mass. 561; 18 Am. Ry. Rep. 418, opinion by Gray, C. J.)

— **Oregon.** See statute of 1885 and decision of Deady, J., in *Exp. Koehler*, 23 Fed. Rep. 529, quoted at length in note (23), *post*, p. 128.

— **Pennsylvania.** Under Pennsylvania Tonnage Commutation Act, 1861, prescribing rates for local freight, a railroad may discriminate in rates between "local freight" and freight coming from outside the state—a case of charging more for "**through**" than "**local**" freight. (*Shipper* v. *Penn. R. Co*, 47 Pa. St. 338.)

But grain bought in another state, and shipped to and stored for sale at Pittsburgh, and afterward reshipped to Philadelphia, is "local freight;" and the excess paid as for "through freight" may be recovered back. (*Penn. R. Co.* v. *Canfield*, 46 Pa. St. 211.)

Grain bought in another state and shipped to Pittsburgh, and reshipped to Philadelphia, but not stored for sale, is not "local freight." (*Rowland* v. *Penn. R. Co.*, 52 Pa. St. 250.)

An act provided that "rates for toll and transportation may be regulated in such manner as the company may deem most advisable; provided, that the average charges for tolls shall not exceed four cents per ton per mile for freight": *Held*, that the company might impose more than four cents per mile on some charges, so that, by making others less, the general average should not exceed four cents. The adjustment need not be made so as to bear on each individual equally. Discriminations may be made in favor of longer distances. The charges against plaintiff, averaged by the whole amount of the business of the company, was less than the four per cent; by that done for him alone they were more than five per cent: *Held*, that the former was the proper estimate, and the charges were not excessive. (*Hersh* v. *North C. Ry. Co.*, 74 Pa. St. 181.)

— **Evidence.** An entire contract to carry between two points, in absence of contrary evidence, implies that the charge is the same on every part of the distance. (*Wabash, etc., Ry. Co.* v. *People*, 105 Ill. 236; but see s. c., 118 U. S. 557.)

As to evidence under Ill. statute, see *St. Louis, etc., R. Co.* v. *Hill*, 14 Bradw. 579.

The fact that cotton shipped from longer distances at lower rates, but under changed conditions, being compressed and thus greatly reduced in bulk, is not evidence that higher rates for shorter distances upon uncompressed cotton are unreasonable. (*Lotspeich* v. *Central R. Co.*, 73 Ala. 306; s. c., 18 Am. & Eng. Cas. 490.)

— **Pleading.** See note to section 8, *post*.

Equal mileage rates. Where a railway company having a right, under their special act, to charge for six miles where the traffic was carried for less than six miles, agreed with B. for a varying scale of charges for certain traffic for distances between three and six miles (under which they charged 7d. per ton for a distance of five miles and fifty-four chains), and refused to apply the like scale to A.'s traffic (which they charged 6*d.* per ton for a distance of three miles and fifty-seven chains), and A. complained of an undue prejudice, it was held that the disproportion was not an undue preference, having regard to the short distance clause of the special act, because the applicants had failed to show that any traffic was being carried for B. for the same distance as that for A. (*Merry* v. *Glasgow and South-western Railway*, 4 Ry. & Can. Traf. Cas. 383.)

There is no requirement of the common law, that when there is a difference of distances, the charge shall be proportioned to the respective distances. (*Railroad Co.* v. *Hill*, 14 Bradw. (Ill. App.) 579 (1884.)

Upon the question of the practicability of equal mileage charges see note, 1 Nev. & Mac. 71.

That congress did not intend to establish the principle of proportionate mileage charges by the "long and short haul" section (section 4), see debates in congress, Dos Passos Inter-state Com. Act, p. 38–9.

(21) "GREATER COMPENSATION IN THE AGGREGATE FOR TRANSPORTATION."

"Transportation" is made by the second paragraph of the first section of the act to "include all instrumentalities of shipment or carriage." Section 6 provides that carriers shall print and keep for public inspection "schedules showing the rates and fares and *charges for transportation*," and also provides that such schedules "shall also state separately the terminal charges and any rules or regulations which in any wise change, affect, or determine any part or the *aggregate* of such aforesaid rates and fares and charges." So that it would seem clear that "greater compensation in the *aggregate*" includes charges for terminal and other facilities in loading and unloading and demurrage and other charges. Stated in another form, the word "*aggregate*" in section 4 means the same as in section 6; it means what it expressly says in the latter section—all "charges and . . . rules or regulations which *in any wise* change, affect, or determine . . . *the aggregate* of such . . . charges," *i. e.*, "charges for transportation."

Then, too, it seems perfectly clear that if the same service is performed, the charges for demurrage, terminal and other facilities must be the same for local as for through traffic (§ 2 of the Act); and the place from which the goods are shipped and the destination thereof are not "circumstances" authorizing any difference in charge. (*Denaby, etc., Co.* v. *Manchester, etc., Ry. Co.*, L. R. 11 App. Cas. 97; *Ransome* v. *Eastern Cos. Ry. Co.* (No. 2) 4 C. B. (N. S.) 135; 1 Nev. &

Mac. 109; *Budd* v. *London and N. W. Ry. Co.*, 36 L. T. (N. S.) 302; 4 Ry. & Can. Traf. Cas. 393; *Oxlade* v. *N. E. Ry. Co.* (No. 1), 1 C. B. (N. S.) 454; 1 Nev. & Mac. 72.)

Therefore, I can not agree with Mr. Easley that "the words 'in the aggregate' do not require the word transportation to include terminal charges, or the like, but such charges may be made where reasons for them exist, even though such charges result in causing higher charges between points nearer each other than between points further apart." (Railway Age, April 8, 1887, p. 237.)

(22) "LIKE KIND OF PROPERTY."

In section 2 the words are "like kind of traffic." I perceive no reason for believing that any different meaning or significance is to be attached to the words in the present section. The substitution of "property" for "traffic" was probably accidental. Reference is made to note to § 2, *ante*, p. 46.

(23) "SUBSTANTIALLY SIMILAR CIRCUMSTANCES AND CONDITIONS."

This is identically the same phrase found in § 2 of the Act (the Equality Clause). The sources from which this language was drawn and the construction put upon it, are so fully set out in the notes to that section that only a brief recapitulation of the points of the decisions will be made, reference being made to the notes themselves for a fuller statement of the cases and a discussion of the principles upon which they proceed. No reason is perceived for giving the same language a different meaning in this section from that which it should have in section 2, notwithstanding the elaborate argument of Mr. Easley to the contrary (Railway Age, April 8 and 15, 1887). Rather the stages through which the bill passed before becoming a law, would seem to indicate a purpose to adopt throughout, language which had received a fixed and well-understood meaning in the English law.

Interests of company. In determining under the second section of the Railway and Canal Traffic Act, 1854, whether a railway company has given an undue and unreasonable preference to a particular person, company or traffic, or subjected a particular person, company or traffic to an undue or unreasonable prejudice or disadvantage, this court may take into consideration the fair interests of the railway itself, and entertain such questions as whether the company might not carry larger quantities, or for longer distances, at lower rates per ton per mile than smaller quantities, or for shorter distances, so as to derive equal profits to itself. (*Ransome* v. *The Eastern Co.'s Ry. Co., etc.*,

1 Nev. & Mac. 63; 1 C. B. (N. S.) 437; *Nicholson* v. *G. W. Ry. Co.*, 5 C. B. 366; 1 Nev. & Mac. 121.)

Cost of service constitutes a real difference in "circumstances." (*Denaby, etc., Co.* v. *Manchester, etc., Ry. Co.*, L. R. 11 App. Cas. 97; *C. & A. Ry. Co.* v. *People*, 67 Ill. 11–24, and cases cited under § 2, p. 48, *supra*, and under § 3, p. 79, *supra*.)

Expense of starting train is the same for a long as for a short haul. (*Ransome* v. *Eastern Co.'s Ry. Co.*, 1 Nev. & Mac. 117.)

"If a company were to make a distinction between terminal traffic and intermediate traffic, there might be very fair and sufficient reasons for their so doing. As, for instance, in respect of terminal, there might be competition with another railway, and in respect of terminal traffic, as distinguished from intermediate traffic, it might well be they could afford to carry goods over the whole line cheaper, or proportionately so, than they could over an intermediate part of the line." (Cockburn, C. J., in *Harris* v. *Railway Co.*, 1 Nev. & Mac. 97, 103.)

The difference in cost must bear some proportion to the difference in cost of service. Otherwise it will amount to an undue preference. (Cases collected in note to § 2, *ante*, p. 49.)

Quantity of freight shipped. Cases collected and principles stated in note to § 2, *ante*, p. 50 *et seq.*, also note to § 3, *ante*, p. 80 *et seq.*

Competition with other lines. The court having shown that railroads can not unjustly discriminate as to individuals, proceeded: "If, then, an unjust discrimination is not to be permitted as between individuals in regard to freights, is it any more permissible as between different communities or localities? We are wholly at a loss to discover the slightest difference in reason or principle. If a farmer, living three miles from the Springfield station upon this company's road, is charged fifteen cents per bushel for shipping his corn to Chicago, is it just that the farmer living twenty miles nearer Chicago should be charged a higher sum? Certainly not, unless the railway company can show a peculiar state of affairs to justify the discrimination, and this must be something more than the mere fact that there are competing lines at one point and not at the other. The discrimination, in such a case, is as much a discrimination between individuals as it would be in reference to two persons living in the same locality, and shipping at the same station, unless, as before stated, a satisfactory reason can be given for discrimination between the points of shipment, and such a reason, in the case supposed, is not very easy to conceive." (Lawrence, C. J., in *C. & A. R. Co.* v. *People*, 67 Ill. 11, 19–20.)

The principle announced in this case was subsequently incorporated into the statute law of the state as follows:

"It shall not be deemed a sufficient excuse or justification of such discriminations (same or greater charge for short haul), on the part of such railroad corporation, that the railway station or point at which it shall charge or receive the same or less rates of toll or compensation for the transportation of such passenger or freight, or for the use and transportation of such railroad car the greater distance, than for the shorter distance, is a railway station or point at which there exists competition with any other railroad or means of transportation." (Act of 1873, § 3; Starr & Curtis' Annotated Statutes Ill., 1885, § 147.)

The settled doctrine of the English courts is the same. (*London, etc., Ry. Co.* v. *Evershed*, L. R. 3 App. Cas. 1029; *Budd* v. *London, etc., Ry. Co.*, 36 L. T. (N. S.) 802; 4 Ry. & Can. Traf. Cas. 393; *Thompson* v. *London & N. W. Ry. Co.*, 2 Nev. & Mac. 115; *Greenop* v. *S. E. Ry.*, *Id.* 319; see also article by Mr. Adelbert Hamilton in 16 Am. Law Rev., p. 833 et seq., and note to § 2, and to § 3.)

By a canal act a company were entitled to demand a fixed sum for goods carried upon any part of the canal, and by 8 and 9 Vict., c. 28, canal companies may vary the tolls, provided that they are equal, for goods conveyed in boats using the same portion of the canal under the like circumstances. *Held*, that it was competent to the company to take a proportionably less toll per ton per mile for goods carried a given distance along any part of a canal, than for goods carried less than that distance; and, also, that it was competent to the company to agree to carry at a lower rate for a particular individual in consideration of a large guaranteed minimum toll in order to enable them to enter into a successful competition with a rival line of railway. (*Strick, etc.,* v. *Swansea Canal Co.*, 16 C. B. (N. S. 245.) This case must be regarded as overruled by the later English cases.

The Oregon Act of February 20, 1885 (Oregon Laws, 1885, p. 38), provides (1) that all charges in transportation shall be reasonable; (2) that no greater or less compensation shall be charged for a "like and contemporaneous service; and (3) prohibits discrimination [§ 1]; (4) prohibits the giving of rebates, drawbacks, etc. [§ 2]; (5) and entering into combinations to prevent transportation from being continuous from place of shipment to place of destination;" and (6) forbids pooling "freights of different and competing roads [§ 3], and also forbids charging or receiving greater compensation for a 'short' than for a 'long haul'" [§ 4]. The act also provides for posting schedules of rates, recovery of damages, allowance of counsel fees, etc. The act expressly excepts from its operation "goods in good faith intended to be shipped to points beyond the limits of this state."

Deady, J., upon an application of a receiver for instructions, said: "If the legislature can not require a railway corporation, formed under the laws of the state, to carry freight for nothing, or at any less rate than a reasonable one, then it necessarily follows that this provision of the act can not be enforced so far as to prevent the railway from competing with the water-craft at Corvallis and other similarly situated points, even if in so doing they are compelled to charge less for a long haul than a short one in the same direction. It is not the fault or contrivance of the railway that compels this discrimination, but it is the necessary result of circumstances altogether beyond its control. It is not done wantonly for the purpose of putting the one place up or the other down, but only to maintain its business against rival and competing lines of transportation. In other words, the matter so far as the railway is concerned, resolves itself into a choice of evils. It must either compete with the boats during the season of water transportation, and carry freight below what the legislature has declared to be a reasonable rate, or abandon the field and let its road go to rust. Nor can the shipper at the non-competing point, as over the short haul complain, so long as his goods are carried at a reasonable rate. It is not the fault of the railway that the shipper who does business at a competing point has the advantage of him. It is a natural advantage which he must submit to unless the legislature will undertake to equalize the matter by prohibiting the carriage of goods by water for a less rate than by rail; and when this is done, the inequalities of distance as well as place may also be overcome by requiring goods to pay the same rate over a short haul as a long one, and then the shipper at Ashland will be as near the market as any one."

And the court ordered the receiver to charge "no more for the carriage of goods for a short haul than a long one in the same direction, except to and from points where the rate attainable is affected by water transportation, in which case he may carry at as low a rate as the water-craft do, without reference to the length of the haul." (*Ex parte Koehler*, 23 Fed. Rep. 529, 533; 21 Am. & E. Ry. Cas. 52.)

The same question re-examined and affirmed. *Ex parte Koehler*, 25 Fed. Rep. 73; s. c., 21 Am. & E. Ry. Cas. 58.

It is to be noted that the question presented in the second case related to transportation of goods from Oregon to California—inter-state commerce. (*Ex parte Koehler*, 25 Fed. Rep. 73.)

Developing trade. The English decisions uniformly hold that the fact that certain goods are shipped to develop a new trade does not constitute a difference in circumstances. (*Denaby, etc., Co.* v. *Man-*

chester, etc., Co., L. R. 11 App. Cas. 97; *Ransome* v. *Eastern Co.'s Ry. Co.*, 1 Nev. & Mac. 63; and other cases cited in notes to § 2, *ante*, p. 57, and to § 3, *ante*, p. 77.)

(24) "OVER THE SAME LINE."

The language of section 90 of the Railways Clauses Consolidation Act, 1845 (see note to section 2, *ante*, p. 43), is "passing only over the same portion of the line of railway." Under that statute and the similar Scotch Act, it has been held that it "applies only to goods passing between the same points of departure and arrival, and passing over no other part of the line." (*Denaby, etc., Co.* v. *Manchester, etc., Ry. Co*, L. R. 11 App. Cas. 97; *Murray* v. *Glasgow, etc., Ry. Co.*, 11 Court Sess. Cas. (4th Ser.) 205; 4 Ry. & Can. Traf. Cas. 456.)

In the Regulation of Railways Act, 1873, § 11, sub. § 5, in the provision as to through traffic, the railway commissioners are to determine not only as to the reasonableness of the rate but of the proposed "route." It is held that "a 'route,' within the meaning of this section, is a route from the station on the sending line where the traffic arises to the station on the forwarding line where such traffic is delivered." (*Junction Ry. Co.* v. *G. W. Ry. Co.*, 1 Nev. & Mac. 331.)

(25) "IN THE SAME DIRECTION."

The necessity of such a limitation is pointed by Lawrence, C. J., in *C. & A. R. Co.* v. *People*, 67 Ill. 11, in the fact that at certain seasons the major portion of the traffic moves in one direction, and what might be a fair rate one way would not be the other way. The act in question in that case having made no limitations in this respect, it afforded one of the grounds for holding that act in conflict with the constitutional limitation that the discrimination must be unjust.

(26) SAME CHARGE FOR SHORTER AS FOR LONGER DISTANCE.

It has been held that the same charge made for a shorter as for a longer distance amounted to an undue preference under section 2 English Railway and Canal Traffic Act, 1854, which has been incorporated into section 3 of the present act. (*Denaby, etc., Colliery Co.* v. *Manchester, etc., Ry. Co.*, 3 Nev. & Mac. 426, 441; 4 Ry. & Can. Traf. Cas. 23; *Ib.* 28; see note, "Group Rates," to § 3, on p. 68, *ante*, and note (20) to this section.)

(27) POWER OF COMMISSION TO SUSPEND THIS SECTION.

Nature of the power. A doubt has been suggested as to whether the power given to the Commission to suspend the operations of section 4 was constitutional; that it was a delegation to it of legislative power. I do not concur in the view taken. The duties of the Commission are administrative, and the power vested in it is only the ascertainment of a fact or condition in which congress itself determined to limit or suspend the operation of the section.

In *Miller* v. *The Mayor of New York*, 109 U. S. 385, congress authorized the construction of the Brooklyn bridge and legalized it as a lawful structure and post road, but empowered the secretary of the treasury to determine what mode of construction should constitute it a lawful structure. In answer to the same constitutional objection that is urged here, the court says (p. 394): "The act in question in requiring the approval of the secretary before the construction of the bridge was permitted, was not essentially different from a great mass of legislation directing certain measures to be taken upon the happening of particular contingencies or the ascertainment of particular information. The execution of a vast number of measures authorized by congress, and carried out under the direction of heads of departments, would be defeated if such were not the case. The efficiency of an act as a declaration of legislative will must, of course, come from congress, **but the ascertainment of the contingency upon which the act shall take effect may be left to such agencies as it may designate.**"

In several cases it has been held that the legislature having a right to provide for the correction and prevention of abuses in the management and conduct of railways, it has the right to select its own agencies for that purpose. It may confer power upon commissioners to require railroads to erect depots at points determined by them to be requisite to meet the demands of public convenience. (*R. Com'rs* v. *Portland, etc., R. Co.*, 63 Me. 269, 285; *Portland, etc., R.* v. *Grand Trunk Ry. Co.*, 46 Me. 69; *Commonwealth* v. *Eastern R. Co.*, 103 Mass. 254; *State* v. *Chicago, etc., R. Co.*, 19 Neb. 476.)

The object of the constitutional provision conferring power upon the legislature to regulate railroad freights and passenger tariffs, to prevent unjust discrimination, and require reasonable and just freights and tariffs, and making it the duty of the legislature to pass laws in furtherance of this provision, was to give proper protection to the citizens against unjust rates for the transportation of freights and passengers over the railroads of the state, and to prevent unjust discrimination, even though the rates might be just. It was not expected that the legislature should do more than pass laws to accomplish the ends in view. Nor were they required to enter into the details of settling freights and tariffs over all the railroads in the state. The railroad commissioners are officers appointed to carry into execution the laws passed by the legislature, and are constitutional officers. The powers of the railroad commissioners are not legislative. The power to adopt rules and regulations to carry into effect a law already passed differs from a power to enact the law. (*Georgia Railroad* v. *Railroad Com'rs*, 70 Ga. 694; 71 Ga. 863.)

In fact the final execution of laws of the nature of the one in question is confided in a great degree to the discretion of boards or officers authorized to administer them, and the law in each particular case is modified in its enforcement by the judgment of such officers or boards. The legislative will has its execution modified in each case by the ministerial agent.

Of like nature is the power delegated by legislative bodies to boards or officers authorized to license business or acts which, without such license, would be illegal. In such cases the effect and operation of the law depends upon their action. In the judgment of congress, in a field of untried legislation, when it could not provide for and foresee all the circumstances in which its act would have operation and effect, it was deemed necessary to vest in the Commission the duty of ascertaining the fact or condition from time to time in each case in which the congressional will should be modified, and the prohibited act be permitted and licensed. It was claimed that an immediate and unconditional enforcement of the rule would work great hardship to investments made upon the faith of previously existing usage, and, as in the case above quoted, the Commission was vested with the authority to determine the fact in each case, and that the will of congress and the intent of the law should be carried into effect accordingly.

Suspension is limited to this section—Other features of the law remain operative—Export trade. One of the questions which has been given a large prominence by the passage of this act is as to the right of railroads to make reductions in rates on account of the destination of the traffic, as whether it is to be exported or is intended for domestic consumption. It appears that the railroads have been accustomed to make reductions in favor of the export trade. No sound reason is perceived for the distinction. Whenever the service of transportation is the same the charge should be the same; the uses or destination of the merchandise are entirely immaterial. (*Twells* v. *Penna. R. Co.*, 3 Am. Law Reg. (N. S.) 728.) It is a discrimination against ourselves. (See *Mo. Pa. Ry. Co.* v. *Tex. & Pac. Ry. Co.*, 30 Fed. Rep. 2.) Rather strangely this discussion has centered around this section. And yet if this section were stricken from the statute altogether, it is clear that sections 2 and 3 would render unlawful a continuance of the practice heretofore prevailing in this regard (*Denaby, etc., Co. v. Manchester, etc., Ry. Co.*, L. R. 11 App. Cas. 97, 1885), unless the doctrine of the English courts in construing language that can not be distinguished from the present act is to be overthrown.

In the matter of the Boston export trade it is clear that if the long and short haul clause be eliminated from the law the discriminations in favor of the export trade would be unlawful, assuming the carriers to be subject to the act. The same question as in the case put, of shipments from Chicago to Boston, goods intended for the local or domestic trade being charged more than the through rate over the same roads between the same points to Liverpool, was before the House of Lords in 1885 in the *Denaby case* and the House was unanimous in holding that no distinction could be made between the the export trade and the domestic trade.

In fact, the doctrine of the English courts is now thoroughly settled that the motives of the shipper, as in opening a new trade (*Denaby, etc., Co. v. Manchester, etc., Ry. Co.*, L. R. 11 App. Cas. 97); or of the railway company as to secure traffic that would otherwise go to other lines (*London, etc., Ry. Co. v. Evershed*, L. R. 3 App. Cas. 1029; *Oxlade v. N. E. Ry. Co.* (No. 1), 1 C. B. (N. S.) 454; 1 Nev. & Mac. 72); or to compete with sea transportation (*Budd v. London & N. W. Ry. Co.*, 36 L. T. (N. S.) 802; 4 Ry. & Can. Traf. Cas. 393); or the origin or place from which the goods are shipped (*Ransome v. Eastern Cos. Ry. Co.* (No. 2), 4 C. B. 135; 1 Nev. & Mac. 109); or their place of destination (*Denaby, etc., Co. v. Manchester, etc., Ry. Co., supra*); or the person who ships them, whether a rival in business or not (*Gt. West. Ry. Co. v. Sutton*, L. R. 4 Eng. & Ir. App. (H. L.) 226), do not change the "circumstances" of transportation so as to warrant discriminations in charges.

Indeed, it would seem clear that discriminations on account of the destination of the property transported are illegal at common law. In the case of *Twells v. Penna. R. Co.*, in the Supreme Court of Pennsylvania, where a difference of charge was made by reason of the destination of the goods, Strong, J., afterward a justice of the Supreme Court of the United States, said that the claim "that the imposition of high rates for carrying the complainant's oil to Philadelphia because it is afterward to be forwarded in some way to New York is necessary to prevent his having an advantage in the New York market over those who employ the defendants to transport all the way, or over those who send oil from Pittsburgh to New York with through bills of lading is a matter outside of their control. It has no proper relation to them as carriers." (p. 733.) "When the service is the same the compensation demanded must be the same." (p. 729; 3 Am. Law Reg. (N. S.) 728.)

The only authority the Commission possesses is to suspend the operation of section 4. It may give authority in "special cases" "to charge less for longer than for shorter distances;" but the other provisions of the statute remain in full force. (*In re Petition of the Order of Railway Conductors*, decided by the Commission April 18, 1887.) It is believed, therefore, that the Commission does not possess any authority to authorize discriminations between export and domestic traffic, as is asked in the Boston case, or between the products of Asia and the produce of this country, as in the case of the Pacific railways. The Commission may say that the railroads are permitted to charge less from San Francisco to New York than from San Francisco to Cincinnati, but they can not say that tea destined for European trade shall enjoy a lower rate than tea intended for consumption in this country.

Insofar as as the action of Judge Pardee upon the petition of the receivers of the Texas and Pacific Railway for instructions under the act indicates a contrary opinion, it may be said that no reasons are given; apparently the cases have not been considered, and it is believed that upon full consideration the rule as above stated will be found to be correct. (1 Ry & Corp. L. J. 428, April 30, 1887.)

In cases of suspension such as that temporarily granted upon the application of the Southern Railway and Steamship Association, it is obvious that all the other provisions of the law continue to operate upon traffic subject to its provisions.

POOLING ARRANGEMENTS PROHIBITED.

Sec. 5. That it shall be unlawful for any common carrier subject to the provisions of this act to enter into any contract, agreement, or combination with any other common carrier or carriers for the pooling of freights of different and competing railroads, or to divide between them the aggregate or net proceeds of the earnings of such railroads, or any portion thereof; and in any case of an agreement for the pooling of freights as aforesaid, each day of its continuance shall be deemed a separate offense. (28).

(28) RAILWAY POOLS.

This section is, it would seem, declarative of the rule already existing at common law. It was aimed against the freight pools existing in this country at the time of the passage of the act. The features of these pools included an agreement to maintain tariffs and to divide the earnings of traffic subject to the arrangement, between the companies upon a basis agreed upon, or to be fixed by the pool, or by an arbitrator. It was an agreement between the transcontinental lines competing for the through traffic of the country to sustain the prices at an agreed figure, and prevent the competition which otherwise would result. A penalty was also provided for a violation of the agreed tariff by any of the roads or their agents. These agreements covered many other features; but the features mentioned are those which are deemed material to the present discussion, and bring the agreements within the class that the courts have held to be contrary to public policy, as tending to create a monopoly, and, therefore, illegal.

A similar statutory prohibition of railway pools is contained in the Oregon act of February 20, 1885, § 3.

This principle of public policy is the same as that which exists as to the consolidation of competing roads. In Ohio, in the somewhat famous *Vanderbilt case*, it was held that the lines of two roads, which are in their general features parallel and competing, can not be consolidated into one corporation under the statute. (*State* v. *Vanderbilt*, 37 O. S. 590.) These statutes and decisions upon the question are fully collected in the brief of Mr. Bristow, pp. 594, 595.

A recent case before the Circuit Court of the United States in the District of Louisiana is particularly instructive. Under the charter of the Texas Pacific Railway Company (16 U. S. St. at Large, 578), and the Texas act of May 2, 1873, granting land to it, which forbid discrimination by it against any connecting or intersecting road, and the latter of which forbids it to enter into any combination in the nature of a partnership with any railroad in the state running parallel with it, or in the same direction, that will give the latter control of rates on it, a pooling and traffic arrangement made by the receivers of the road, or of its successor, the Texas and Pacific Railway Company, with the Missouri Pacific Railway Company, which has 200 miles of road parallel to its road in Texas, relating to business interchanged in Texas, and giving the Missouri Pacific a preference in rates, is illegal, and will be ordered to be abrogated upon objection made by other lines connecting with the Texas and Pacific Railway Company's road in Louisiana, although the receivers are willing to make the same arrangement with the objecting companies, if they will furnish their road with the same amount of business under the same conditions, and although the arrangement is satisfactory to the traffic agents of the objecting companies, and operates to the benefit of the property in the receivers' hands. Likewise membership in a traffic association is improper, and the receivers will be ordered to withdraw therefrom, if the association has power to make discriminating rates for or against the Texas and Pacific Railway Company. (*Missouri Pacific Railway Co.* v. *Texas and Pacific Railway Co.*, 30 Fed. Rep. 2.)

Any agreement to maintain prices or rates, and which tends to deprive the public of the natural and legitimate fruits of competition, seems to be contrary to public policy. (*Central Ohio Salt Co.* v. *Guthrie*, 35 Ohio St. 666; *Crawford* v. *Wick*, 19 *Ib.* 190; *Pullman, etc., Co.* v. *Texas, etc., Ry. Co.*, 11 Fed. Rep. 625–631; Wald's Pollock on Contracts, 309; *Menacho* v. *Ward*, 27 Fed. Rep. 529–534; 23 Am. & E. Ry. Cas. 647.)

In England two railroad companies made an agreement to divide their receipts in given proportions. An injunction was granted restraining the execution of the agreement. Wood, V. C., said: "An agreement that the profits and loss shall be brought into one common fund, and the net receipts divided into two shares of nine-tenths and one-tenth, without an authority of an act of parliament, appears to me so clearly and palpably illegal that I do not think the court ought to hesitate in its views in that respect; otherwise, it might be that all the railways in the kingdom might be collected into one large joint stock concern." (*Charlton* v. *Newcastle, etc., R. Co.*, 5 Jur. (N. S.) 1100.) And such is understood to be the result of the Trunk Line pool as to all through freight to or from the eastern seaboard. A contrary view was expressed in the case of *Hare* v. *London, etc., R. Co.*, 2 Johns. & H. 80, in which two groups of railway companies, being respectively the owners of independent co-terminus routes, agreed to divide the profits of the whole traffic in certain fixed proportions, calculated on the experience of the past course of traffic. It was said: "With regard to the argument against the validity of the agreement, I may clear the ground of one objection by saying that I see nothing in the alleged injury to the public arising from the prevention of competition. I find no indication in the course taken by the legislature of an intention to create competition by authorizing various lines. From my own experience in parliamentary committees I should rather be disposed to say that the legislature wisely inclined to avoid authorizing the construction of two lines which would necessarily compete with each other. It is a mistaken notion that the public is benefited by pitting two railroad companies against each other till one is ruined, the result being at last to raise fares to the highest possible standard."

The leading case in this country is *Staunton* v. *Allen*, 5 Denio, 440.

The proprietors of boats on the Erie & Oswego Canals formed a pooling association, by which they agreed to regulate and fix the price of freight and passage, and to divide the profits of their business according to the number of boats employed by each. The Court of Appeals of New York held the agreement unlawful, saying: "It is nothing else than the attainment of an exemption of the standard of freights and the facilities and accommodations to be rendered to the public from the wholesome influence of rivalry and competition."

It has been held that where a pooling contract between railroads "has been fully executed, and the defendant road has availed itself of all the benefits to be derived from it, that corporation is now estopped to deny its validity." (*Nashua, etc., R. Corp.* v. *Boston, etc., R. Corp.*, 19 Fed. Rep. 804.)

A voluntary association of salt manufacturers was formed for the purpose of selling and transporting that commodity. By the articles of association all salt manufactured or owned by the members, when packed in barrels, became the property of the company, whose committee was authorized and required to regulate the price and grade thereof, and also to control the manner and time of receiving salt from the members; and each member was prohibited from selling any salt during the continuance of the association, except by retail at a factory, and at prices fixed by the company.

Held, that such agreement was in restraint of trade, and void as against public policy. McIlvain, C. J., said: "The clear tendency of such an agreement is to establish a monopoly and to destroy competition in trade, and for that reason, on grounds of public policy, courts will not aid in its enforcement." It has been said, with reference to the railroad freight pools, that they have not in fact prevented competition in rates, and that they have been beneficial, rather than injurious to the public. In answer to this argument the same judge continued: "It is no answer to say that competition in the salt trade was not, in fact, destroyed, or that the price of the commodity was not unreasonably advanced. Courts will not stop to inquire as to the degree of injury inflicted upon the public; it is enough to know that the inevitable tendency of such contracts is injurious to the public." (*Central Ohio Salt Co.* v. *Guthrie*, 35 O. S. 666–672.)

In *Morris Run Coal Co.*, 68 Pa. St. 173, a pooling agreement between five coal corporations, made in New York, and agreeing to divide two coal regions in Pennsylvania, of which they had the control; to appoint a committee to take charge of their interests, which was to decide all questions and appoint a general agent at Watkins, New York; the coal mined to be delivered through him; each corporation to deliver its proportion at its own cost in the different markets at such time and to such persons as the committee might direct; the committee to adjust the prices, rates of freight, etc.; enter into agreements with anthracite companies; the five companies might sell their coal themselves only to the extent of their proportion, and at prices adjusted by the committee; the agent to suspend shipments to either beyond their proportion; frequent detailed reports to be made by companies, and settlements monthly by the committee; prices to be averaged and payments made to those in arrear by those in excess; neither to sell coal otherwise than agreed upon; and the regulations of the committee to be carried out faithfully. A statute of New York made it a misdemeanor for "persons to conspire to commit any act injurious to trade or commerce." The Supreme Court of Pennsylvania decided that this agreement was in contravention of that statute, and also against public policy, and therefore illegal and void. Judge Agnew said: "The effects produced on the public interests lead to the consideration of another feature of great weight in determining the illegality of the contract, to wit, the combination resorted to by these five companies. Singly each might have suspended deliveries and sales of coal to suit its own interests, and might have raised the price, even though this might have been detrimental to the public interests. There is a certain freedom which must be allowed to every one in the management of his own affairs. When competition is left free individual error or folly will generally find a correction in the conduct of others. But here is a combination of all the companies operating in the Blossburg and Barclay mining regions, and controlling their entire productions. They have combined together to govern the supply, and the price, and the price of coal in all the markets from the Hudson to the Mississippi rivers, and from Pennsylvania to the lakes. This combination has a power in its confederated form which no individual action can confer. The public interest must succumb to it, for it has left no competition free to correct its baleful influence. When the supply of coal is suspended the demand for it becomes importunate and prices must rise. Or, if the supply goes forward, the price fixed by the confederates must accompany it. The domestic hearth, the furnaces of the iron master, and the fires of the manufacturer, all feel the restraint, while many dependent hands are paralyzed and hungry mouths are stinted. The influence of a lack of supply or a rise in the price of an article of such prime necessity can not be measured. It permeates the entire mass of the community, and leaves few of its members untouched by its withering blight. Such a combination is more than a contract; it is an offense. 'I take it,' said Gibson,

J., 'a combination is criminal whenever the act to be done has a necessary tendency to prejudice the public or to oppress individuals by unjustly subjecting them to the power of confederates, and giving effect to the purpose of the latter, whether of extortion or mischief.' *Com.* v. *Carlisle*, Brightly, 40. In all such combinations, where the purpose is injurious or unlawful, the gist of the offence is conspiracy. Men can often do, by the combination of many, what severally no one could accomplish, and even what, when done by one, would be innocent."

See an excellent discussion of this question by Mr. Adelbert Hamilton in note to 15 Feb. Rep. 667–672; also *Central Ry. Co.* v. *Collins*, 40 Ga. 582.

Printed Schedules of Freight Rates and Passenger Fares Must be Kept in Every Depot and Station.(29)

Sec. 6, Par. 1. That every common carrier subject to the provisions of this act shall print and keep for public inspection schedules showing the rates and fares and charges for the transportation of passengers and property which any such common carrier has established and which are in force at the time upon its railroad, as defined by the first section of this act. The schedules printed as aforesaid by any such common carrier shall plainly state the places upon its railroad between which property and passengers will be carried, and shall contain the classification of freight(30) in force upon such railroad, and shall also state separately the terminal charges and any rules or regulations which in any wise change, affect, or determine any part or the aggregate of such aforesaid rates and fares and charges(31). Such schedules shall be plainly printed in large type, of at least the size of ordinary pica, and copies for the use of the public shall be kept in every depot or station(32) upon any such railroad, in such places and in such form that they can be conveniently inspected.

(29) The English Regulation of Railways Act, 1873, § 14 (see Appendix, *post*), requires every railway company to keep at each of their stations a book showing the rates charged for the carriage of traffic other than passengers and their baggage.

(30) Under Underwood's Ill. St., ch. 114, § 19, which requires railroad and warehouse commissioners to make and publish for each rail-

road company a schedule of maximum rates, the classification of freights is a part of the schedule, and must be published to be operative. (*St. Louis and Cairo R. R. Co.* v. *Blackwood*, 14 Ill. App. 503.)

(31) TERMINAL CHARGES AND RULES AFFECTING THE AGGREGATE CHARGE.

Section 6 above requires that the printed schedules show "the terminal charges and any rules or regulations which in any wise change, affect, or determine any part or the aggregate of such aforesaid rates and fares and charges." The English Regulation of Railways Act, 1873, § 14 (see Appendix), did not require this in the first instance, but provided that the commissioners might require the company to "distinguish in such book how much of each rate is for the conveyance of the traffic, . . . including tolls (etc.) . . . and *how much is for other expenses, specifying the nature and detail of such other expenses.*"

Under English act—Terminal charges—Section 14 of the Regulation of Railways Act, 1873, enacts (*inter alia*): "The Commissioners may from time to time, on the application of any person interested, make orders with respect to any particular description of traffic, requiring a railway company or canal company to distinguish in such book how much of each rate is for the conveyance of the traffic on the railway or canal, including therein tolls for the use of the railway or canal, for the use of carriages or vessels, or for locomotive power, and how much is for other expenses, specifying the nature and detail of such other expenses."

Held, that the words "specifying the nature and detail of such other expenses" require a railway company to state in their rate book, to which the order made applies, what terminal services they undertake to perform with regard to the particular traffic, and how much they charge for each of such terminal services, and that a railway company does not sufficiently comply with the section by giving a list of the various terminal services which they perform, and stating what their total charge is for the whole of these services. (*Colman* v. *G. E. Ry. Co.*, 4 Ry. & Can. Traf. Cas. 108; see note to § 3, Par. 1, *ante*, p. 92.)

—When entitled to make. A railway company worked a line for the carriage of minerals, which was connected with collieries by junctions to private sidings. The company had no power to make a terminal charge for services at the junctions of their line with the sidings. The company's trains called for trucks standing in the different sidings. At each junction the engine was detached and ran off the main line into the siding beyond the company's lands, from which it drew out any trucks ready to start and attached them to the train. The engine had, besides, frequently to perform shunting and marshaling, so as to pick out of a number of trucks, full and empty, such as were to be added to the train. The railway company charged for the work done on the sidings a fixed sum of 3*d.* per ton, in addition to the mileage rate for conveyance on the railway company's own line: *Held*, that the company were not entitled to make such charge, and that, as the plan of each siding, as well as its junction, had received the approval of the engineer of the railway company, the owners of the sidings did all that was necessary to entitle them to have their traffic taken by the railway company at the mileage rate, and free of any charge for terminal services, if they placed their trucks as near to the junctions as they could be brought with safety to the main line, arranged in proper order, and clear of any obstacles to their being moved away. (*Watkinson, etc.* v. *Wrexham, etc., Ry. Co.*, 3 Nev. & Mac. 5.)

Semble, that a railway company can not make any terminal charge for merely unloading into a depot where they have no sidings for delivery. (*Locke, etc.* v *N. E. Ry. Co.*, 3 Nev. & Mac. 44.)

— **Collection and delivery charges.** Upon the application of a carrier, who collected and carted parcels to the terminus of a railway company for conveyance, for an order requiring the railway company to distinguish in their book of rates how much of their parcels' rates was for conveyance on the railway and how much for collection or cartage:—

Held, that, as the railway company's parcel rates included charges for other services beside conveyance, they must distinguish in the book of rates at the terminus where the applicant's parcels were received for conveyance, how much of the parcels' rates was for conveyance on the railway, and how much for other expenses, and must specify the nature and detail of such other expenses. (*Robertson* v. *Great S. & W. Ry. Co.* 2 Nev. & Mac. 374.)

Where a complaint is made that a railway company does not allow a sufficient rebate from a cartage rate or gross rate, including the charge for collection and delivery of goods conveyed upon their line, to those who cart to or from the company's stations for themselves, the application should, as a general rule, in the first instance, be for an order requiring the company to distinguish in the books kept at each of their stations, and open to the inspection of the public, how much of the rate is for the conveyance of the traffic on the railway and how much is for other expenses, specifying the nature and details thereof under section 15 of the Regulation of Railways Acts, 1873.

After such separation of the cartage rate from the gross rate, if the company do not allow carriers performing the cartage the same amount as they charge to the public for such service when performed by the company, or if the charge be made too low, for the purpose of preventing competition, the same amount as the service costs the company, any person injured by the insufficient allowance may apply to the Commissioners for an injunction under section 2 of the Railway and Canal Traffic Act, 1854, or for an order under section 15 of the Regulation of Railways Acts, 1873.

Quaere, whether the company is not bound to allow, in such cases, the charge made by them to the public for the same service, or, in cases where there is not a satisfactory test, the actual cost to the company of the service and any profit which may accrue thereon to the company, or be estimated by them in respect thereof.

The company must allow to carriers for the cartage of parcels and empties the same amounts which they charge to the public and allow to their own agents in respect of such cartage. It is no ground of complaint that the company give credit to, or have a monthly ledger account with, certain of their customers, and refuse the same to persons for whom goods are collected and delivered by carriers, unless it be shown that the difference was made for the purpose of preventing competition, or of otherwise injuring the complainant. (*Goddard* v. *London, etc., Ry. Co., etc.*, 1 Nev. & Mac. 308.)

— **Demurrage.** The rule of the company as to demurrage charges would be a "rule . . . affecting . . . the aggregate of such . . . charges," and should be stated in the printed schedule. (See *Diphwys, etc., Co.* v. *Festiniog Ry. Co.*, 2 Nev. & Mac. 73.)

— **Practice under English act.** It being the duty of a railway company to inform any person interested, and applying to it for information, how much of each local and through rate in its entirety is for conveyance, and how much is for other expenses, specifying the nature and detail of such other expenses, if the information is withheld the railway commissioners will, on an application under section 14 of the Regulation of Railways Act, 1873, order it to be given, and to be made public by proper entries in the rate book, and will order the railway company to pay the costs of the proceedings which became necessary for the purpose of obtaining such information. (*Cairns* v. *N. E. Ry. Co.*, 4 Ry. & Can. Traf. Cas. 221.)

It is the duty of a railway company to inform any person interested, and applying to it for information, how much of each local or through rate in its entirety is for conveyance, and how much is for other expenses, specifying the nature and detail of such other expenses, and if the information is withheld it will be ordered by the railway commissioners to be given, and to be made public by proper entries in the rate book. (*Watkinson* v. *Wrexham, etc., Ry. Co.*, 3 Nev. & Mac. 446.)

A company refusing to show their rate books at their stations will have to pay the costs of any proceedings which the parties, in the absence of information which the rate books would have afforded, had "reasonable and probable cause" for taking. (*Clonmel Traders* v. *Waterford, etc., Ry. Co.*, 4 Ry. & Can. Traf. Cas. 92.)

(32) Depots and Stations—What Are?

The Regulation of Railways Act, 1873, § 14 (Appendix) provides that every railway company and canal company shall keep "at each of their stations and wharves a book" of rates, etc. The question has arisen as to what are stations within the statute and the power of the companies to arrange traffic into districts, etc.

A railway company arranged their mineral traffic into three districts, and in each district had a principal or central station, at which the mineral rate books were kept. No books of mineral rates were kept at any other stations, although many of such stations were close to large iron works, quarries, and coal mines, and a very considerable traffic in coal was brought down by rail to the main line, and sent forward from such stations, or from sidings near them. The mineral traffic from the local stations was charged and booked at the central stations only.

Held, that this arrangement was a contravention of section 14 of the Regulation of Railways Act, 1873, which requires a railway company to keep "at each of their stations a book or books showing every rate for the time being charged for the carriage of traffic, other than passengers and their luggage, from that station to any place to which they book," and that the obligation to keep books of rates at the station from which the rates are charged attaches equally whether the booking is done there or elsewhere.

Semble, that the words "to which they book" in section 14 of the Regulation of Railways Act, 1873, mean "to which they quote a rate." (*Jones* v. *Northeastern Ry. Co.*, 2 Nev. & Mac. 208.)

The 14th section of the Regulation of Railways Act, 1873, requires railway companies to keep at their stations books of rates charged for the carriage of traffic (other than passengers and their luggage) from such stations to places where they book. The L. & N. W. Ry. Co. carried coals in owner's wagons from certain collieries; the wagons were loaded and made into trains by the colliery owners and placed by them in coal sidings, whence they were taken by the railway company's engines, and the company contended that they were not bound to keep books of rates in respect of such traffic.

Held, that for the purpose of coal trafic the said coal sidings were "stations," within the meaning of the above section, and that the companies were bound to keep books of rates for the conveyance of coals therefrom, such books to be kept either at the sidings (if accessible to the public), or, for the greater convenience of the company and the public, at the station where the general merchandise traffic of the district was conducted. (*Harborne Ry. Co.* v. *London, etc., Ry. Co.,* 2 Nev. & Mac. 169.)

The book of rates which a railway company are required by the 14th section of the Regulation of Railways Act, 1873, to keep at their stations should show all rates, local as well as through, which are being charged from the station where the book is kept.

Through rates need not be shown, in whole or in part, at any other station than the one from which the traffic carried at through rates is forwarded in the first instance. (*Oxlade* v. *North Eastern Ry. Co.,* 3 Nev. & Mac. 35.)

SPECIAL PROVISION AS TO FREIGHT SHIPPED FROM UNITED STATES THROUGH FOREIGN COUNTRY INTO UNITED STATES.

Sec. 6, Par. 2. Any common carrier subject to the provisions of this act receiving freight in the United States to be carried through a foreign country to any place in the United States shall also in like manner print and keep for public inspection, at every depot where such freight is received for shipment, schedules showing the through rates established and charged by such common carrier to all points in the United States beyond the foreign country to which it accepts freight for shipment; and any freight shipped from the United States through a foreign country into the United States, the through rate on which shall not have been made public as required by this act, shall, before it is admitted into the United States from said foreign country, be subject to customs duties as if said freight were of foreign production; and any law in conflict with this section is hereby repealed.

§ 6, PAR. 4.]   INTER-STATE COMMERCE ACT.   145

NO ADVANCE IN RATES, FARES, OR CHARGES SO PUBLISHED SHALL BE MADE WITHOUT TEN DAYS' NOTICE—REDUCTIONS SHALL BE POSTED IMMEDIATELY.

Sec. 6, Par. 3. No advance shall be made in the rates, fares, and charges which have been established and published as aforesaid by any common carrier in compliance with the requirements of this section, except after ten days' public notice, which shall plainly state the changes proposed to be made in the schedule then in force, and the time when the increased rates, fares, or charges will go into effect; and the proposed changes shall be shown by printing new schedules, or shall be plainly indicated upon the schedules in force at the time and kept for public inspection. Reductions in such published rates, fares, or charges may be made without previous public notice; but whenever any such reduction is made, notice of the same shall immediately be publicly posted and the changes made shall immediately be made public by printing new schedules, or shall immediately be plainly indicated upon the schedules at the time in force and kept for public inspection.(33)

(33) **Under English act.** Upon complaint and proof that a railway company had at different times reduced particular rates of traffic from G. to L., but had not given the applicant's traffic the benefit of such reductions till long after the authorized dates of their coming into operation, and after the dates when they took effect for similar traffic from other traders in G. carrying on the same business as the applicant: *Held*, that the applicant had been subjected to an undue prejudice and disadvantage in and about the sale and disposal of his goods in competition with the other traders in G. carrying on a similar business with himself. (*MacFarlane* v. *North British Railway C..* (No. 2), 4 Ry. & Can. Traf. Cas. 269.)

ALL CHARGES GREATER OR LESS THAN THOSE NAMED IN PUBLISHED SCHEDULE FORBIDDEN.

Sec. 6, Par. 4. And when any such common carrier shall have established and published its rates, fares, and charges in compliance with the provisions of this section, it shall be unlawful for such common carrier to charge, demand, collect, or receive from any person or persons a greater or less compensation for the transportation of passengers or property, or for any services in connection therewith, than is specified in such published schedule of rates, fares, and charges as may at the time be in force.

SCHEDULES, CONTRACTS, JOINT TARIFFS, ETC., TO BE FILED WITH THE COMMISSION, TO BE PUBLISHED WHEN DIRECTED BY THE COMMISSION.

Sec. 6, Par. 5. Every common carrier subject to the provisions of this act shall file with the Commission hereinafter provided for copies of its schedules of rates, fares, and charges which have been established and published in compliance with the requirements of this section, and shall promptly notify said Commission of all changes made in the same. Every such common carrier shall also file with said Commission copies of all contracts, agreements, or arrangements with other common carriers in relation to any traffic affected by the provisions of this act to which it may be a party. And in cases where passengers and freight pass over continuous lines or routes operated by more than one common carrier, and the several common carriers operating such lines or routes establish joint tariffs of rates, or fares, or charges for such continuous lines or routes, copies of such joint tariffs shall also, in like manner, be filed with said Commission. Such joint rates, fares, and charges on such continuous lines so filed as aforesaid shall be made public by such common carriers when directed by said Commission, in so far as may, in the judgment of the Commission, be deemed practicable;(34) and said Commission shall from time to time prescribe the measure of publicity which shall be given to such rates, fares, and charges, or to such part of them as it may deem it practicable for such common carriers to publish, and the places in which they shall be published; but no common carrier party to any such joint tariff shall be liable for the failure of any other common carrier party thereto to observe and adhere to the rates, fares, or charges thus made and published.

(34) **Division of through rates.** A railway company is not required, under section 14 of the Regulation of Railways Act, 1873, to show how the through rates quoted by it are divided between the rail-

way companies receiving them. (*Watkinson v. Wrexham, etc., R. Co.,* 3 Nov. & Mac. 446.)

REMEDIES FOR VIOLATIONS OF THIS SECTION—PENALTIES.

Sec. 6, Par. 6. If any such common carrier shall neglect or refuse to file or publish its schedules or tariffs of rates, fares, and charges as provided in this section, or any part of the same, such common carrier shall, in addition to other penalties(36) herein prescribed, be subject to a writ of mandamus, to be issued by any circuit court of the United States in the judicial district wherein the principal office of said common carrier is situated, or wherein such offense may be committed, and if such common carrier be a foreign corporation, in the judicial circuit wherein such common carrier accepts traffic and has an agent to perform such service, to compel compliance with the aforesaid provisions of this section; and such writ shall issue in the name of the people of the United States, at the relation of the Commissioners appointed under the provisions of this act; and failure to comply with its requirements shall be punishable as and for a contempt; and the said Commissioners, as complainants, may also apply, in any such circuit court of the United States, for a writ of injunction against such common carrier, to restrain such common carrier from receiving or transporting property among the several states and territories of the United States, or between the United States and adjacent foreign countries, or between ports of transhipment and of entry and the several states and territories of the United States, as mentioned in the first section of this act, until such common carrier shall have complied with the aforesaid provisions of this section of this act.

(36) The provisions of this paragraph are remedial rather than penal. See *Stockwell* v. *U. S.*, 13 Wall. 531; and see note to § 8, on p. 163, *post*.

COMBINATIONS TO PREVENT CARRIAGE BEING CONTINUOUS FORBIDDEN—BREAK OF BULK, ETC., SHALL NOT PREVENT CARRIAGE BEING CONTINUOUS.(37)

Sec. 7. That it shall be unlawful for any common carrier subject to the provisions of this act to enter into any combination, contract, or agreement, expressed or implied, to prevent, by change of time schedule, carriage in different cars, or by other means or devices, the carriage of freights from being continuous(38) from the place of shipment to the place of destination;(39) and no break of bulk, stoppage, or interruption made by such common carrier shall prevent the carriage of freights from being and being treated as one continuous carriage from the place of shipment to the place of destination, unless such break, stoppage, or interruption was made in good faith for some necessary purpose, and without any intent to avoid or unnecessarily interrupt such continuous carriage or to evade any of the provisions of this act.(40)

(37) The general duties of connecting carriers, both at common law and by statute, are discussed in the notes to the second paragraph of the third section, *supra*, p. 96, et seq. The third clause of sec. 2 of the Railway and Canal Traffic Act of 1854 (Appendix) was evidently before congress in framing this section. It provides, as quoted by the supreme court in 110 U. S. 685, "that every railway company . . . working railways . . . which form part of a continuous line of railway . . . communication . . . shall afford all due and reasonable facilities for receiving and forwarding by one of such railways . . . all the traffic arriving by the other, without any unreasonable delay, and without any . . . preference or disadvantage, or prejudice and disadvantage . . . and so that no obstruction may be offered to the public desirous of using such railways . . . as a continuous line of communication; and so that all reasonable accommodation may, by means of the railways . . . of the several companies, be at all times afforded to the public in that behalf."

Chief Justice Waite, after holding that at common law a railroad common carrier is not bound to carry beyond its own line, and if it contracts to do so, "it may, in the absence of statutory regulations, determine for itself what agencies it will employ," and is not bound to stop its trains and exchange traffic at a junction with another road where it has not established a station, said: "Were there such a statute in Colorado, this case would come before us in a different aspect. As it is, we know of no power in the judiciary to do what the parliament of Great Britain has done, and what the proper legislative authority ought, perhaps, to do for the relief of the parties to this controversy." (*Atchison, T. & S. F. R. Co.* v. *Denver & N. O. R. Co.*, 110 U. S. 667, 685; see, also, notes to Par. 2, § 3, *ante*.)

In the absence of a special contract a railroad company can not be compelled to undertake the carriage of persons or property beyond its own line, and in the absence of contract its liability terminates with the delivery to the connecting carrier. (*Myrick* v. *Mich. C. R. Co.*, 107 U. S. 102; *Stewart* v. *Terre Haute, etc., R. Co.*, 3 Fed. Rep. 768; 1 McCrary, 312; *Ogdensburg, etc., R. Co.* v. *Mineral Springs Mfg. Co.*, 16 Wall. 318; *Burroughs* v. *Railroad Co.*, 100 Mass. 26; *Railroad Co.* v. *Berry*, 68 Pa. St. 272; *Babcock* v. *Railroad Co.*, 49 N. Y. 491; *Converse* v. *Trans. Co.*, 33 Conn. 166; *Perkins* v. *Railroad Co.*, 47 Me. 573; *Bintuall* v. *Railroad Co.*, 32 Vt. 673; *Express Co.* v. *Rush*, 24 Ind. 403; *McMillan* v. *Railroad Co.*, 10 Mich. 119; *Coates* v. *Express Co.*, 45 Mo. 238; *Bussey* v. *Memphis, etc., R. Co.*, 13 Fed. Rep. 330.)

"Nor can a railroad corporation be compelled to give a bill of lading for delivery beyond its line." (*Lotspeich* v. *Railroad Co.*, 73 Ala. 306; 18 Am. & E. R. Cas. 491.) Because the issuing of such bill of lading requires the carrier to provide means of transportation to the ultimate destination to which the goods are billed, unless the carrier expressly restricts its liability. (*Bussey* v. *Memphis, etc., Co.*, 13 Fed. Rep. 330.) The making of a through fare does not render the company liable for the carriage beyond its own line. (*Myrick* v. *Mich. Cent. R. Co.*, 107 U. S. 102, 108.)

Many facilities for through transportation over connecting lines may be afforded without rendering the carrier giving them liable beyond the terminus of its own line. For instance, the posting, making, or taking of a through fare to the point of destination (*Myrick* v. *Mich. C. R. Co.*, 107 U. S. 102, 108.); and the giving of a receipt reciting the destination of the goods. (*Ib.*; *Stewart* v. *Terre Haute, etc., R. Co.*, 3 Fed. Rep. 768; 1 McCrary, 312; see Redfield Carr., §§ 443, 449.)

Decisions under English Railway and Canal Traffic Act. See notes to Par. 2, § 3, *ante*, p. 96, et seq. To justify the interference of the court to enforce the running of through trains on a continuous line of railways, it must be shown that public convenience requires it, and that it can reasonably be done. (*Barret* v. *Gt. Northern Ry. Co.*, 1 C. B. (N. S.) 423; 26 L. J., C. P. 83; 1 Nev. & Mac. 38.)

The court will not interfere, at the instance of an individual, where there is a continuous line by which through tickets may be obtained, though by a somewhat longer route, no additional cost or serious loss of time being thereby incurred, and no substantial inconvenience being thereby occasioned to the public, and it appearing that no complaints have been made of the inadequacy of the existing accommodation. (*Ib.*)

The court refused to grant an injunction on the complaint of a company having a branch on a trunk line, to restrain the parent company from charging higher rates for the conveyance of passengers to the complainant's terminus than they charged for the conveyance of passengers to the terminus of another branch line (in which they themselves were interested), extending over the same number of miles. (*Caterham Railway Co.* v. *London, etc., Ry. Co.*, 1 C. B. (N. S.) 410; 26 L. J., C. P. 16; 1 Nev. & Mac. 32.)

(38) CONTINUOUS SHIPMENT IN SAME CARS—BREAKING BULK—ACT OF CONGRESS, JUNE 15, 1866.

"By an act of congress, approved July 1, 1862 (12 Stat. at Large, 496; § 5257, Rev. Stat.), other railroad companies are authorized to connect their roads with the Union Pacific Railroad or any of its branches. The Act of June 15, 1866 (14 Stat. at Large, 66; Rev. Stat., § 5258), provides that 'every railroad company in the United States . . . is hereby authorized to carry upon and over its road, boats, bridges and ferries, all passengers, . . . freight and property on their way from any state to another state, and to receive compensation therefor, and to connect with roads of other states, so as to form **continuous lines** for the transportation of the same to the place of destination.' Under these statutes the defendant is authorized to connect its railroad with the Union Pacific Railroad, so as to form a continuous line for the transportation of passengers and freight to the places of their destination. The conneċtion indicated by the language of these acts of congress is that whereby the cars of one road may be transported over the other, so that passengers and freight may be carried as upon a continuous line of railway without change of cars. The provision last quoted expresses this thought by direct and plain language, and the first implies the same, for it is hardly probable that congress meant no more by the word "**conneċt**," used in the provision, than that freight and passengers may be transferred from the cars of one railroad to those of another. On the contrary, it was intended that the cars themselves, with their burdens, should be transferred from one road to another, so that passengers and freight might be transported from ocean to ocean without change of cars or breaking bulk, as upon one continuous line of road. The purpose of the statutes is evidently in the interest of commerce, intended to promote speedy and unobstructed transportation, and intended to relieve the products and merchandise of the country of the indirect tax of breaking bulk and reshipping at the various railroad termini, when being transported by rail. Nothing tends more effectually to produce these results than continuous lines for the carriage of commerce. The delay, expense and loss attending the breaking of bulk and reshipment is a serious embarrassment and impediment to commerce. These congressional enactments, under the interpretation given them, tend to remedy these evils; any other interpretation would destroy their force and defeat their evident purpose." (Miller, C. J., in *Council Bluffs* v. *Ks. City, etc., R. Co.*, 45 Iowa, 338, 351-2 (1876); see *Hardy* v. *A. T. & S. F. R. Co.*, 32 Kans. 698, 717.)

Railroads are bound at common law to receive and haul cars of other roads. (*Vermont, etc., R.* v. *Fitchburg R.*, 14 Allen (Mass.) 462, 469; *Mackin* v. *Boston & A. R.*, 135 Mass. 201, 206; *Peoria, etc., R. Co.* v. *Chicago, etc., R. Co.*, 109 Ill. 135; *s. c.*, 19 Cent. L. J. 111, and elaborate note thereto; *s. c.*, 18 Am. & Eng. R. Cas. 506, and note.)

Statutes of a number of states have expressly so provided. (Michigan Gen. Laws, 1873, p. 99; Georgia Act, Feb. 14, 1874, and see statutes and decisions collected in note to 19 Central L. J. 113.)

See, also, decision of Supreme Court of Georgia under statute of that state, in note to Par. 2, § 3, *ante*, pp. 116-117; *Logan* v. *Central R.*, 74 Ga. 684.

(39) "PLACE OF SHIPMENT TO PLACE OF DESTINATION."

Property brought to a depot for purpose of transportation outside of the state, while remaining there is not the subject of inter-state commerce, but after its transportation from one state to another has begun, it continues to be subject to the control of congress as inter-state commerce, although it may be detained in the state from which it was shipped by temporary causes. (*Coe* v. *Errol*, 116 U. S. 517.)

Coal, mined in Pennsylvania, and sent by water to New Oleans to be sold in open market there on account of the owners in Pennsylvania, becomes intermingled, on arrival there, with the general property in the State of Louisiana, and is subject to taxation under general laws of that state, although it may be, after arrival, sold from the vessel on which the transportation was made, and without being landed, and for the purpose of being taken out of the country on a vessel bound to a foreign port. (*Brown* v. *Houston*, 114 U. S. 622.)

The place of shipment of grain bought in another state and shipped to, and stored for sale at Pittsburgh, and afterward reshipped to Philadelphia, is Pittsburgh, and is classed as "local freight" under the Pennsylvania statute. (*Penn. R. Co.* v. *Canfield*, 46 Pa. St. 211.)

But grain bought in another state and shipped to Pittsburgh and reshipped to Philadelphia, but not stored for sale, has for its place of shipment the point from which it was originally shipped, and is not "local freight" under said statute. (*Rowland* v. *Penn. R. Co.*, 52 Pa. St. 250.)

(40) CASES UNDER § 11, ENGLISH ACT, 1873—"THROUGH TRAFFIC" DEFINED—PRINCIPLES UPON WHICH THROUGH ROUTES AND RATES ARE GRANTED.

The Regulation of Railways Act, 1873, § 11 (Appendix), enlarged and extended the Railway and Canal Traffic Act, 1854, § 2, as to "through traffic," giving the railway commissioners power to compel the opening of new "through" routes, and the giving of through rates. Some of the cases arising under this section are subjoined.

The C. W. Railway Company applied to the commissioners for an order under section 11 of the Regulation of Railways Act, 1873, allowing through rates in respect of the traffic in certain goods between Chester and Haverfordwest, the route proposed being from Chester over lines owned and worked by the L. & N. W. Railway Company, and over the applicants' own line, which was worked by the same company under an agreement with the applicants, and thence to Haverfordwest over G. W. Railway Company's line, which was worked and owned exclusively by that company, and *vice versa* from Haverfordwest to Chester. The through route proposed consequently commenced and terminated off the line of the company proposing the through rate.

The applicants had no rolling-stock, and did not work their railway, but maintained and managed their line, and collected, forwarded, and delivered their own traffic, the whole of the staff at their stations being employed and paid by them, and subject to their orders. *Held*, by the Queen's Bench Division (affirming the judgment of the railway commissioners, and in accordance with the judgment of the Court of Session in the *Greenock and Wemyss Bay Railway Company* v. *The Caledonian Railway Company*, 5 Sc. Sess. Ca. (4th Ser.) 995; 3 Nev. & Mac. 145), that the traffic required to be forwarded was "through traffic to or from" the applicants' railway, and that the applicants were a railway company entitled to apply for a through rate in respect of such traffic, within the meaning of section 11.

Upon an application for a through route or rate, it was proved that the proposed route was fifty-six miles shorter than the route over which the traffic was being carried, and was worked not less conveniently as regards the railway companies by whom the traffic was handled before it got to its destination, and that the proposed rate was of less amount, and presumably, therefore, more beneficial to the public, while at the same time being more in proportion to distance than the rate by the other route, it yielded a larger sum per mile to the companies carrying, and was therefore not obviously unreasonable as against them. The commissioners inferred from those facts that the route was a reasonable one, and that the public were interested in the rate being granted; and *held*, that where a good *prima facie* case of public interest existed on general considerations, it was not necessary to bring evidence to prove a special case as well. (*Cen. Wales & Carmarthen Junc. Ry. Co.* v. *G. W. Ry. Co. et al.*, 4 Ry. & Can. Traf. Cas. 110.)

On an application by the C. W. Railway Company for through rates for traffic carried between Haverfordwest and Chester, Liverpool, Manchester, Leeds, Burton, Birmingham, and Wolverhampton, required to be forwarded via the C. W. route, it appeared that that route was shorter and more direct than the G. W. route, via Hereford (on which through rates were in force): the saving of distance by the C. W. route, from Chester, Liverpool, Manchester, and Leeds, being fifty-seven miles; from Burton, thirty-two miles; from Wolverhampton, twenty-two; and from Birmingham, seven. The G. W. Company contended that the proposed rates were not in the public interest, because the quantity of traffic to which they could apply was small; because no time would be saved if the traffic were carried by the proposed route; and that the number of exchanges on the portion of the proposed through route worked by other companies was great: *Held*, that these were not reasons for refusing through rates any more than they would be for withholding facilities under section 2 of the Railway and Canal Traffic Act, 1854. That through rates exist by an alternative route, and that to maintain competition by the proposed route a similar facility is necessary, is a reason for granting through rates. That the distance between the points of arrival and departure of two through routes is the same, is too vague a ground for deciding that the rates charged in respect of these routes should be the same. (*Central Wales & Car. Junc. Ry. Co.* v. *London & N. W. Ry. Co.*, 4 Ry. and Can. Traf. Cas. 211.)

By section 11 of the Regulation of Railways Act, 1873, it is enacted (*inter alia*): "That every railway company and canal company . . . having or working railways or canals, which form part of a continuous line of railway or canal . . . communication, . . . shall afford all due and reasonable facilities for receiving and forwarding, by one of such railways or canals, all the traffic arriving by the other, without any unreasonable delay, . . . and so that no obstruction may be offered to the public desirous of using such railways or canals . . . as a continuous line of communication, and so that all reasonable accommodation may, by means of the railways and canals of the several companies, be at all times afforded to the public in that behalf;" and that the said facilities shall include the due and reasonable receiving, forwarding, and delivering by every railway and canal company, at the request of any other such company, of through traffic at through rates, and that if any objection be made to the granting of the rate or to the route, the railway commissioners shall consider whether the granting of the rate is a due and reasonable facility in the interest of the public, and whether, having regard to the circumstances, the route proposed is a reasonable route, and shall allow or refuse the rate accordingly; and that, in apportioning the through rate, the commissioners shall take into consideration all the circumstances of the case, including any special expense incurred in respect of the construction, maintenance, or working of the route, or any part of the route, as well as any special charges which any company may have been entitled to make in respect thereof.

A sending company having two alternative routes for through traffic, one eight miles longer than the other, proposed, for the purpose of a through rate, to carry by the longer one, at a double cost and labor in working and maintaining the junctions, with the object of making their own mileage more and the mileage of the forwarding company less: *Held*, that such longer route was not a reasonable route, within the meaning of section 11, sub-section 5, of the Regulation of Railways Act, 1873.

A "route" within the meaning of this section, is a route from the station on the sending line, where the traffic arises, to the station on the forwarding line where such traffic is delivered. (*East, etc., Ry. Co.* v. *Gt. Western, etc., Ry. Co.*, 1 Nev. & Mac. 331.)

Where it is doubtful whether a junction which is sought by applicants as a reasonable facility would be allowed by the Board of Trade to be used, if ordered by the commissioners and constructed by the company, and where the mode of working such junction would be unsatisfactory and obstructive to the other traffic on the main line, such a junction is not a due facility within the meaning of section 2 of the Railway and Canal Traffic Act, 1854.

An injunction against a company to work traffic will only be issued where there is a well-founded ground of complaint in respect of past working, and the question of proper facilities for the receipt, etc., of traffic at a junction does not arise until the junction exists.

If a junction could not be reasonably worked when constructed, a company could not be enjoined to construct it as a reasonable facility.

§ 7.] INTER-STATE COMMERCE ACT. 155

(*Dublin Whis. Dis. Co. Lim.*, etc., v. *Midland G. W. Ry. Co.*, 4 Ry. and Can. Traf. Cas. 32.)

The S. and M. Company were the owners of a railway in two sections, connected by lines belonging to two other companies, which were worked by the Great Western Railway Company. The S. and M. Company did not book or work traffic between their two sections, and the Great Western Railway Company did not book from the stations on the lines worked by them to stations on either section of the S. and M. Company's Railway. To permit the exchange of traffic required by the applicants, sidings and other accommodation at one of the junctions was necessary: *Held*, that the failure to provide these between the 25th April and the 29th June, during which time the companies were considering the alterations which were necessary to enable the S. and M. Company to exercise their running powers over those connecting lines, was not a failure to provide facilities for the receiving, forwarding, and delivery of traffic: *Held*, that the route, until so completed and sanctioned by the Board of Trade, was not a continuous line of railway communication. (*Hammans et al.* v. *G. W. Ry. Co. et al.*, 4 Ry. & Can. Traf. Cas. 181.)

The existence of through booking and through rates over one route which is fifty-six miles longer than another route, of which the applicant company's line (which is run over and used under an agreement by the L. & N. W. Rail. Co.) forms a part, is no ground for an application against the L. & N. W. Rail. Co. under § 2 of the Railway and Canal Traffic Act, 1854. (*Cen. Wales & Carmarthen Junc. Ry. Co.* v. *L. & N. W. Ry. Co.*, 4 Ry. & Can. Traf. Cas. 101.)

Under an act in 1846 the B. Canal Company were authorized to charge certain tolls, rates, and dues for goods traffic in respect of the canals and other works of the company, and were prohibited from making an order to reduce, advance, or otherwise vary all or any of such tolls, rates, or dues, without the consent of a railway company, who guaranteed that, if the income of the canal company in any year was insufficient to pay a dividend of 4*d*. per cent on the capital of the canal company, the railway company would make up the deficiency. The B. Canal Company was one link in a chain of canals owned by various companies, and forming a continuous line of navigation between two points. In pursuance of an application made to them by one of those companies, the railway commissioners, under the Regulation of Railways Act, 1873, § 11, made an order allowing through rates for goods traffic between those two points, the effect of which would be to reduce the tolls of the B. Canal Company below the maximum allowed by the act of 1846, and below the amounts thereto-fore charged by the company. The railway company were not represented before the commissioners, and did not consent to the order or to any variation of the tolls: *Held*, that the order was made without jurisdiction, and must be restrained by prohibition. By Kelly, C. B., because the commissioners could not make an order affecting the liability of the railway company under their guaranty without at least hearing them. By Pollock, B., and Hawkins, J., because the consent of the railway company had not been obtained, and the Regulation of Railways Act, 1873, gave the commissioners no power without such consent to reduce the tolls, rates, or dues as authorized by the act of 1846. (*Warwick Can. Co.* v. *Birmingham Can. Co.*, 5 L. R., Exch. Div. 1; 48 L. J., Exch. Div. 550; 40 L. T. (N. S.) 846.)

CARRIER LIABLE IN DAMAGES TO PERSONS INJURED FOR VIOLATIONS OF ACT—COSTS, INCLUDING COUNSEL FEE.(41)

Sec. 8. That in case any common carrier subject to the provisions of this act shall do, cause to be done, or permit to be done any act, matter, or thing in this act prohibited or declared to be unlawful, or shall omit to do any act, matter, or thing in this act required to be done, such common carrier shall be liable to the person or persons injured thereby for the full amount of damages(42) sustained in consequence of any such violation of the provisions of this act, together with a reasonable counsel or attorney's fee, to be fixed by the court in every case of recovery, which attorney's fee shall be taxed and collected as part of of the costs in the case(43).

(41) ENGLISH DECISIONS.

Railway and Canal Traffic Act, 1854. Section 2 of the English Railway and Canal Traffic Act, 1854, having imposed a duty upon carriers beyond that imposed by the common law or previous statutes, and section 6 giving a remedy by injunction or interdict, the weight of English authority is that no action lies for a breach of it; that the "only remedy to enforce performance of the new duty was by injunction or interdict." (*Denaby Main Colliery Co.* v. *Manchester, etc., Ry. Co.*, L. R. 11 H. L. 97. Such was the decision of the Queen's Bench Division in this case (Mathew and Day, JJ.) and of the Court of Appeal (the Master of the Rolls, Cotton, L. J., and Lindley, L. J., 14 Q. B. D. 209); and in the House of Lords, Lord Blackburn (L. R. 11 H. L. 121), the Earl of Selborne (*Ib.*, page 113), and Lord Fitzgerald, were of this opinion, while Lord Chancellor Halsbury reserved his opinion upon the question (*Ib.*, page 112). The

Court of Session of Scotland also held that no action would lie. (*Murray* v. *Glasgow, etc., Ry. Co.*, 11 Court Sess. Cas., 4 Ser. 205; 4 Ry. & Can. Traf. Cas. 456.)

Recovery—Action for money had and received at common law. If a shipper is compelled to pay more than is reasonable, he may recover back, in an action for money had and received, the excess over a reasonable charge. (*Gt. Western Ry. Co.* v. *Sutton*, L. R. 4 Eng. & Ir. App. 226, 237.)

The plaintiff, a carrier, sent goods by the defendants to be carried on their line, as also on that of the Great Western, a continuous line; he objected to the charges as excessive, but paid the amount claimed under protest, making no tender of any sum as a reasonable charge. *Held*, that he was entitled to recover back the amount paid above what was a fair and reasonable charge in an action for money had and received, and that the whole sum so overpaid was recoverable against the defendants, though a portion of it was received by them as agents for the Great Western Railway Company. (*Parker* v. *The Bristol, etc., Ry. Co.*, 6 Ry. Ca. 776.)

If inequality of charge was known to a shipper and paid without objection, he could not recover. (*Evershed* v. *Lond. & N. W. R. Co.*, L. R. 3 Q. B. Div. 144; s. c., L. R. 3 App. Cas. 1029; *Lancashire R. Co.* v. *Gidlow*, L. R. 7 H. L. Cas. 517; *Parker* v. *Gt. Western R. Co.*, 7 Man. & G. 253; see *Hillme* v. *Railroad Co.*, 100 N. Y. 395, 401.)

Measure of recovery. The question arises where an unjustifiable inequality in charge has been made as to what is the measure of recovery; whether the complaining shipper can recover the excess paid upon all goods shipped by him, or merely upon the amount of goods up to but not beyond the quantity of goods shipped by the favored shipper. The latter rule was laid down by the House of Lords in the *Denaby case.* The Earl of Selborne said: "The appellants ought to have been charged at the same reduced rate up to but not beyond the same total quantity during the same period of time (of Bannister the favored shipper's shipments), and that is the true measure of overcharge for which the arbitrator ought to give them credit." (L. R. 11 App. Cas. 117.) Lord Blackburn in the same case said: "I think it can not be right to calculate the amount of overcharge on all the coal sent by the defendants from their colliery to Grimsby for shipment without reference to the quantity of coal on which, or the times during which, the less rate was charged to Bannister for coal carried from the defendant's colliery." (p. 124). (*Denaby, etc., Co.* v. *Manchester, etc., Ry. Co.*, L. R. 11 App. Cas. 97.)

Costs. The railway commissioners have no jurisdiction under the

Regulation of Railways Act, 1873, § 28, to order a defendant, in whose favor they have decided, to pay costs to the unsuccessful applicant.

The discretion as to costs given to the commissioners under section 28 is not greater than that given to the High Court under Order LV., Rule 1 of the Rules of the Supreme Court.

The commissioners, in dismissing an application, ordered the defendant to pay half the costs of the applicants, on the ground that the defendants were responsible for the litigation, because they had not given public notice that they had ceased to be owners or managers of a certain canal. *Held*, by the Court of Appeals (Brett and Cotton, L. JJ.), reversing the judgment of the Queen's Bench Division (Field, Mainsty, and Bowen, JJ.), that the commissioners in making such an order had exceeded the jurisdiction as to costs given to them by section 28 of the Regulation of Railways Act, 1873. (*Foster, etc. v. G. W. Ry. Co.*, 4 Ry. & Can. Traf. Cas. 58.)

(42) ACTION AGAINST CARRIERS FOR DAMAGES.

Recovery—Money had and received. At common law, excessive charges paid could be recovered in an action for money had and received. (*Johnson* v. *Railroad Co.*, 16 Fla. 623; Angell on Carriers, § 124: see English Decisions, *supra*.)

An action lies in New Hampshire for damage caused by an unreasonable discrimination practiced in Maine in violation of the law of that state. (*McDuffie* v. *Portland & Rochester R. R. Co.*, N. H. 430, 1873.)

If by reason of bribes or other improper motives, railway employes give preference to one person over another, the company may be held liable for damage thereby sustained. (*Galena & C. R. Co.* v. *Rae*, 18 Ills. 488.)

A recovery may be had by a party who paid the excessive fare simply for the purpose of suing for the penalty. (*Fisher* v. *N. Y. C. & H. R. R. Co.*, 46 N. Y. 644.)

Where parties are equally at fault in having violated the law against extortionate charges, as the railroad agent, as shipper making payments to himself as agent, there can be no recovery. (*Steever* v. *Ills. Cent. Ry. Co.*, 62 Iowa, 371.)

— Protest. Where a common carrier demands and receives an excessive charge (made so by statute), the shipper has a right at common law to recover the excess and no protest is necessary. (*Heiserman* v. *Burlington, etc., Ry. Co.*, 63 Iowa, 732; *Fuller* v. *Chicago, etc., R. Co.*, 31 Iowa, 187.)

§ 8.] INTER-STATE COMMERCE ACT. 159

— **Payment—Duress.** If the shipper had no other outlet for shipment, payments will be deemed to be under duress, and excess can be recovered back. (*C. & A. R. Co.* v. *Chicago, etc., Coal Co.*, 79 Ill. 121; *W. Va. Transp. Co.* v. *Sweetser*, 25 W. Va. 434; s. c., 22 Am. & Eng. R. Cas. 469.)

Demand not necessary before institution of suit. (*W. Va. Transp. Co.* v. *Sweetser, supra.*)

— **Not in equity.** The action to recover back overcharge is at law. Bill in equity will not lie even where proportional part is to be recovered of each of several roads. (*Scott* v. *Erie Ry. Co.*, 34 N. J. Eq. 354.)

Pleading. In an action under § 3 of the Illinois Act of May 2, 1873 (Laws Ill., 1873, 136), prohibiting charges of a greater amount for any distance than is at the same time charged "for the transportation in the same direction of any passenger **or like quantity of freight of the same class** a greater distance of the same railroad": *Held*, that the declaration must show that the respective freights mentioned were of like quantity, of the same class, and that, in respect to such freight, there was a higher charge for a less than for a greater distance. The description of the respective freights merely as one car load of ponies, and one car load of horses, does not sufficiently show them to be "like quantities of freight of the same class." (*C. B. & Q. R. Co.* v. *People*, 77 Ill. 443.)

— **Like conditions.** Under Iowa statutes (Laws 1874, ch. 68, § 10), providing that "no railroad company shall charge any person, company, or corporation for the transportation of any property a greater sum than it shall charge and collect from any other person, company, or corporation for a like service from the same place, and upon like conditions, and all concessions of rates, drawbacks, and contracts for special rates founded upon the demands of commerce and transportation shall be open to all persons, companies, and corporations alike": *Held*, that no recovery can be had from a railroad company under this section for discrimination in charges for cars between different shippers of stock, unless it is shown that the shipments were made under like conditions. (*Paxon* v. *Ill. Cent. R. Co.*, 56 Iowa, 427.)

The petition in this case set out that plaintiff had shipped from Manchester to Chicago car loads of hogs, upon defendant's road, for which it had charged him $56 per car; that during the same time defendant allowed another shipper rebates and drawbacks of from $6 to $16 per car; and that defendant charged plaintiff $104 "over what the defendant charged the said Gannon *for the same service* during the same time; but there was no allegation that the shipments of plaintiff and Gannon were made under *like conditions*."

The court said: "Cases, we incline to think, may be supposed where it would be competent for the carrier, under the statute, to charge one person more than another for a like service. For instance, suppose the cars loaded by one person were attached to express trains and those of another to ordinary freight trains." (*Paxon* v. *Ill. Cent. R. Co., supra*, 430.)

Also, in an action under a statute prohibiting extortion and **unjust discrimination,** the declaration must allege not only a discrimination in rates, but that the discrimination was *unjust*. (*St. Louis, etc., R. Co.* v. *Hill*, 11 Bradw. 248.)

See further as to pleading: *Burkholder* v. *Union Trust Co.*, 82 Mo. 572; s. c., 23 Am. & Eng. R. Cas. 656; *Dwyer* v. *Gulf, etc., R. Co.*, 23 Am & Eng. R. Cas. 654.

(43) Counsel or Attorney's Fee.

The provision for "a reasonable counsel or attorney's fee, to be fixed by the court in every case of recovery," is criticised on the ground that it is imposed only upon the defendant, and on account of this inequality, its constitutionality has been doubted. But provisions of this character are not unusual. It is a means of making the law efficient. In many cases the recovery would be more than consumed in counsel fees. Congress may well have thought that such a provision was necessary to secure obedience to the law and its prompt and efficient enforcement. Can it be questioned that congress has power to make this provision, any more than to provide that in all cases of recovery, the court shall add from ten to three hundred per cent in its discretion? Provisions for ten per cent penalty, double damages and treble damages are now of established validity. The present provision seems more reasonable and better adapted to its purpose. The amount of the fee is left entirely to the discretion of the court, so that all the circumstances of each case may be considered.

The unanimous judgment of the Supreme Court of Kansas upon a similar statute seems to put the question upon the right basis. (*Kans. Pac. Ry. Co.* v. *Mower*, 16 Kans. 573.)

The **Kansas Stock Law** of 1874 provided that "in case such railway company or corporation, or the assignee or lessee thereof, shall fail for thirty days after demand made therefor by the owner of such animal, or his agent or attorney, to pay such owner or his agent or attorney the full value of such animal if killed, or damages thereto if wounded, such owner may sue and recover from such railway company or corporation, or the assignee or lessee thereof, the full value of such animal, or damages thereto, **together with a reasonable attorney fee for the prosecution of the suit,** and all costs," etc. (Laws of Kans., 1874, ch. 94, § 2.) *Held,* constitutional.

Counsel for the railroad contended that "a law which gives a successful plaintiff in a civil action his attorney's fees, and denies them to defendant, is a gross violation" of the constitutional guarantees of equality of rights and remedies for injury by due course of law. The court were unanimously of the opinion that the contention of counsel could not be sustained. Brewer, J., said: "While the law may be harsh and rigorous (and yet its rigor may have seemed to the legislature as essential to its value, for, if a claimant for stock killed was compelled to pay his own attorney's fees, it might well happen that in all cases that the amount of his claim—such amounts being uniformly small—would be consumed by attorney's fees, and so leave the claimant in no better condition than before), we see no reason to hold it beyond the power of the legislature. It is no uncommon thing for legislatures to provide, in cases where failure to pay seems to imply more than ordinary wrong, that such failure should carry with it something in the nature of a penalty. Sometimes double or treble damages are given. The Iowa Stock Law gave double damages. Our Trespass Act provides for both double and treble damages. Ten per cent may sometimes be added in the discretion of the court. Other illustrations might be suggested." (*Kans. Pac. Ry. Co.* v. *Mower*, 16 Ks. 573, 582; also, *Atchison, etc., R. Co.* v. *Harper*, 19 Ks. 529.)

In New Hampshire, by statute of December 23, 1840, ch. 584, § 2, land-owners are authorized to employ counsel at expense of railroad corporations, when the corporation has taken land without fully compensating the owner. The statute was before the supreme court in 1845, but no question raised as to its constitutionality. (*Boston & M. R.* v. *Wentworth*, 20 N. H. 406.)

The Pennsylvania Act of May 3, 1866, requiring corporations to pay the counsel fees of plaintiffs in suits against them in certain cases, was by a majority of the court held inapplicable to a case to recover upon unpaid coupons, the company defending on the ground that they had not been presented. No question of the constitutionality of the law was raised. (*N. Pa. R. Co.* v. *Adams*, 54 Pa. St. 94.)

In actions for damages for the infringement of a patent it is provided that "whenever in any such action a verdict is rendered for the plaintiff, the court may enter judgment thereon for any sum above the amount found by the verdict as the actual damages sustained, according to the circumstances of the case, not exceeding three times the amount of such verdict, together with costs." (§ 4919 Rev. Stat. U. S.) The validity of this statute has been recognized and its provisions enforced in numerous cases by the Supreme Court of the United States. (*Birdsall* v. *Coolidge*, 93 U. S. 64, and cases collected in Walker on Patents, § 567, 568.)

An owner of capital stock in a corporation who sues for himself and all other share-holders, and successfully prosecutes the action for a wrong done to the corporation, is entitled to be reimbursed his actual and necessary expenditures, including attorney's fees, out of the corporate funds. (*Meeker* v. *Winthrop Iron Co.*, 17 Fed. Rep. 48.)

Appeals. "Any corporation, person, or persons, owning or controlling any railroad in this state, or any complainant against such corporation, person, or persons, taking an appeal from a decision rendered by a justice of the peace in a suit for damages brought under [the law for killing live stock], and failing to sustain such appeal, or to reduce or increase the judgment before the appellate court, shall be liable for a reasonable attorney's fee incurred by reason of such appeal, to be assessed by the court, not to exceed $20; and the attorney's fee shall be part of the cost and collected as such." (Alabama Code, § 1715.)

Held, unconstitutional, "being violative of that equality and uniformity of rights and privileges, which, by the fundamental principles of the constitution, state and federal, are secured to all persons, and creating unequal and unjust discrimination against a particular *class of litigants*." (*S. & N. Ala. R. Co.* v. *Morris*, 65 Ala. 193.

The Mississippi Act, March 9, 1882, providing "that whenever an appeal shall be taken from the judgment of any court in any action for damages brought by any citizen of this state against any corporation, a reasonable attorney's fee for the appellee shall be assessed by the court," etc. *Held*, that "this act discriminates between **classes of persons** as to the incidents of an appeal from the judgment of an inferior court, and is, therefore, unconstitutional because violative of that principle of personal equality before the law" guaranteed by the constitution. (*S. & N. Ala. R. Co.* v. *Morris, supra*, followed; *Chicago, etc., R. Co.* v. *Moss*, 60 Miss. 641; see, also, *Durkee* v. *Janesville*, 28 Wis. 464.)

Attorney's fee—Practice. In an action under the Kansas stock law of 1874, *supra*, the railroad company recovered judgment before the justice. On appeal the plaintiff recovered judgment, and in it the court included the fees of plaintiff's attorney on the trial before the justice. *Held*, no error. (*Mo. Riv., etc., R. Co.* v. *Shirley*, 20 Kans. 660.)

— **Evidence.** On the trial of an action under said law, the opinion of a witness as to the value of the services rendered by the plaintiff's attorney in prosecuting the case, is competent, if such opinion is founded upon the character of the case set out in the bill of particulars filed in the action, or upon a hypothetical case put to the witness, corresponding with the real case. (*Cent. B. U. P. R. Co.* v. *Nichols*, 24 Kans. 242.)

Remedial or penal? The act of congress of March 3, 1823, providing that a person illegally importing goods shall "forfeit and pay a sum double the amount or value of the goods," etc., is **remedial** and not strictly penal in its character, and a civil action of debt will lie. (*Stockwell* v. *U. S.*, 13 Wall. 531.)

A statute providing for a "forfeiture" or penalty is criminal rather than remedial; it indicates more than compensation—it inflicts punishment. (*Herriman* v. *Burlington, etc., R. Co.*, 57 Iowa, 187.)

The statute of Iowa (Laws, 1878, chap. 77, § 13) providing for treble damages and costs, including counsel fee, for the violation of the statute as to "extortion and unjust discrimination," is a penal statute and must be strictly construed. (*Bond* v. *Wabash, etc., Ry. Co.*, 67 Iowa, 712; 23 Am. & E. Ry. Cas. 608, 610.)

The liability to treble damages imposed by statute upon railroad corporations for extortion and unjust discrimination is a statutory penalty. (*St. Louis, etc., R. Co.* v. *Hill*, 11 Bradw. (Ill. App.) 248.)

ACTIONS FOR DAMAGES: WHERE TO BE BROUGHT(43)—CRIMINATING EVIDENCE.

Sec. 9. That any person or persons claiming to be damaged by any common carrier subject to the provisions of this act may either make complaint to the Commission as hereinafter provided for, or may bring suit in his or their own behalf for the recovery of the damages for which such common carrier may be liable under the provisions of this act, in any district or circuit court of the United States of competent jurisdiction; but such person or persons shall not have the right to pursue both of said remedies, and must in each case elect which one of the two methods of procedure herein provided for he or they will adopt. In any such action brought for the recovery of damages the court before which the same shall be pending may compel any director, officer, receiver, trustee, or agent of the corporation or company defendant in such suit to attend, appear, and testify in such case, and may compel the production of the books and papers of such corporation or company party to any such suit; the claim that any such testimony or evidence may tend to criminate the person giving such evidence shall not excuse such witness from testifying, but such evidence or testimony shall not be used against such person on the trial of any criminal proceeding.(44)

(43) Under the Nebraska Act, June 6, 1885, complaint must first be made to the Railroad Commission. (*State* v. *Chicago, etc., R. Co.*, 19 Neb. 476.)

(44) CRIMINATING EVIDENCE.

General rules. Witnesses are not bound to make any discovery which would expose them to a prosecution or penalty. (*U. S.* v. *Saline Bank*, 1 Pet. 100.)

The foundation of this rule is that the evidence which the witness is called upon to give subjects the witness to danger of prosecution. (*R.* v. *Boyes*, 9 Cox, 32; 1 B. & S. 311.)

The danger must be real, not imaginary. (*Ib.*; Wharton, Crim. Ev., § 469.)

The question of privilege is for the determination of the court. (Wharton, Crim. Ev., § 469.)

The privilege is personal to the witness. (*Boyle* v. *Wiseman*, 19 Ex. 647.)

The constitutional power of the legislature to prescribe rules of evidence is well settled. (*Holmes* v. *Hunt*, 122 Mass. 505, Gray, C. J.; *Kendall* v. *Kingston*, 5 Mass. 524, 534, Parsons, C. J.; *Ogden* v. *Saunders*, 12 Wheat. 213, 262, 349, and see note to § 14.)

But if the statute requiring a witness to testify expressly provides that "such evidence or testimony shall not be used against such person in the trial of any criminal proceeding," it takes away the privilege, because no danger can exist of such testimony being used against the witness in a criminal prosecution. (*U. S.* v. *McCarthy*, 18 Fed. Rep. 87; *Kendrick* v. *Commonwealth*, 17 Va. 490.)

"If a **pardon** has been issued by the proper authorities so as to relieve the witness from any penal responsibility for the offense as to which he is asked, he will be compelled to answer; and so when the **statute of limitations** has interposed a bar." (Wharton, Crim. Ev., § 471.

Fifth amendment. The provision in the fifth amendment to the constitution that no person "shall be compelled in any criminal case to be a witness against himself" being a constitutional provision for the security of person and property should be liberally construed. (*Boyd* v. *U. S.*, 116 U. S. 616.)

"Criminal case," what is. A proceeding to forfeit a person's goods for an offense against the laws, though civil in form, and whether *in rem* or *in personam* is a "criminal case" within the meaning of that part of the fifth amendment which declares that no person "shall be compelled, in any criminal case, to be a witness against himself." (*Ib.*)

Production of papers. The seizure or compulsory production of a man's private papers, to be used in evidence against him, is equivalent to compelling him to be a witness against himself, and, in a prosecution for a crime, penalty, or forfeiture, is equally within the prohibition of the fifth amendment. (*Ib.*)

Statutes requiring the giving of criminating evidence. Such a statute as § 9 in the present act does not violate the constitutional guaranty that no person "shall be compelled, in any criminal case, to be a witness against himself." (5th Amendt. U. S. Const.) (*U. S.* v. *McCarthy*, 18 Fed. Rep. 87; 21 Blatchf. C. C. 469; *People* v. *Kelly* (*In re Hackley*), 24 N. Y. 74; *State* v. *Warner*, 13 La. (Tenn.) 52; *U. S.* v. *Brown*, 1 Sawy. 531, 536; *U. S.* v. *Williams*, 15 Int. Rev. Rec. 199; *In re Phillips*, 2 Am. Law Times, 154; Wharton, Crim. Ev., § 471.)

So held as to the act of February 15, 1868 (15 Stat. at Large, 37; § 860, Revised Statutes), providing that such evidence shall not be used against the witness, and the witness was compelled to testify. (*U. S.* v. *McCarthy*, *supra*.)

But where the constitutional guaranty is that no person "shall be compelled to accuse or *furnish evidence against himself*," the statute must not only provide that the testimony shall not be used against him, but also that he shall not thereafter be prosecuted for any offense so disclosed by him. (*State* v. *Nowell*, 58 N. H. 514; 9 Reporter, 577; *Emery's case*, 107 Mass. 172.)

The line of distinction between the cases is that the language "to be a witness against himself" does not protect the witness from the indirect and incidental consequences of a disclosure which he might be called upon to make (*People* v. *Kelly, supra*), while the words "furnish evidence against himself," require a broader signification and entitle the witness to immunity from future liability as fully as if he had not testified. (*Emery's case, supra*, p. 185; *State* v. *Nowell, supra*.)

Under the 5th amendment is not the witness entitled to be relieved of the collateral results of his testimony, as well as from the use of the testimony itself? And yet is it not going too far to say "he is to be *secured against all liability* to future prosecution *as effectually* as if he were wholly innocent?" (*State* v. *Nowell, supra.*) If he refuses to testify he may still be prosecuted. But, on the other hand, is the mere immunity against the use of his testimony as a confession a full protection? If he claims and is awarded the privilege of refusing to testify, he furnishes no information whatever that can be used against himself; while if he testifies, he necessarily discloses the sources of other evidence against himself. Should he not be relieved from all the consequences of giving evidence, as well as secured from the use of his own testimony? Can this immunity be fully secured except by exemption from prosecution as to the matters concerning which he testifies?

Penalty for Violation of Act—Directors, Officers, and Employes Liable to Prosecution.

Sec. 10. That any common carrier subject to the provisions of this act, or, whenever such common carrier is a corporation, any director or officer thereof, or any receiver, trustee, lessee, agent, or person acting for or employed by such corporation, who, alone or with any other corporation, company, person, or party, shall willfully (45) do or cause to be done, or shall willingly suffer or permit to be done, any act, matter, or thing in this act prohibited or declared to be unlawful, or who shall aid or abet therein, or shall willfully omit or fail to do any act, matter, or thing in this act required to be done, or shall cause or willingly suffer or permit any act, matter, or thing so directed or required by this act to be done not to be so done, or shall aid or abet any such omission or failure, or shall be guilty of any infraction of this act, or shall aid or abet therein, shall be deemed guilty of a misdemeanor, and shall, upon conviction thereof in any district court (46) of the United States within the jurisdiction of which such offense was committed, be subject to a fine of not to exceed five thousand dollars for each offense.

(45) The word "**willfully**" as used in Iowa statute (Act 1862, ch. 169, § 2), does not imply the idea of malice; and if it be shown that the railroad company designedly omitted to do the things enjoined by the act, it will be sufficient to fix its liability to the penalty prescribed.

Whether such omission was by design or through mistake or inadvertence is a question of fact for the jury. (*Fuller* v. *Chicago, etc., R. Co.*, 31 Iowa, 187; see *U. S.* v. *Claypool*, 14 Fed. Rep. 127.)

(46) Section 629, Revised Statutes, provides that "Circuit courts shall have original jurisdiction as follows: Twentieth. Exclusive cognizance of all crimes and offences cognizable under the authority of the United States, except where it is or may be otherwise provided by law, *and concurrent jurisdiction with the district courts of crimes and offenses cognizable therein.*"

In many districts, indictments have been uniformly found in the circuit court, and defendants have had no opportunity to secure a review of the rulings of the trial judge, except where the trial judge has requested the presence of another judge at the hearing of a motion for new trial or in arrest of judgment. In my judgment, the liberty of a citizen should never be in the hands of a single judge, however able or upright he may be. The statutes defining crimes against the United States and prescribing the procedure for their prosecution are very incongruous and unsystematic. The fact that no appeal or error can be taken in criminal cases to the supreme court, and no review provided where indictments or informations are filed in the circuit court, is not creditable to the wisdom or justice of congress. Provisions should be made so that proceedings in error could be prosecuted in any criminal case before an appellate court composed entirely of different judges. The statutes of the United States respecting crimes need thorough revision and codification.

Inter-State Commerce Commission Established—Appointment, Terms, Removal, and Qualifications of Commissioners.

Sec. 11. That a Commission is hereby created and established to be known as the Inter-State Commerce Commission, which shall be composed of five Commissioners, who shall be appointed by the President, by and with the advise and consent of the Senate. The Commissioners first appointed under this act shall continue in office for the term of two, three, four, five, and six years, respectively, from the first day of January, Anno Domini eighteen hundred and eighty-seven, the term of each to be designated by the President; but their successors shall be appointed for terms of six years, except that any person chosen to fill a vacancy shall be appointed only for the unexpired time of the Commissioner whom he shall succeed. Any Commissioner may be removed by the President for inefficiency, neglect of duty, or malfeasance in office. Not more than three of the Commissioners shall be appointed from the same political party. No person in the employ of or holding any official relation to any common carrier subject to the provisions of this act, or owning stock or bonds thereof, or who is in any manner pecuniarily interested therein, shall enter upon the duties of or hold such office. Said Commissioners shall not engage in any other business, vocation, or employment. No vacancy in the Commission shall impair the right of the remaining Commissioners to exercise all the powers of the Commission.(45)

(45) Corresponding provisions are found in the Regulation of Railways Act, 1873, §§ 4 and 5 in Appendix.

POWERS OF THE COMMISSION.

Sec. 12, Par. 1. That the Commission hereby created shall have authority to inquire into the management of the business of all common carriers subject to the provisions of this act, and shall keep itself informed as to the manner and method in which the same is conducted, and shall have the right to obtain from such common carriers full and complete information necessary to enable the Commission to perform the duties and carry out the objects for which it was created; and for the purposes of this act the Commission shall have power to require the attendance and testimony of witnesses and the production of all books, papers, tariffs, contracts, agreements, and documents relating to any matter under investigation, and to that end may invoke the aid of any court of the United States in requiring the attendance and testimony of witnesses and the production of books, papers, and documents under the provisions of this section.(46)

(46) See somewhat similar provisions in the Mississippi Railroad Commission Act, 1884, §§ 12, 14, and 21, before the Supreme Court in *Stone* v. *Farmers' L. & T. Co.*, 116 U. S. 307, 310–313, 331 et seq.

See, also, § 25 Regulation of Railways Act, 1873.

As to the right of congress to confer such powers upon the Commission, see *Miller* v. *New York*, 109 U. S. 385; *R. Comrs.* v. *Portland, etc., R. Co.*, 63 Me. 269; *Commonwealth* v. *Eastern R. Co.*, 103 Mass. 254; *State* v. *Chicago, etc., R. Co.*, 19 Neb. 476; *Georgia R.* v. *R. Comrs.*, 70 Ga. 694; see note (27) to § 4 *ante*.

That a charter right to manage the business of the company through its board of directors is not violated by such provisions. (See *Stone* v. *Farmers' L. & T. Co.*, 116 U. S. 307, 331–333.)

The Maine Act of 1871, empowering the railroad commissioners to direct a railroad corporation to erect and maintain a depot at a specified place on the line of its road, determined by them to be proper and in accordance with the demands of public convenience and necessity, is constitutional, and is not inconsistent with a charter which provided that "the corporation shall be obliged to receive at all proper times and places, and convey persons and articles;" and is a proper regulation of the public use of the road. (*R. Comrs.* v. *Portland, etc., R. Co.*, 63 Me. 269.)

The Massachusetts statute providing for the appointment of commissioners to fix the compensation to be paid by one railroad for drawing its merchandise and cars over another railroad, does not infringe the charter rights of the latter to regulate its tolls. (*V. & M. R. Co.* v. *Fitchburg R. Co.*, 9 Cush. 369.)

U. S. CIRCUIT COURTS MAY COMPEL OBEDIENCE TO SUBPŒNA.

Sec. 12, Par. 2. And any of the circuit courts of the United States within the jurisdiction of which such inquiry is carried on may, in case of contumacy or refusal to obey a subpœna issued to any common carrier subject to the provisions of this act, or other person, issue an order requiring such common carrier or other person to appear before said Commission (and produce books and papers if so ordered) and give evidence touching the matter in question; and any failure to obey such order of the court may be punished by such court as a contempt thereof. The claim that any such testimony or evidence may tend to criminate the person giving such evidence shall not excuse such witness from testifying; but such evidence or testimony shall not be used against such person on the trial of any criminal proceeding.(47)

(47) As to the constitutionality and effect of this provision requiring the giving of criminating evidence, see note to § 9, *ante*, p. 164.

Complaints of Violations of Act and Proceedure Thereon by the Commission.

Sec. 13. That any person, firm, corporation, or association, or any mercantile, agricultural, or manufacturing society, or any body politic or municipal organization complaining of any thing done or omitted to be done by any common carrier subject to the provisions of this act in contravention of the provisions thereof, may apply to said Commission by petition, which shall briefly state the facts(48); whereupon a statement of the charges thus made shall be forwarded by the Commission to such common carrier, who shall be called upon to satisfy the complaint or to answer the same in writing within a reasonable time, to be specified by the Commission. If such common carrier, within the time specified, shall make reparation for the injury alleged to have been done, said carrier shall be relieved of liability to the complainant only for the particular violation of law thus complained of.(49) If such carrier shall not satisfy the complaint within the time specified, or there shall appear to be any reasonable ground for investigating said complaint, it shall be the duty of the Commission to investigate the matters complained of in such manner and by such means as it shall deem proper.(50)

(48) See § 6 of the Regulation of Railways Act, 1873. By § 13 of the same act, municipal and other public corporation, local or harbor board, may also make complaints. (See 4 Nev. & Mac. 20; *Ib.* 137; *Ib.* 564; 4 Ry. & Can. Traf. Cas. 44; *Ib.* 69.)

(49) See § 7 of the Regulation of Railways Act, 1873.

(50) THE DUTIES OF THE COMMISSION—NATURE AND SCOPE OF THE ACT, AND THE OBLIGATION OF CARRIERS SUBJECT TO IT.

The Commission has already put a construction upon this section, and has given quite a full statement of the nature and character of the power conferred upon it by the act. A number of applications had been made to the Commission for its answer to certain questions as to the proper interpretation of the law. The Commisson, in its opinion, says:

"It is obvious from the tenor of such applications as these, which reach us by every mail, that the impression is generally prevalent that this Commission has power to construe, interpret, and apply the law by preliminary judgment. We are continually appealed to for decisions in advance as to whether common carriers, said to be willing to adopt certain methods of dealing with respect to inter-state commerce, can do so without subjecting themselves to the penalties denounced by the statute for violating its provisions.

"A careful reading of the 'act to regulate commerce,' under which this Commission is organized, will show to the petitioners and others who have made similar applications that no jurisdiction has been given us to answer questions like those under consideration. An expression of our opinion on these subjects at this time, being neither a duty imposed nor a power conferred by the statute, would carry with it no judicial efficacy or sanction; in fact, would be no more useful to the public or the carrier than the opinion of other men upon the same points.

"Two sections of the law confer power upon the Commission to entertain and decide applications and petitions. Section 4 empowers us upon applications by a common carrier to authorize such common carrier in special cases to charge less for longer than for shorter distances, over the same line; and also to prescribe the extent of relief from the operation of the former part of the same section which a designated common carrier may from time to time enjoy. A large number of petitions have been filed under this section, the consideration of which is at this time engaging the attention of the Commission, and nothing said in this opinion is to be treated as in any manner bearing thereon. It is obvious that applications like those of the Railway Conductors' and the Traders' and Travelers' Union have no relation whatever to the duties imposed upon us by section 4. And this is the only section of the law which the Commission has power to suspend or relax.

"Section 13 authorizes complaints to the Commission and confers jurisdiction to entertain the same. It provides that any person complaining of any thing done or omitted to be done by any common carrier subject to the provisions of this act in contravention of the provisions thereof may apply to said Commission by petition, which shall briefly state the facts, notice, and opportunity for answer having been given. Unless satisfaction is made an investigation is required. Upon such an investigation the Commission will necessarily entertain the consideration of the question whether the conduct complained of is or is not in contravention of the provisions of the law; and if it so adjudge it is authorized to issue a notice enjoining the carrier from further violation of the law and to award reparation for the injury done, or both. But neither the Railway Conductors' nor Traders' and Travelers' Union complain that any common carrier has violated the law. On the contrary, they both aver that the railroad companies do not now violate the law, and do not wish to do so. The conductors say that they fear they will not receive passes as heretofore, and the Traders and Travelers' say that they fear commercial travelers will not be allowed free transportation for 150 pounds of extra baggage, as was allowed last year. They present no complaint of the provisions of the law. If a railroad company should issue a pass to a conductor and his family to attend the approaching convention, or should transport three hundred pounds of baggage free for a commercial traveler, under the registry and indemnity system, and some person feeling aggrieved should make complaint of unjust discrimination, it would then be proper for the Commission to entertain the question of whether such conduct was or was not in violation of the law, and if so whether it was or was not within the exceptions as stated in section 22. Complaints may also be presented if the charges made by the carriers are not considered reasonable and just. But until questions of this kind come before us in the way clearly indicated by the statute, it would be worse than useless for us to express our opinions or give advice. We should not only lay ourselves justly open to the charge of assuming unwarranted authority, but should also run great risk of involving all concerned in what the courts might afterward hold to be breaches of the law, by hasty and ill-considered conclusions, based upon *ex parte* statements and arguments. Although it might be desirable, or at least convenient, in respect to any piece of new legislation to have a tribunal established to which inquirers might apply for instruction and advice regarding the meaning of the law and its application to suggested 'circumstances and conditions,' a moment's reflection will show that no such tribunal could be properly erected. Congress has not taken the management of the railroads out of the hands of the railroad companies. It has simply established certain general principles under which inter-state commerce must be conducted.

"It has enacted in section 1 that all charges for inter-state transportation 'shall be reasonable and just;' has prohibited in section 2 all manner of unjust discriminations; has forbidden in section 3 all undue and unreasonable preferences and advantages; has required in the same section reasonable and equal facilities for the interchange of traffic, and has prohibited in section 5 the pooling of freights. That in substance is the inter-state commerce law.

"There is nothing novel in these provisions. They simply bring back the business of the common carriers to the well-settled principles of the common law. Yet no one can deny that there was urgent need of their statutory formulation. Alleged difficulties in putting them in operation only disclose examples of the extent to which they have been violated in the past. These sections of the act are expressed in plain words. A construction must be given to them in the first instance by the carriers and their patrons. When a course of conduct has been adopted, of which complaint is made that it violates the law, the decision of the question will rest with the courts or with the Commission, as the complaining party may elect. This is the orderly method in which all legislation is administered and applied, and the statute in question presents no exception.

"One more suggestion may properly be added. It appears from the numerous petitions that have been laid before us for preliminary advice, many of them obviously upon the suggestion if not by the procurement of the carriers themselves, that common comment on the law, by the carriers and those who have heretofore enjoyed special favors at their hands, describe the system of penalties which the law provides as extreme, and the risks imposed upon unintentional and unwitting violators of its provisions as enormous. Such comment seems to us neither fair nor just. It is true that section 8 provides that for violations of the law, and for failure to do an act which the law requires, the offending carrier shall be liable to the injured party for the actual damages sustained, together with a reasonable counsel or attorney's fee, to be fixed by the court, and collected with the costs in the case. It is also true section 10 imposes a fine of "not to exceed $5,000" upon common carriers and their officers, agents, and servants who willfully do or cause to be done, or willingly suffer or permit to be done, any prohibited act, or upon conviction in a district court of the United States. The civil remedy described in section 8 adds an attorney fee to the existing common-law right of any injured party to recover the full amount of his damages, a condition of affairs which can not greatly alarm corporations disposed to fair dealing; while the criminal remedy given in section 10 obviously pertains to intentional violators of the law, and is in these cases to be graduated by the court according to the enormity of the offense.

"Good faith, exhibited in an honest effort to carry out the requirements of the law, will involve reasonable and fair-minded officials in no danger of damages or fine. The elasticity of the statute in their favor is noticeable. The unjust discrimination of section 2 must be 'in a like and contemporaneous service in the transportation of a like kind of traffic, under substantially similar circumstanced conditions.'

"The preference or advantage of section 3 must be 'undue or unreasonable.' Throughout the act, as it now stands in confessedly experimental form, there is exhibited an obvious and generous purpose to allow to the corporations ample scope in the conduct of their business as common carriers for the people, and fair consideration of every reasonable claim, while insisting upon just, impartial, open, and consistent rates of charge to which every citizen shall be subjected alike whose situation is the same. Surely the people could not ask for less. The language and the tenor of the act wholly fail to justify railroad managers, if any such there be, who refuse to accept responsibility, decline to offer rates, neglect to announce conditions of traffic, embarrass the customary interchange of business, and impose stagnation upon trade, while they 'stick in the bark' of the phrases and expressions of the law, inventing doubts and imagining dangers. It is still more unjustifiable for railroad companies to make use of the general clauses of the law, ignoring its modifying and enlarging words and formulas, in order to impose additional burdens upon localities, trades, professions, manufacturers, consumers, classes of travelers, or employes, straining and representing every construction in favor of the corporate treasury, and quoting the new law as their authority for all manner of petty exactions.

"The powers of the Commission are entirely adequate to cope with such conduct, the existence of which is not affirmed, although it has been somewhat publicly suggested. The same statute which enacts that charges for like service shall be uniform to all, also provides that charges in every case, and for every kind and class of service, shall be reasonable and just. As the law is practically applied, it is said to contain many elements of advantage to the economical and profitable management of the business of the carriers, which they have not been slow to apprehend and take the benefit of. The Commission venture to express the hope that with this explanation respecting the mutual functions of the carriers, and the Commissioners in carrying the law into effect according to its true intent and meaning, there will be no lack of good faith and active co-operation in continuing the normal activity of every kind of reputable industry and traffic throughout the land, under favorable, fair, and reasonable terms, conceding frankly to the people all the rights, benefits, advantages, and equal privileges which the 'act to regulate commerce' was intended to secure." (*In re Petition of the Order of Railway Conductors; In re Petition of Traders and Travelers' Union, April* 18, 1887, **Railway Age,** April 22, 1887, p. 282.)

This construction of the power given the Commission is in consonance with the construction placed upon the English Act of 1873 as to the power of the railway commissioners by Lord Chancellor Selborne in his opinion quoted at length on page 98 et seq., *supra*.

The Railway Commissioners have full power of permitting the proceedings before them to be amended; and will exercise the power liberally to give effect to the statute. (*Mayor, etc.*, v. *S. E. Ry. Co.*, 1 Nev. &. Mac. 349.)

Railroad commissioners under state statutes, such as that of **Iowa**, **are executive** and not **judicial officers**. (*In re Railroad Commissioners*, 15 Neb. 679.)

INVESTIGATION AT THE REQUEST OF STATE OR TERRITORIAL RAILROAD COMMISSIONERS, OR UPON ITS OWN MOTION.

Sec. 13, Par. 2. Said Commission shall in like manner investigate any complaint forwarded by the Railroad Commissioner or Railroad Commission of any state or territory, at the request of such Commissioner or Commission, and may institute any inquiry on its own motion in the same manner and to the same effect as though complaint had been made.

WANT OF DIRECT DAMAGE TO THE COMPLAINANT.

Sec. 13, Par. 3. No complaint shall at any time be dismissed because of the absence of direct damage to the complainant(51).

(51) The Regulation of Railways Act, 1873, § 13 (see Appendix) provides that "a complaint . . . may be made . . . by a municipal or other public corporation, local or harbor board, *without proof that the complainants are aggrieved by the contravention*; provided, that a complaint shall not be entertained by the Commissioners in pursuance of this section, unless such complaint is accompanied by a certificate of the board of trade to the effect that in their opinion the case in respect of which the complaint is made is a proper one to be submitted for adjudication to the Commissioners, by such municipal or other public corporation, local or harbor board."

WRITTEN REPORT OF INVESTIGATIONS TO BE MADE; AND FINDINGS OF FACT THEREIN TO BE PRIMA FACIE EVIDENCE.

Sec. 14, Par. 1. That whenever an investigation shall be made by said Commission, it shall be its duty to make a report in writing in respect thereto, which shall include the findings of fact upon which the conclusions of the Commission are based, together with its recommendation as to what reparation, if any, should be made by the common carrier to any party or parties who may be found to have been injured; and such findings so made shall thereafter, in all judicial proceedings, be deemed *prima facie* evidence as to each and every fact found(52).

(52) PRIMA FACIE EVIDENCE.

Constitutionality of such statutes. It has been questioned whether statutes giving *prima facie* force to certain proof are constitutional.

The weight of authority is certainly very strongly in their favor. (See elaborate review of the question and the decisions thereon, by Gray, C. J., in *Holmes* v. *Hunt*, 122 Mass. 505.)

Justice Gray, now on the bench of the Supreme Court of the United States, there says, in deciding this case, which arose under the Massachusetts statute of 1817, that the making of the **report of an auditor** *prima facie* evidence, upon such matters as are embraced in the order to him, is constitutional. That it is *prima facie* evidence, not only of the result of the accounts, but of the facts or inferences stated in his report as derived from the evidence before him and involved in the determination of the issues submitted to him, even if they include a finding upon the general question whether the defendant is or is not liable to the plaintiff.

In *Allen* v. *Hawks*, 11 Pick. 359, Shaw, C. J., says: "The Massachusetts statute of 1817, which makes the report of an auditor appointed by the court *prima facie* evidence, introduced a new species of competent evidence often very useful, and intended to facilitate, not to supersede jury trials."

The ground upon which the constitutionality of such statutes is questioned seems to be that they infringe upon the right of trial by jury. It is claimed that an examination by an auditor, and, perhaps by a commission likewise, has all the insignia of a trial of the rights of the parties.

The Massachusetts statute above referred to does not technically change the burden of proof; it simply obliges the other party to offer evidence to rebut or control it, or else it will be conclusive. (*Allen* v. *Hawks*, 11 Pick. 359; *Morgan* v. *Morse*, 13 Gray, 150; *Fanning* v. *Chadwick*, 3 Pick. 420.)

That the **report of an auditor** may be *prima facie* evidence seems to be settled by a series of decisions. (*Lazarus* v. *Commonwealth Ins. Co.*, 19 Pick. 81; *Lock* v. *Bennett*, 7 Cush. 445, 453; *Nolan*

v. *Collins*, 112 Mass. 12; *Fair* v. *Manhattan Ins. Co.*, 112 Mass. 320, 328–332; *Lowe* v. *Pimental*, 115 Mass. 44; *Corbett* v. *Greenlaw*, 117 Mass. 167.)

It was said, in *Holmes* v. *Hunt*, 122 Mass. 505, of the provisions of the Massachusetts statute above referred to, that they have been constantly applied by this court, without a doubt of their validity being suggested, for nearly sixty years. After so long a practical construction and acquiescence by the legislature, by the courts, and by all parties to judicial proceedings, it would require a very clear case to warrant the court in setting them aside as unconstitutional. (See, also, *Stewart* v. *Laird*, 1 Cranch, 299, 309; *Packard* v. *Richardson*, 17 Mass. 122, 144; *Commonwealth* v. *Parker*, 2 Pick. 550, 557; *Copp* v. *Henniker*, 55 N. H. 179, 209.)

Justice Gray says further, "but it does not appear to us that, if these statutes had just been enacted for the first time, there would be any ground for holding them unconstitutional. While the right of trial by jury in actions at law is secured by the constitution, the forms of proceeding and the rules of evidence are within the control of the legislature."

The constitutional power of the legislature to prescribe **rules of evidence** is well settled. (Parsons, C. J., in *Kendall* v. *Kingsdon*, 5 Mass. 524, 534; Washington, J., and Marshall, C. J., in *Ogden* v. *Saunders*, 12 Wheat. 213, 262, 349; *Board* v. *Merchant*, 103 N. Y. 143; s. c., 34 Albany L. J. 394.)

This power to prescribe rules of evidence has been often exercised by the legislature, with the sanction of the courts, so as to change the burden of proof, or to effect the question as to what shall be deemed *prima facie* evidence at the trial before a jury. (*Goshen* v. *Richmond*, 4 Allen, 458; *Monson* v. *Palmer*, 8 Allen, 551, 556; *Howard* v. *Moot*, 64 N. Y. 262, 268; *Doyle* v. *Doyle*, 56 N. H. 567; *Perkins* v. *Scott*, 57 N. H. 55; *Brown* v. *Kemball*, 12 Vt. 617; *Stoddard* v. *Chapin*, 15 Vt. 443; see *Lee* v. *Tillotson*, 24 Wend. 337, in connection with 2 Paine, 583.)

The legislature may enact that the deed of a collector of taxes shall be *prima facie* evidence that the land has been sold for non-payment of taxes, at a time and in a manner authorized by law. (*Pillow* v. *Roberts*, 13 Howard, 472, 476; *Callanan* v. *Hurley*, 93 U. S. 387; *Hand* v. *Ballou*, 2 Kernan 541; Cooley Const. Lim. (3d ed.) 367, 368.)

So it may enact that the record of a deed shall be evidence that it has been duly acknowledged or proved before a magistrate, without any record of the certificate or of proof of acknowledgment. (*Webb* v. *Den*, 17 How. 376.)

A statute providing that a notary's protest of a note should be evidence of the facts stated therein has been held to be constitutional by the Supreme Court of Maine. (*Fales* v. *Wadsworth*, 23 Maine, 553.)

The recorded certificate of two witnesses is made sufficient evidence of an entry to foreclose a mortgage, and the affidavit of the mortgagee himself evidence that the requisitions of a power of sale have been complied with. (*Hawkes* v. *Bingham*, 16 Gray, 561; *Ellis* v. *Drake*, 8 Allen, 161, 163; *Thompson* v. *Kenyon*, 100 Mass. 108; *Childs* v. *Dolan*, 5 Allen, 319; *Field* v. *Gooding*, 106 Mass. 310, 312.)

Justice Story gave the fullest effect to an act of congress which provided that the certificate of a vice-consul, that a master had refused to take a destitute seaman on board, should be *prima facie* evidence in a suit against the master for a penalty imposed on him for such refusal. (U. S. Stat., Feb. 28, 1803, § 4; U. S. Rev. Stat., § 4578; *Matthews* v. *Offley*, 3 Sumner, 115, 123.)

Where a license is relied on in defense, the burden of proving it in criminal actions is on defendant by the statute of Massachusetts, which would otherwise have to be disproved by the commonwealth. (Stats., 1844, c. 102; 1864, c. 121; Gen. Stats., c. 172, § 10; *Commonwealth* v. *Thurlow*, 24 Pick. 374; *Commonwealth* v. *Kelly*, 10 Cush. 69; *Commonwealth* v. *Latry*, 8 Gray, 459; *Commonwealth* v. *Carpenter*, 100 Mass. 204.)

Even statutes providing that in prosecutions for unlawful **sales of intoxicating liquors** delivery in or from any building or place other than a dwelling-house shall be deemed *prima facie* evidence of sale have been held constitutional. (*Commonwealth* v. *Williams*, 6 Gray, 1; *Commonwealth* v. *Rowe*, 14 Gray, 47; *Commonwealth* v. *Wallace*, 7 Gray, 15; see *State* v. *Higgins*, 13 R. I. 330; *State* v. *Mellor*, 13 R. I. 667; *State* v. *Thomas*, 47 Conn. 546.)

Similar statutes, however, have been held unconstitutional. (*People* v. *Lyon*, 27 Hun, 180; *s. c.*, 1 N. Y. Rep. 400; *State* v. *Beswick*, 13 R. I. 211; *s. c.*, 43 Am. Rep. 26, and note.)

The inhibition in this case was against evidence of mere reputation of the premises and of those frequenting them. (See *State* v. *Higgins*, 13 R. I. 330.)

A statute providing that where a person is seen to drink intoxicating liquors on the premises of a vendor, who is only licensed to sell such liquors not to be drunk on the premises, it shall be *prima facie* evidence that the liquor was sold by the occupant of the premises with intent to be drunk thereon, is constitutional. (*Board* v. *Merchant*, 103 N. Y. 143; *s. c.*, 34 Alb. L. J. 394.)

See on this question article in 26 Alb. L. J. 63; 35 Alb. L. J. 300; *Plimpton* v. *Somerset*, 33 Vt. 283.

Railway regulation statutes. The Mississippi Railroad Commission Act, March 11, 1884, § 19, provides that the report of the commission shall be *prima facie* evidence of the correctness of the determination therein stated. (See *Stone* v. *Farmers' L. & T. Co.*, 116 U. S. 307, 312.)

The Illinois statute makes all discriminations in rates *prima facie* evidence of unjust discrimination as prohibited by the statute. (Rev. Stat. Ill. 1883, § 125; see *C. & A. R. Co.* v. *People*, 67 Ill. 11, in note on page 28, *supra*, where a statute was held unconstitutional because it made certain facts conclusive evidence of guilt.)

When a statute declares certain things *prima facie* evidence, the defendant may transverse them and prove the contrary. (*St. Louis, etc., R. Co.* v. *Hill*, 11 Bradw. 248.)

REPORTS OF INVESTIGATIONS TO BE ENTERED OF RECORD AND COPIES FURNISHED.

Sec. 14, Par. 2. All reports of investigations made by the Commission shall be entered of record, and a copy thereof shall be furnished to the party who may have complained, and to any common carrier that may have been complained of.

ORDERS OF THE COMMISSION TO CARRIERS FOUND VIOLATING THE ACT—EXONERATION UPON COMPLIANCE.

Sec. 15. That if in any case in which an investigation shall be made by said Commission it shall be made to appear to the satisfaction of the Commission, either by the testimony of witnesses or other evidence, that any thing has been done or omitted to be done in violation of the provisions of this act, or of any law cognizable by said Commission, by any common carrier, or that any injury or damage has been sustained by the party or parties complaining, or by other parties aggrieved in consequence of any such violation, it shall be the duty of the Commission to forthwith cause a copy of its report in respect thereto to be delivered to such common carrier together with a notice to said common carrier to cease and desist from such violation, or to make reparation for the injury so found to have been done, or both, within a reasonable time, to be specified by the Commission; and if, within the time specified, it shall be made to appear to the Commission that such common carrier has ceased from such violation of law, and has made reparation for the injury found to have been done, in compliance with the report and notice of the Commission, or to the satisfaction of the party complaining, a statement to that effect shall be entered of record by the Commission, and the said common carrier shall thereupon be relieved from further liability or penalty for such particular violation of law.(53)

(53) Under the Regulation of Railways Act, 1873, § 6, the English Railway Commissioners are vested with the jurisdiction formerly possessed by the court of common pleas, and enforce their own orders by injunction and other process as specified in § 3 of the Railway and Canal Traffic Act, 1854.

PROCEDURE IN CIRCUIT COURT TO ENFORCE OBEDIENCE TO ORDERS—APPEAL TO SUPREME COURT.(54)

Sec. 16. That whenever any common carrier, as defined in and subject to the provisions of this act, shall violate or refuse or neglect to obey any lawful order or requirement of the Commission in this act named, it shall be the duty of the Commission, and lawful for any company or person interested in such order or requirement, to apply, in a summary way, by petition, to the Circuit Court of the United States sitting in equity in the judicial district in which the common carrier complained of has its principal office, or in which the violation or disobedience of such order or requirement shall happen, alleging such violation or disobedience, as the case may be; and the said court shall have power to hear and determine the matter, on such short notice to the common carrier complained of as the court shall deem reasonable; and such notice may be served on such common carrier, his or its officers, agents, or servants, in such manner as the court shall direct; and said court shall proceed to hear and determine the matter speedily as a court of equity, and without the formal pleadings and proceedings applicable to ordinary suits in equity, but in such manner as to do justice in the premises; and to this end such court shall have power, if it think fit, to direct and prosecute, in such mode and by such persons as it may appoint, all such inquiries as the court may think needful to enable it to form a just judgment in the matter of such petition; and on such hearing the report of said Commission shall be *prima facie* evidence of the matters therein stated(55); and if it be made to appear to such court, on such hearing or on report of any such person or persons, that the lawful order or requirement of said Commission drawn in question has been violated or disobeyed, it shall be lawful for such court to issue a writ of injunction or other proper process, mandatory or otherwise, to restrain such common carrier from further continuing such violation or disobedience of such order or requirement of said Commission, and enjoining obedience to the same; and in case of any disobedience of any such writ of injunction or other proper process, mandatory or otherwise, it shall be lawful for such court to issue writs of attachment, or any other process of said court incident or applicable to writs of injunction or other proper process, mandatory or otherwise, against such common carrier, and if a corporation, against one or more of the directors, officers, or agents of the same, or against any owner, lessee, trustee, receiver, or other person failing to obey such writ of injunction or other proper process, mandatory or otherwise; and said court may, if it shall think fit, make an order directing such common carrier or other person so disobeying such writ of injunction or other proper process, mandatory or otherwise, to pay such sum of money not exceeding for each carrier or person in default the sum of five hundred dollars for every day after a day to be named in the order that such carrier or other person shall fail to obey such injunction or other proper process, mandatory or otherwise; and such moneys shall be payable as the court shall direct, either to the party complaining, or into court to abide the ultimate decision of the court, or into the Treasury; and payment thereof may, without prejudice to any other mode of recovering the same, be enforced by attachment or order in the nature of a writ of execution, in like manner as if the same had been recovered by a final decree *in personam* in such court. When the subject in dispute shall be of the value of two thousand dollars or more, either party to such proceeding before said court may appeal to the Supreme Court of the United States, under the same regulations now provided by law in respect of security for such appeal; but such appeal shall not operate to stay or supersede the order of the court or the execution of any writ or process thereon; and such court may, in every such matter, order the payment of such costs and counsel fees as shall be deemed reasonable(56). Whenever any such petition shall be filed or presented by the Commission it shall be the duty of the District Attorney, under the direction of the Attorney-General of the United States, to prosecute the same; and the cost and expenses of such prosecution shall be paid out of the appropriation for the expenses of the courts of the United States. For the purposes of this act, excepting its penal provisions, the circuit courts of the United States shall be deemed to be always in session.

(54) ENGLISH STATUTES AND DECISIONS.

Even the procedure for enforcing the provisions of this Act seems to have been modeled after the English statute. Section 3 of the Railway and Canal Traffic Act, 1854, provided that the court or judge, in case of violations of the Act, should issue an injunction or interdict to the company; obedience to the same was enforceable by writs of attachment or other proper process; and, if the court or judge think fit, they or he may make an order for the payment of money not exceeding 200 pounds for each day the company shall fail to obey such injunction or interdict; and such moneys shall be payable as may be directed by the court or judge, either to the party complaining, into court to abide its ultimate decision, or to her Majesty; and payment thereof, without prejudice to any other mode of recovering the same, may be enforced by attachment or order in the nature of a writ of execution. By § 6 of the Regulation of Railways Act, 1873, the jurisdiction under § 3 above was transferred to the railway commissioners. (See these statutes in full in Appendix.)

Statute aimed at individual grievances—Public duties and remedies unaffected. It is held that the statute of 1854 was intended to afford a remedy against an undue preference or undue prejudice to a particular individual or class in respect of railway or canal traffic, and was not intended to apply to breaches of public duties already susceptible of redress by mandamus or indictment. All remedies heretofore existing continue unabridged (*Bennett* v. *Man-*

chester, etc., *Ry. Co.*, 6 C. B. (N. S.) 707; *Atty. Genl.* v. *Gt. North. Ry. Co.*, 1 Drew & S. 154); nor by giving concurrent jurisdiction to courts of law, does it abridge the jurisdiction of the court of chancery. (*Baxendale* v. *West Mid. Ry. Co.*, 3 Giff. 650; 7 L. T. (N. S.) 297; *Atty. Genl.* v. *Gt. North. Ry. Co.*, *supra.*)

Practice. A rule calling on a railway company to show cause why it should not act in compliance with the Railway and Canal Traffic Act, is too vague. (*Marriot* v. *London, etc., Ry. Co.*, 3 Jur. (N. S.) 493; 26 L. J., C. P. 154.)

Previously to an application for an injunction to a railway company, the complainant ought to make a full representation of the grievance of which he seeks redress to the company, and in general it is only on the failure of such application that he is to come to the court. (*Cooper* v. *London, etc., Ry. Co.*, 4 Jur. (N. S.) 762, C. P.)

(55) As to provision that the report of the Commission shall be **prima facie evidence** of the matters therein stated, see note to § 14, *ante*, p. 176, et seq.

(56) As to the taxing of **counsel fees**, the validity of such provisions, and the practice thereunder, see note to § 8, *ante*, p. 160.

REGULATION OF THE PROCEEDINGS OF THE COMMISSION.

Sec. 17. That the Commission may conduct its proceedings in such manner as will best conduce to the proper dispatch of business and to the ends of justice(57). A majority of the Commission shall constitute a quorum for the transaction of business, but no Commissioner shall participate in any hearing or proceeding in which he has any pecuniary interest(58). Said Commission may, from time to time, make or amend such general rules or orders as may be requisite for the order and regulation of proceedings before it, including forms of notices and the service thereof, which shall conform, as nearly as may be, to those in use in the courts of the United States(59). Any party may appear before said Commission and be heard, in person or by attorney. Every vote and official act of the Commission shall be entered of record, and its proceedings shall be public upon the request of either party interested(60). Said Commission shall have an official seal, which shall be judicially noticed(61). Either of the members of the Commission may administer oaths and affirmations.

(57) See section 27 Regulation of Railways Act, 1873, in Appendix.

(58) See paragraph second of section 5 of the same act.

(59) See § 29 of the Regulation of Railways Act, 1873. The rules or general orders adopted by the Railway Commissioners under this provision will be found in 2 Nev. & Mac. Ry. Cas. 2–10.

(60) Section 27 of the Regulation of Railways Act, 1873, provides that "any complaint made to them [the Railway Commissioners] shall, on the application of any party to the complaint, be heard and determined in open court."

(61) The Railway Commissioners "shall have an official seal which shall be judicially noticed." (§ 4 Regulation of Railways Act, 1873.)

Salaries of Commissioners, Secretary, and Employes — Offices and Office Supplies — Witness Fees — Expenses.

Sec. 18. That each Commissioner shall receive an annual salary of seven thousand five hundred dollars, payable in the same manner as the salaries of judges of the courts of the United States.(62) The Commission shall appoint a Secretary, who shall receive an annual salary of three thousand five hundred dollars, payable in like manner. The Commission shall have authority to employ and fix the compensation of such other employes as it may find necessary to the proper performance of its duties, subject to the approval of the Secretary of the Interior.

The Commission shall be furnished by the Secretary of the Interior with suitable offices and all necessary office supplies. Witnesses summoned before the Commission shall be paid the same fees and mileage that are paid witnesses in the courts of the United States. All of the expenses of the Commission, including all necessary expenses for transportation incurred by the Commissioners, or by their employes under their orders, in making any investigation in any other place than in the city of Washington, shall be allowed and paid, on the presentation of itemized vouchers therefor approved by the chairman of the Commission and the Secretary of the Interior.

(62) Each of the English Railway Commissioners is paid such salary

§ 20.] INTER-STATE COMMERCE ACT. 185

as the Treasury may determine, not exceeding three thousand pounds a year. (Regulation of Railways Act, 1873, § 21.)

PRINCIPAL OFFICE OF THE COMMISSION—SESSIONS ELSEWHERE.

Sec. 19. That the principal office of the Commission shall be in the city of Washington, where its general sessions shall be held; but, whenever the convenience of the public or of the parties may be promoted or delay or expense prevented thereby, the Commission may hold special sessions in any part of the United States(63). It may, by one or more of the Commissioners, prosecute any inquiry necessary to its duties, in any part of the United States, into any matter or question of fact pertaining to the business of any common carrier subject to the provisions of this act.(64)

(63) See § 27 of the Regulation of Railways Act, 1873, in Appendix.
(64) See § 25 of the same act.

CARRIERS TO MAKE ANNUAL REPORTS TO THE COMMISSION IF REQUIRED.

Sec. 20. That the Commission is hereby authorized to require annual reports from all common carriers subject to the provisions of this act, to fix the time and prescribe the manner in which such reports shall be made, and to require from such carriers specific answers to all questions upon which the Commission may need information. Such annual reports shall show in detail the amount of capital stock issued, the amounts paid therefor, and the manner of payment for the same; the dividends paid, the surplus fund, if any, and the number of stockholders; the funded and floating debts and the interest paid thereon; the cost and value of the carrier's property, franchises, and equipment; the number of employes and the salaries paid each class; the amounts expended for improvements each year, how expended, and the character of such improvements; the earnings and receipts from each branch of business and from all sources; the operating and other expenses; the balances of profit and loss; and a complete exhibit of the financial operations of the carrier each year, including an annual balance sheet. Such reports shall also contain such information in relation to rates or regulations concerning fares or freights, or agreements, arrangements, or contracts with other common carriers, as the Commission may require; and the said Commission may, within its discretion, for the purpose of enabling it the better to carry out the purposes of this act, prescribe (if in the opinion of the Commission it is practicable to prescribe such uniformity and methods of keeping accounts) a period of time within which all common carriers subject to the provisions of this act shall have, as near as may be, a uniform system of accounts, and the manner in which such accounts shall be kept.(65)

(65) REPORTS OF CARRIERS SUBJECT TO THE ACT.

The question will probably arise whether congress has the power to require corporations incorporated under state laws to give information as to its capital stock and financial condition, and to make an exhibit of all its business, that which is wholly domestic as well as that which comes within the purview of the Act. The question presents considerable difficulty. Both congress and the states are sovereign within their respective jurisdictions.

One of the grounds upon which the power of congress to make these inquiries will probably be rested is that such information is necessary to enable the Commission (and through it congress) to see in what manner carriers are discharging the duties imposed by the Act.

The Mississippi Railroad Commission Act required " the company: 1. To furnish the commissioners with copies of its tariffs for all kinds of transportation. 2. To post in some conspicuous place at each of its depots the tariff approved by the commissioners, with the certificate of approval attached. 3. To conform to the tariff as approved without discrimination in favor of or against persons or localities. 4. To furnish the commissioners with all the information they require relative to the management of its line, and particularly with copies of all leases, contracts, and agreements for transportation with express, sleeping-car, or other companies to which they are parties. . . . 6. To make quarterly returns of its business to the commissioners, which returns shall embrace all the receipts and expenditures of its railroad. . . . The second and third of these requirements relate only to the duty of the company to keep its charges within the limit of the tariff approved by the commissioners without discrimination in favor of or against persons or localities. The first, fourth, and sixth are clearly intended as a means of furnishing the commissioners with the information necessary to enable them to act understandingly in fixing the tariff. Whether under these provisions the company can be required to make a report of or give information about its business outside of Mississippi is a question we do not now undertake to decide." (Waite, C. J., in *Stone* v. *Farmers' L. & T. Co.*, 116 U. S. 307, 331-2.)

Annual Reports of the Commission.(66)

Sec. 21. That the Commission shall, on or before the first day of December in each year, make a report to the Secretary of the Interior, which shall be by him transmitted to congress, and copies of which shall be distributed as are the other reports issued from the Interior Department. This report shall contain such information and data collected by the Commission as may be considered of value in the determination of questions connected with the regulation of commerce, together with such recommendations as to additional legislation relating thereto as the Commission deem necessary.

(66) Section 31 of the Regulation of Railways Act, 1873, requires the railway commissioners to make annual reports of their proceedings, which shall be laid before Parliament. The several state Railroad Commission Acts require reports to be made, with recommendations as to such additional legislation as may be deemed necessary.

Savings from the Operation of the Act.

Sec. 22. That nothing in this act shall apply to the carriage, storage, or handling of property free or at reduced rates for the United States, state, or municipal governments, or for charitable purposes, or to or from fairs and expositions for exhibition thereat(67), or the issuance of mileage, excursion, or commutation passenger tickets(68); nothing in this act shall be construed to prohibit any common carrier from giving reduced rates to ministers of religion(69); nothing in this act shall be construed to prevent railroads from giving free carriage to their own officers and employes, or to prevent the principal officers of any railroad company or companies from exchanging passes or tickets with other railroad companies for their officers and employes; and nothing in this act contained shall in any way abridge or alter the remedies now existing at common law or by statute, but the provisions of this act are in addition to such remedies(70): *Provided*, That no pending litigation shall in any way be affected by this Act.

(67) Judge Baxter, in *Hays* v. *Penn. Co.*, 12 Fed. Rep. 309, speaking of the duty of railroads at common law, said: "Harmless discrimination may be indulged in. For instance, the carrying of one person, who is unable to pay fare, free, is no injustice to other passengers who may be required to pay the reasonable and regular rates fixed by the company. Nor would the carrying of supplies at nominal rates to communities scourged by disease, or rendered destitute by floods or other casualty, entitle other communities to have their supplies carried at the same rate. It is the custom, we believe, for railroad companies to carry fertilizers and machinery for mining and manufacturing purposes to be employed along the lines of their respective roads, to develop the country and stimulate productions, as a means of insuring a permanent increase of their business, at lower rates than are charged on other classes of freight, because such discrimination, while it tends to advance the interests of all, works no injustice to any one." (p. 311.)

(68) MILEAGE, EXCURSION, AND COMMUTATION PASSENGER TICKETS.

The terms "mileage," "excursion," and "commutation," as used in this section of the Act, have received in a great measure from usage a definite signification, and it is with this meaning that the words are to be understood in the statute, and not in their general sense as employed in common use. Since the adoption of the Inter-state Commerce Law numerous attempts have been made by railroad officers and counsel to define the meaning of these terms as applied to passenger tickets, some of which are as follows:

At a meeting of the general passenger agents of the principal railroads, held in New York city in March, the following was adopted as the sense of the meeting:

"Section 22 states that nothing in this act shall apply to the issuance of mileage, excursion, or commutation passenger tickets. We understand from this that while nothing prevents the issuance of **mileage tickets,** the issue must still be in accordance with the general non-discriminating spirit of the act, and, if continued at all, they must be sold under uniform rates and conditions to all persons who may wish to purchase them.

"First. We define the term **"excursion tickets,"** as used in section 22, to mean a round trip ticket sold at a reduced rate to a person

§ 22.] INTER-STATE COMMERCE ACT. 189

who, under certain conditions, desires to make a journey within a given time to a given point and return.

"Second. We believe that it is the intention of the law to leave all the questions of restriction, limitation, place, and fares, for the sale of excursion tickets, in the discretion of the railway companies interested, respectively, within reasonable limits."

The general counsel of the Boston and Maine, Boston and Lowell and Fitchburg railroads, in reply to the question, What constitutes an excursion ticket under the law? have said:

"An excursion ticket means a round trip ticket sold at a reduced rate to any person who, for a special purpose or at a particular season, desired to make a special journey within a given time to a given point and return."

These definitions, however, it must be stated, were not those uniformly understood among railroad men, or by the public using such tickets, at the time and previous to the passage of the act, but are the result of a compromise in part of conflicting opinions. The words in the act will receive the meaning which they had in fact in common use among railroads and their patrons, as applied to passenger tickets, at the time the act was adopted. This section is, in substance and effect, a proviso to the sections generally governing the rates as to passenger tickets, and as such it will be strictly construed. (Potter's Dwarris on Statutes, 118, note 11.) Justice Story says: "We are led to the general rule of law which has always prevailed, and become consecrated almost as a maxim in the interpretation of statutes, that where the enacting clause is general in its language and objects, and a proviso is afterward introduced, that proviso is construed strictly and takes no case out of the enacting clause which does not fall fairly within its terms. In short, a proviso carves special exceptions only out of the enacting clause; and those who set up any such exception must establish it as being within the words as well as within the reason thereof." (*U. S.* v. *Dickson*, 15 Pet. 165.)

The meaning of these terms being governed by their usage in the business to which they relate, it will be limited to such meaning as may be ascribed to them by a usage that is certain, uniform, and general, and must be such as existed at the time of the passage of the act. (*Wood* v. *Wood*, 1 Carr. & P. 59; *Womersley* v. *Dally*, 26 L. J. (Exch.) 219; Lawson on Usage, p. 32, § 10; p. 40, § 17; p. 53, § 24; as to words, p. 367, § 181, *passim*.) It can not include tickets which were not generally understood by railroad officers and employes, and the public dealing with them, as being embraced within the description of mileage, excursion, and commutation tickets. Wherever uncertainty or diversity existed at the passage of this Act as to their usage and understanding in this respect as to whether a ticket is embraced within these terms, such ticket must be excluded from the exemption of section 22. And the mere agreement of the agents or officers of railroads subsequently to the passage of the Act that such tickets shall be held and considered as described by such terms, will not bring them within the exemptions of the section. It is a question of fact existing at the time of the passage of the Act, and not of agreement or usage since.

It would perhaps be unsafe to attempt a definition of these terms as fixed by usage, and yet there is so much of agreement and certainty as to the meaning of these phrases as used in the Act, that I feel warranted in part in undertaking to define them. The term "**excursion ticket**" will include a round trip ticket, at a reduced price, issued to the public, to a body, or association of persons, for a special occasion, at a designated time, and to be used in the manner, within the time, or on the trains prescribed in the terms of their issue.

It does not include, it is believed, a round trip ticket issued to a single individual having no reference to any special occasion, public or social, whether such a ticket is confined to a particular route or destination, or is, or is not, limited as to the time of its use.

Tourists' tickets, so far as I can ascertain, have been treated and understood to be excursion tickets. They are round trip tickets, providing for a return to the starting point, either upon the outgoing or other line of travel, and are usually to the north and seaboard in the summer, and to the south and California in winter, for purposes of health and pleasure. The practical difficulty that arises with respect to these tickets will be in maintaining a limitation as to their use, so as to preserve the purview of the Act. A tourist ticket may be issued to one or many, and is only to be distinguished from any other return ticket, issued for purposes of business, by the purpose of the traveler in purchasing it; for one may take the same route and return for purposes of pleasure and health that another at the same time takes for purposes of business. No one will insist or desire that the ticket office shall be charged by the law with the duty of ascertaining whether a man is traveling for business or pleasure, in order to determine whether he can sell to him an excursion ticket or not. Even if they are confined to the trip tours named, there being almost no limit as to the direction or points to which they may go, what is to prevent them from being used for general purposes of travel, in the north during the summer, and in the south and California during the winter, entirely exempt from the operation of the provisions of the Act?

This difficulty is suggested, and, in solving it, the rule is to be kept in view that the proviso which includes the exemption in question must be strictly construed with the view to preserve and give effect to the general intent and purpose of the Act.

If a construction of the proviso shall be claimed that will imperil the purposes of the Act, it may be assumed that that construction is erroneous. Judge Sherman says: "A statute should be so construed that the several parts will not only accord with the general intent of the legislature, but also harmonize with each other, *and a construction of a particular clause that will destroy or render useless any other provision of the same statute, can not be correct.*" (*Allen* v. *Parish*, 3 Ohio, 193; *Savings Bank* v. *U. S.*, 19 Wall. 229.) "A saving clause in a statute is to be rejected when it is directly repugnant to the purview or body of the Act, and could not stand without rendering the act inconsistent and destructive to itself." (1 Kent's Commentaries, 462.)

Mileage tickets are those issued to a person named in the ticket, for a given number of miles, usually one thousand, with coupons attached for each mile, at a uniform and reduced rate per mile, to be used at the option of the holder between any points upon the line of the road issuing them.

A commutation ticket is one issued at reduced rates, authorizing the holder to travel for a given number of times or a given length of time, or both, between given points, upon the road issuing them. These are usually issued to residents upon the road transacting business at other points upon it.

The last edition of Webster's Dictionary defines the verb "commute" as "to pay less for in the gross than would be paid for separate trips; —used in reference to the privilege of traveling upon a certain route for a specified time; as to *commute* the passage for a year." Also "commutation," the adjective—"pertaining to or obtained by the purchase of a right called *commutation*, as *commutation tickets.*" "Commutation" the noun—"the purchase of a right to go upon a certain route during a specified period, for a less amount than would be paid in the aggregate for separate trips."

(69) At a meeting of the general passenger agents of the principal railroads held in New York city in March, the following was adopted as the sense of the meeting: "In defining the term 'ministers of religion,' we accept the definition given by Webster's Dictionary, as follows: 'One who serves at the altar; one who performs sacerdotal duties; the pastor of a church duly authorized or licensed to preach the gospel and administer the sacraments.'"

(70) Even without this provision, the common-law right of action to recover back excessive charges paid would have remained. (See *Fuller* v. *Chicago & N. W. R. Co.*, 31 Iowa, 187.)

Appropriation for Purposes of this Act.

Sec. 23. That the sum of one hundred thousand dollars is hereby appropriated for the use and purposes of this act for the fiscal year ending June thirtieth, anno Domini eighteen hundred and eighty-eight, and the intervening time anterior thereto.

Time at which the Act Takes Effect.

Sec. 24. That the provisions of sections eleven and eighteen of this act, relating to the appointment and organization of the Commission herein provided for, shall take effect immediately, and the remaining provisions of this act shall take effect sixty days after its passage.

Approved, February 4, 1887.

APPENDIX.

ENGLISH STATUTES.

THE RAILWAY AND CANAL TRAFFIC ACT, 1854.
(17 & 18 Vict., c. 31.)

AN ACT for the better Regulation of the Traffic on Railways and Canals. (10th July, 1854.)

Whereas, it is expedient to make better provision for regulating the traffic on railways and canals: *Be it enacted, etc.*, as follows:

1. In the construction of this act "the board of trade" shall mean the lords of the committee of her Majesty's privy council for trade and foreign plantations.

The word "traffic" shall include not only passengers and their luggage and goods, animals and other things conveyed by any railway company or canal company, or railway and canal company, but also carriages, wagons, trucks, boats, and vehicles of every description, adapted for running or passing on the railway or canal of any such company.

The word "railway" shall include every station of or belonging to such railway used for the purposes of public traffic; and,

The word "canal" shall include any navigation whereon tolls are levied by authority of Parliament, and also the wharves and landing places of and belonging to such canal or navigation, and used for the purposes of public traffic.

The expression "railway company," "canal company," or "railway and canal company," shall include any person being the owner or lessee of, or any contractor working any railway or canal or navigation, constructed or carried on under the powers of any act of Parliament.

A station, terminus, or wharf shall be deemed to be near another station, terminus, or wharf, when the distance between such stations,

APPENDIX.

termini, or wharves shall not exceed one mile, such stations not being situate within five miles from St. Paul's church, in London.

2. Every railway company, canal company, and railway and canal company, shall, according to their respective powers, afford all reasonable facilities for the receiving and forwarding and delivering of traffic upon and from the several railways and canals belonging to, or worked by, such companies respectively, and for the return of carriages, trucks, boats, and other vehicles, and no such company shall make or give any undue or unreasonable preference or advantage to or in favor of any particular person or company, or any particular description of traffic, in any respect whatsoever, nor shall any such company subject any particular person or company, or any particular description of traffic, to any undue or unreasonable prejudice or disadvantage in any respect whatsoever; and every railway company and canal company and railway and canal company having or working railways or canals which form part of a continuous line of railway or canal or railway and canal communication, or which have the terminus, station, or wharf of the one near the terminus, station or wharf of the other, shall afford all due and reasonable facilities for receiving and forwarding all the traffic arriving by one of such railways or canals by the other, without any unreasonable delay, and without any such preference or advantage, or prejudice or disadvantage as aforesaid, and so that no obstruction may be offered to the public desirous of using such railways or canals or railways and canals as a continuous line of communication, and so that all reasonable accommodations may, by means of the railways and canals of the several companies, be at all times afforded to the public in that behalf.

3. It shall be lawful for any company or person complaining against any such companies or company of any thing done, or of any omission made in violation or contravention of this act, to apply in a summary way, by motion or summons, in England to her Majesty's court of common pleas at Westminster, or in Ireland to any of her Majesty's superior courts in Dublin, or in Scotland to the court of session in Scotland, as the case may be, or to any judge of any such court; and upon the certificate to her Majesty's attorney-general in England or Ireland, or her Majesty's lord advocate in Scotland, of the Board of Trade alleging any such violation or contravention of this act by any such companies or company, it shall also be lawful for the said attorney-general, or lord advocate, to apply in like manner to any such court or judge, and in either of such cases it shall be lawful for such court or judge to hear and determine the matter of such complaint; and for that purpose, if such court or judge shall think fit, to direct and pros-

ecute, in such mode and by such engineers, barristers, or other persons as they shall think proper, all such inquiries as may be deemed necessary to enable such court or judge to form a just judgment on the matter of such complaint; and if it be made to appear to such court or judge on such hearing, or on the report of any such person, that any thing has been done or omission made in violation or contravention of this act by such company or companies, it shall be lawful for such court or judge to issue a writ of injunction or interdict, restraining such company or companies from further continuing such violation or contravention of this act, and enjoining obedience to the same; and in case of disobedience of any such writ of injunction or interdict, it shall be lawful for such court or judge to order that a writ or writs of attachment, or any other process of such court incident or applicable to writs of injunction or interdict, shall issue against any one or more of the directors of any company, or against any owner, lessee, contractor, or other person, failing to obey such writ of injunction or interdict; and such court or judge may also, if they or he shall think fit, make an order directing the payment by any one or more of such companies of such sum of money as such court or judge shall determine, not exceeding for each company the sum of two hundred pounds for every day, after a day to be named in the order, that such company or companies shall fail to obey such injunction or interdict; and such moneys shall be payable as the court or judge may direct, either to the party complaining, or into a court to abide the ultimate decision of the court, or to her Majesty; and payment thereof may, without prejudice to any other mode of recovering the same, be enforced by attachment or order in the nature of a writ of execution, in like manner as if the same had been recovered by decree or judgment in any superior court at Westminster or Dublin, in England or Ireland, and in Scotland by such diligence as is competent on an extracted decree of the court of session; and in any such proceeding as aforesaid, such court or judge may order and determine that all or any costs thereof or thereon incurred shall and may be paid by or to the one party or the other, as such court or judge shall think fit; and it shall be lawful for any such engineer, barrister, or other person, if directed so to do by such court or judge, to receive evidence on oath relating to the matter of any such inquiry, and to administer such oath.

4. It shall be lawful for the said court of common pleas at Westminster, or any three of the judges thereof, of whom the chief justice shall be one, and it shall be lawful for the said courts in Dublin, or any nine of the judges thereof, of whom the Lord Chancellor, the Master of the Rolls, the Lords Chief Justice of the Queen's Bench

and common pleas, and the Lord Chief Baron of the Exchequer, shall be five, from time to time to make all such general rules and orders as to the forms of proceedings and process, and all other matters and things touching the practice and otherwise in carrying this act into execution before such courts and judges as they may think fit, in England or Ireland, and in Scotland it shall be lawful for the court of session to make such acts of sederunt for the like purpose as they shall think fit.

5. Upon the application of any party aggrieved by the order made upon any such motion or summons as aforesaid, it shall be lawful for the court or judge, by whom such order was made, to direct, if they think fit so to do, such motion or application on summons to be reheard before such court or judge, and upon such rehearing to rescind or vary such order.

6. No proceeding shall be taken for any violation or contravention of the above enactments, except in the manner herein provided; but nothing herein contained shall take away or diminish any rights, remedies, or privileges of any person or company against any railway or canal, or railway and canal company, under the existing law.

7. Every such company as aforesaid shall be liable for the loss of, or for any injury done to any horses, cattle, or other animals, or to any articles, goods, or things, in the receiving, forwarding, or delivering thereof, occasioned by the neglect or default of such company or its servants, notwithstanding any notice, condition, or declaration made and given by such company contrary thereto or in any wise limiting such liability; every such notice, condition, or declaration being hereby declared to be null and void; provided, always, that nothing herein contained shall be construed to prevent the said companies from making such conditions with respect to the receiving, forwarding, and delivering of any of the said animals, articles, goods, or things as shall be adjudged by the court or judge before whom any question relating thereto shall be tried, to be just and reasonable; provided always, that no greater damages shall be recovered for the loss of, or for any injury done to, any of such animals beyond the sums hereinafter mentioned; that is to say, for any horse, fifty pounds; for any neat cattle, per head, fifteen pounds; for any sheep or pigs, per head, two pounds; unless the person sending or delivering the same to such company shall, at the time of such delivery, have declared them to be respectively of higher value than as above mentioned, in which case it shall be lawful for such company to demand and receive, by way of compensation for the increased risk and care thereby occasioned, a reasonable percentage upon the excess of the

value so declared above the respective sums so limited as aforesaid, and which shall be paid in addition to the ordinary rate of charge; and such percentage or increased rate of charge shall be notified in the manner prescribed in the Statute Eleventh George Fourth, and First William Fourth, chapter sixty-eight, and shall be binding upon such company in the manner therein mentioned; provided, also, that the proof of the value of such animals, articles, goods, and things and the amount of the injury done thereto, shall in all cases lie upon the person claiming compensation for such loss or injury; provided, also, that no special contract between such company and any other parties respecting the receiving, forwarding, or delivering of any animals, articles, goods, or things as aforesaid shall be binding upon or affect any such party unless the same be signed by him or by the person delivering such animals, articles, goods, or things respectively for carriage; provided, also, that nothing herein contained shall alter or affect the rights, privileges, or liabilities of any such company under the said act of the Eleventh George Fourth and First William Fourth, chapter sixty-eight, with respect to articles of the descriptions mentioned in the said act.

8. This act may be cited for all purposes as the "Railway and Canal Traffic Act, 1854."

THE REGULATION OF RAILWAYS ACT, 1868.
(31 & 32 Vict., c. 119.)

SEC. 2. In this act the term "railway" means the whole or any portion of a railway or tramway, whether worked by steam or otherwise.

The term "company" means a company incorporated either before or after the passing of this act for the purpose of constructing, maintaining, or working a railway in the United Kingdom (either alone or in conjunction with any other purpose), and includes, except when otherwise expressed, any individual or individuals not incorporated who are owners or lessees of a railway in the United Kingdom, or parties to an agreement for working a railway in the United Kingdom.

The term "person" includes a body corporate.

SEC. 16. Where a company is authorized to build, or buy, or hire, and to use, maintain, and work, or to enter into arrangements for using, maintaining, or working steam vessels for the purpose of carrying on a communication between any towns or ports, and to take tolls in respect of such steam vessels, then and in every such case tolls shall be at all times charged to all persons equally and after the same rate in respect of passengers conveyed in a like vessel passing between the same places under like circumstances; and no reduction or advance in the tolls shall be made in favor of or against any person using the steam vessels in consequence of his having traveled or being about to travel on the whole or any part of the company's railway, or not having traveled or not being about to travel on any part thereof, or in favor of or against any person using the railway in consequence of his having used or being about to use, or his not having used or not being about to use the steam vessels, and where an aggregate sum is charged by the company for conveyance of a passenger by a steam vessel and on the railway, the ticket shall have the amount of toll charged for conveyance by the steam vessel distinguished from the amount charged for conveyance on the railway.

The provisions of the Railway and Canal Traffic Act, 1854, so far as the same are applicable, shall extend to the steam vessels and to the traffic carried on thereby.

THE REGULATION OF RAILWAYS ACT, 1873.

(36 & 37 Vict., c. 48.)

AN ACT to make better provision for carrying into effect the Railway and Canal Traffic Act, 1854, and for other purposes connected therewith. (21st July, 1873.)

Be it enacted as follows:

PRELIMINARY.

1. This act may be cited as the Regulation of Railways Act, 1873.

2. This act shall, except as herein is otherwise expressly provided, come into operation on the first day of September, one thousand eight hundred and seventy-three, which date is in this act referred to as the commencement of this act.

3. In this act the term "railway company" includes any person being the owner or lessee of or working any railway in the United Kingdom constructed or carried on under the powers of any act of parliament.

The term "canal company" includes any person being the owner or lessee of, or working, or entitled to charge tolls for the use of any canal in the United Kingdom constructed or carried on under the powers of any act of parliament.

The term "person" includes a body of persons corporate or unincorporate.

The term "railway" includes every station, siding, wharf, or dock of or belonging to such **railway and** used for the purposes of public traffic.

The term "canal" includes any navigation which has been made under or upon which tolls may be levied by authority of parliament, and also the wharves and landing-places of and belonging to such canal or navigation and used for the purposes of public traffic.

The term "traffic" includes not only passengers and their luggage, goods, animals, and other things conveyed by any railway company or canal company, but also carriages, wagons, trucks, boats, and vehicles of every description adapted for running or passing on the railway or canal of any such company.

The term "mails" includes mail bags and post-letter bags.

The term "special act" means a local or local and personal act, or an act of a local and personal nature, and includes a provisional order of the board of trade confirmed by act of parliament, and a certificate granted by the Board of Trade under the Railways Construction Facilities Act, 1864.

The term "the treasury" means the commissioners of her Majesty's treasury for the time being.

The term "superior court" means in England any of her Majesty's superior courts at Westminster; in Ireland, any of her Majesty's superior courts at Dublin, and in Scotland, the court of session.

APPOINTMENT AND DUTIES OF RAILWAY COMMISSIONERS.

4. For the purpose of carrying into effect the provisions of the Railway and Canal Traffic Act, 1854, and of this act, it shall be lawful for her Majesty, at any time after the passing of this act, by warrant under the royal sign manual, to appoint not more than three commissioners, of whom one shall be of experience in the law and one of experience in railway business, and not more than two assistant commissioners; and upon the occurrence of any vacancy in the office of any such commissioner or assistant commissioner from time to time in like manner to appoint some fit person to fill the vacancy. It shall be lawful for the lord chancellor, if he think fit, to remove for inability or misbehavior any commissioner appointed in pursuance of this act.

The three commissioners appointed under this act (and in this act referred to as the commissioners), shall be styled the railway commissioners, and shall have an official seal, which shall be judicially noticed. They may act notwithstanding any vacancy in their number. The said assistant commissioners shall hold office during the pleasure of her Majesty.

5. Any person appointed a commissioner under this act shall, within three calendar months after his appointment, absolutely sell and dispose of any stock, share, debenture stock, debenture bond, or other security of any railway or canal company in the United Kingdom which he shall at the time of his appointment own or be interested in for his own benefit; and it shall not be lawful for any person appointed a commissioner under this act, so long as he shall hold office as such commissioner, to purchase, take, or become interested in for his own benefit, any such stock, share, debenture stock, debenture bond, or other security; and if any such stock, share, debenture stock, debenture bond, or other security, or any interest therein, shall come to or vest in such commissioner by will or succession, for his own benefit, he shall, within three calendar months after the same shall so come to or vest in him, absolutely sell and dispose of the same or his interest therein.

It shall not be lawful for the commissioners, except by consent of the parties to the proceedings, to exercise any jurisdiction by this act conferred upon them in any case in which they shall be directly or indirectly interested in the matter in question. The commissioners shall devote the whole of their time to the performance of their duties under this act, and shall not accept or hold any office or employment inconsistent with this provision.

6. Any person complaining of any thing done or of any omission made in violation or contravention of section two of the Railway and Canal Traffic Act, 1854, or of section sixteen of the Regulation of Railways Act, 1868, or of this act, or of any enactment amending or applying the said enactments respectively, may apply to the commissioners, and upon the certificate of the Board of Trade alleging any such violation or contravention, any person appointed by the Board of Trade in that behalf may in like manner apply to the commissioners; and for the purpose of enabling the commissioners to hear and determine the matter of any such complaint, they shall have and may exercise all the jurisdiction conferred by section three of the Railway and Canal Traffic Act, 1854, on the several courts and judges empowered to hear and determine complaints under that act; and may make orders of like nature with the writs and orders authorized to be issued and made by the said courts and judges; and the said courts and judges shall, except for the purpose of enforcing any decision or order of the commissioners, cease to exercise the jurisdiction conferred on them by that section.

7. Where the commissioners have received any complaint alleging the infringement by a railway company or canal company of the pro-

visions of any enactment in respect of which the commissioners have jurisdiction, they may, if they think fit, before requiring or permitting any formal proceedings to be taken on such complaint, communicate the same to the company against whom it is made, so as to afford them an opportunity of making such observations thereon as they may think fit.

8. Where any difference between railway companies, or between canal companies, or between a railway and a canal company, is, under the provisions of any general or special act, passed either before or after the passing of this act, required or authorized to be referred to arbitration, such difference shall, at the instance of any company party to the difference, and with the consent of the commissioners, be referred to the commissioners for their decision in lieu of being referred to arbitration; provided, that the power of compelling a reference to the commissioners in this section contained shall not apply to any case in which any arbitrator has in any general or special act been designated by his name, or by the name of his office, or in which a standing arbitrator having been appointed under any general or special act, the commissioners are of opinion that the difference in question may more conveniently be referred to him.

9. Any difference to which a railway company or canal company is a party, may, on application of the parties to the difference, and with the assent of the commissioners, be referred to them for their decision.

10. The following powers and duties of the Board of Trade shall be transferred to the commissioners, namely:

(1.) The powers of the Board of Trade under Part III. of the Railway Clauses Act, 1863, or under any special act, with respect to the approval of working agreements between railway companies; and,

(2.) The powers and duties of the Board of Trade under section thirty-five of the Railway Clauses Act, 1863, with respect to the exercise by railway companies of their powers in relation to steam vessels.

And the provisions of the said acts conferring such powers or imposing such duties, or otherwise referring to such powers or duties, shall, so far as is consistent with the tenor thereof, be read as if the commissioners were therein named instead of the Board of Trade.

Explanation and Amendment of Law.

11. Whereas, by section two of the Railway and Canal Traffic Act, 1854, it is enacted that every railway company and canal company and railway and canal company shall, according to their respective power afford all reasonable facilities for the receiving and forwarding and delivering of traffic upon and from the several railways and canals

belonging to or worked by such companies respectively, and for the return of carriages, trucks, boats, and other vehicles; and that no such company shall make or give any undue or unreasonable preference or advantage to or in favor of any particular person or company, or any particular description of traffic, in any respect whatsoever, or shall subject any particular person or company, or any particular description of traffic, to any undue or unreasonable prejudice or disadvantage in any respect whatsoever; and that every railway company and canal company, and railway and canal company having or working railways or canals which form a part of a continuous line of railway, or canal, or railway and canal communication, or which have the terminus, station, or wharf of the one, near the terminus, station, or wharf of the other, shall afford all due and reasonable facilities for receiving and forwarding by one of such railways or canals all the traffic arriving by the other, without any unreasonable delay, and without any such preference or advantage or prejudice or disadvantage as aforesaid, and so that no obstruction may be offered to the public desirous of using such railways or canals or railways and canals as a continuous line of communication, and so that all reasonable accommodation may by means of the railways and canals of the several companies be at all times afforded to the public in that behalf:

And whereas, it is expedient to explain and amend the said enactment, be it therefore enacted, that—

Subject as hereinafter mentioned, the said facilities to be so afforded are hereby declared to and shall include the due and reasonable receiving, forwarding, and delivering by every railway company and canal company and railway and canal company, at the request of any other such company, of through traffic to and from the railway or canal of any other such company at through rates, tolls, or fares (in this act referred to as through rates).

Provided as follows:

(1.) The company requiring the traffic to be forwarded shall give written notice of the proposed through rate to each forwarding company, stating both its amount and its apportionment, and the route by which the traffic is proposed to be forwarded.

(2.) Each forwarding company shall, within the prescribed period after the receipt of such notice, by written notice, inform the company requiring the traffic to be forwarded whether they agree to the rate and route; and, if they object to either, the grounds of the objection.

(3.) If at the expiration of the prescribed period no such objection has been sent by any forwarding company, the rate shall come into operation at such expiration.

(4.) If an objection to the rate or route has been sent within the prescribed period, the matter shall be referred to the commissioners for their decision.

(5.) If an objection be made to the granting of the rate or to the route, the commissioners shall consider whether the granting of the rate is a due and reasonable facility, in the interest of the public, and whether, having regard to the circumstances, the route proposed is a reasonable route, and shall allow or refuse the rate accordingly.

(6.) If the objection be only to the apportionment of the rate, the rate shall come into operation at the expiration of the prescribed period, but the decision of the commissioners as to its apportionment shall be retrospective; in any other case, the operation of the rate shall be suspended until the decision is given.

(7.) The commissioners, in apportioning the through rate, shall take into consideration all the circumstances of the case, including any special expense incurred in respect of the construction, maintenance or working of the route, or any part of the route, as well as any special charges which any company may have been entitled to make in respect thereof.

(8.) It shall not be lawful for the commissioners in any case to compel any company to accept lower mileage rates than the mileage rates which such company may for the time being legally be charging for like traffic carried by a like mode of transit on any other line of communication between the same points, being the points of departure and arrival of the through route.

(9.) The prescribed period mentioned in this section shall be ten days, or such longer period as the commissioners may from time to time, by general order, prescribe.

Where a railway company or canal company use, maintain, or work, or are party to an arrangement for using, maintaining, or working steam vessels for the purpose of carrying on a communication between any towns or ports, the provisions of this section shall extend to such steam vessels and to the traffic carried thereby.

12. Subject to the provisions in the last preceding section contained, the commissioners shall have full power to decide that any proposed through rate is due and reasonable, notwithstanding that a less amount may be allotted to any forwarding company out of such through rate than the maximum rate such company is entitled to charge, and to allow and apportion such through rate accordingly.

13. A complaint of a contravention of section 2 of the Railway and Canal Traffic Act, 1854, as amended by this act, may be made to the commissioners by a municipal or other public corporation, local or

harbor board, without proof that the complainants are aggrieved by the contravention; provided, that a complaint shall not be entertained by the commissioners in pursuance of this section unless such complaint is accompanied by a certificate of the Board of Trade to the effect that in their opinion the case, in respect of which the complaint is made, is a proper one to be submitted for adjudication to the commissioners by such municipal or other public corporation, local or harbor board.

14. Every railway company and canal company shall keep at each of their stations and wharves a book or books showing every rate for the time being charged for the carriage of traffic, other than passengers and their luggage, from that station or wharf to any place to which they book, including any rates charged under any special contract, and stating the distance from that station or wharf of every station, wharf, siding, or place to which any such rate is charged.

Every such book shall, during all reasonable hours, be open to the inspection of any person without the payment of any fee.

The commissioners may from time to time, on the application of any person interested, make orders with respect to any particular description of traffic requiring a railway company or canal company to distinguish in such book how much of each rate is for the conveyance of the traffic on the railway or canal, including therein tolls for the use of the railway or canal, for the use of carriages or vessels, or for locomotive power, and how much is for other expenses, specifying the nature and detail of such other expenses.

Any company failing to comply with the provisions of this section shall, for each offense, and in the case of a continuing offense, for every day during which the offense continues, be liable to a penalty not exceeding five pounds, and such penalty shall be recovered and applied in the same manner as penalties imposed by the Railways Clauses Consolidation Act, 1845, and the Railways Clauses Consolidation (Scotland) Act, 1845 (as the case may require), are for the time being recoverable and applicable.

15. The commissioners shall have power to hear and determine any question or dispute which may arise with respect to the terminal charges of any railway company, where such charges have not been fixed by any act of parliament, and to decide what is a reasonable sum to be paid to any company for loading and unloading, covering collection, delivery, and other services of a like nature; any decision of the commissioners under this section shall be binding on all courts and in all legal proceedings whatsoever.

16. No railway company or canal company, unless expressly author-

ized thereto by any act passed before the passing of this act, shall, without the sanction of the commissioners, to be signified in such manner as they may by general order or otherwise direct, enter into any agreement whereby any control over or right to interfere in or concerning the traffic carried or rates or tolls levied on any part of a canal is given to the railway company, or any persons managing or connected with the management of any railway; and any such agreement made after the commencement of this act without such sanction shall be void.

The commissioners shall withhold their sanction from any such agreement which is in their opinion prejudicial to the interests of the public.

Not less than one month before any such agreement is so sanctioned, copies of the intended agreement certified under the hand of the secretary of the railway company or one of the railway companies party or parties thereto, shall be deposited for public inspection at the office of the commissioners, and also at the office of the clerk of the peace of the county, riding, or division in England or Ireland, in which the head office of any canal company party to the agreement is situate, and at the office of the principal sheriff clerk of every such county in Scotland, and notice of the intended agreement, setting forth the parties between whom or on whose behalf the same is intended to be made, and such further particulars with respect thereto as the commissioners may require, shall be given by advertisement in the London, Edinburgh, or Dublin Gazette, according as the head office of any canal company party to the agreement is situate in England, Scotland, or Ireland, and shall be sent to the secretary or principal officer of every canal company any of whose canals communicate with the canal of any company party to the agreement; and shall be published in such other way, if any, as the commissioners for the purpose of giving notice to all parties interested therein by order direct.

17. Every railway company owning or having the management of any canal or part of a canal shall at all times keep and maintain such canal or part, and all the reservoirs, works, and conveniences thereto belonging, thoroughly repaired and dredged and in good working condition, and shall preserve the supplies of water to the same, so that the whole of such canal or part may be at all times kept open and navigable for the use of all persons desirous to use and navigate the same without any unnecessary hindrance, interruption, or delay.

[The next three sections relate to the "Conveyance of Mails."]

Sec. 21 prescribes the duties of "assistant commissioners," and section 22 the salaries of the commissioners and their assistants; while sections 23 and 24 provide for the appointment of assessors and subordinate officers and clerks.

25. For the purposes of this act the commissioners shall, subject as in this act mentioned, have full power to decide all questions, whether of law or of fact, and shall also have the following powers; that is to say:

(*a*) They may, by themselves or by any person appointed by them to prosecute an inquiry, enter and inspect any place or building, being the property or under the control of any railway or canal company, the entry or inspection of which appears to them requisite;

(*b*) They may require the attendance of all such persons as they think fit to call before them and examine, and may require answers or returns to such inquiries as they think fit to make;

(*c*) They may require the production of all books, papers, and documents relating to the matters before them;

(*d*) They may administer an oath;

(*e*) They may, when sitting in open court, punish for contempt in like manner as if they were a court of record.

Every person required by the commissioners to attend as a witness shall be allowed such expenses as would be allowed to a witness attending on subpœna before a court of record; and in case of dispute as to the amount to be allowed, the same shall be referred to a master of one of the superior courts, who, on request, under the hands of the commissioners, shall ascertain and certify the proper amount of such expenses.

26. Any decision or any order made by the commissioners for the purpose of carrying into effect any of the provisions of this act may be made a rule or order of any superior court, and shall be enforced either in the manner directed by section three of the Railway and Canal Traffic Act, 1854, as to the writs and orders therein mentioned, or in like manner as any rule or order of such court.

For the purpose of carrying into effect this section, general rules and orders may be made by any superior court in the same manner as general rules and orders may be made with respect to any other proceedings in such court.

The commissioners may review and rescind or vary any decision or order previously made by them, or any of them.

The commissioners shall, in all proceedings before them under sections 6, 11, 12 and 13 of this act, and may, if they think fit, in all other proceedings before them under this act, at the instance of any party to the proceedings before them, and upon such security being given by the appellant as the commissioners may direct, state a case in writing for the opinion of any superior court determined by the commissioners upon any question which, in the opinion of the commissioners, is a question of law.

The court to which the case is transmitted shall hear and determine the question or questions of law arising thereon, and shall thereupon reverse, affirm, or amend the determination in respect of which the case has been stated, or remit the matter to the commissioners with the opinion of the court thereon, or may make such other order in relation to the matter, and may make such order as to costs as to the court may seem fit, and all such orders shall be final and conclusive on all parties: *Provided*, that the commissioners shall not be liable to any costs in respect or by reason of any such appeal.

The operation of any decision or order made by the commissioners shall not be stayed pending the decision of any such appeal, unless the commissioners shall otherwise order. Save as aforesaid, every decision and order of the commissioners shall be final.

27. The commissioners shall sit at such times and in such places and conduct their proceedings in such manner as may seem to them most convenient for the speedy dispatch of business; they may, subject as in this act mentioned, sit either together or separately, and either in private or in open court, but any complaint made to them shall, on application of any party to the complaint, be heard and determined in open court.

28. The costs of and incidental to any proceeding before the commissioners shall be in the discretion of the commissioners.

29. The commissioners may at any time after the passing of this act, and from time to time, make such general orders as may be requisite for the regulation of proceedings before them, including applications for and the stating of cases for appeal, and also for prescribing, directing, or regulating any matter which they are authorized by this act to prescribe, direct, or regulate by general order, and also for enabling the commissioners in cases to be specified in such general orders to exercise their jurisdiction by any one or two of their number: *Provided*, that any person aggrieved by any decision or order made in any case so specified may require a rehearing by all the commissioners. They may further make regulations for enabling them to carry into effect the provisions of this act, and may from time to time revoke and alter any general orders or regulations made in pursuance of this act. Every general order, and every alteration in a general order, made in pursuance of this section, shall be submitted to the lord chancellor for approval, **and shall not come into force until it shall be approved by him.**

Every general order purporting to be made in pursuance of this act shall, immediately after the making thereof, be laid before both houses of parliament, if parliament be then sitting, or if parliament be not then sitting, within seven days after the then next meeting of parliament, and if either house of parliament, by a resolution passed within two months after such general order has been so laid before the said house, resolve that the whole or any part of such general order ought not to continue in force, the same shall, after the date of such resolution, cease to be of any force, without prejudice nevertheless to the making of any other general order in its place, or to any thing done in pursuance of such general order before the date of such resolution; but, subject as aforesaid, every general order purporting to be made in pursuance of this act shall be deemed to have been duly made and within the powers of this act, and shall have effect as if it had been enacted in this act.

30. Every document purporting to be signed by the commissioners, or any one of them, shall be received in evidence without proof of such signature, and until the contrary is proven shall be deemed to have been so signed and to have been duly executed or issued by the commissioners.

31. The commissioners shall, once in every year, make a report to her Majesty of their proceedings under this act during the past year, and such report shall be laid before both houses of parliament within fourteen days after the making thereof if parliament is then sitting, and if not, then within fourteen days after the next meeting of parliament.

[Sections 32–37 make provision as to fees, notices, etc.]

Rules. Under the Regulation of Railways Act, 1873, the railway commissioners adopted rules or general orders regulating the procedure before them, which will be found in 2 Nev. & Mac. 2–10.

Forms. The forms for application, answer, and reply, and other proceedings before the railway commissioners, are to be found in 2 Nev. & Mac. Ry. Cas. 11–14.

Reports. Many of the decisions under the Railway and Canal Traffic Act, 1854, and the decisions of the Railway Commissioners under the Regulation of Railways Act, 1873, are collected in a series of reports, the first three volumes of which are known as "Neville and MacNamara's Railway Cases," vol. 1 covering the period from 1855 to 1874; vol. 2 from 1874 to 1876; vol. 3 from 1876 to 1881; vol. 4 of the series is known as "Railway and Canal Traffic Cases," covering the period from 1881 to 1885.

INDEX.

ACQUIESCENCE, Effect of, 37.

ACT to Regulate Commerce, An, 19.
    Existing contracts, Effect on, 25.
    Sources of, 29.
    Rules of construction of, 29, 187.
    Carriers Liable in damages for violation of, 156.
    Nature and scope of, 170,
    Savings from, § 22, 187.
    Appropriation for purposes of, 192
    Time when, takes effect, 192.

ACTIONS to recover illegal charges paid, 157
    Against carriers for damages, 158.
    Recovery at common law and under English statutes, 156-158.
    Money had and received, 156, 158.
    Protest not necessary, 158.
    Payment—Duress 159.
    Where to be brought, 163.

ADVANCE, No, in rates, etc., except upon ten days' notice, 145

ADVANTAGE. See UNDUE PREFERENCE.
    Company can not destroy natural 74.

AGENT of Company compelled to testify, 164.

AGNEW, J., on pooling agreements, 138.

AGREEMENT, Pooling, 134.
    Copies of, with other carriers to be filed with Commission, 146
    To prevent carriage being continuous 147.

"AGGREGATE," Meaning of, 125, 134.
    Earnings can not be pooled, 134.
    Traffic of a place, 91.

ALASKA, Legislation for, 18.

AMENDMENT, Fifth, 164.
    Of pleadings, 175.

ANNUAL reports of carriers, 185.
    Commission, 187.

APPEALS, Attorney's fees on, 162.
    To Supreme Court, § 16, 181.

APPENDIX, 193-208.
    English Statutes—
    Railway and Canal Traffic Act, 1854, 193-197.
    Regulation of Railways Act, 1868, 197-8.
    Regulation of Railways Act, 1873, 198-208.
    Rules, 208.
    Forms, 208.
    Reports, 208.

APPOINTMENT of Commissioners, § 11, 167.

APPROPRIATION to carry out provisions of Act, 192.

"ARRANGEMENT," Meaning of, 19, 32-35.
    Pooling, 134 *et seq.*
    Copies of, with carriers to be filed with Commission, 146.

ASSOCIATION may complain to Commission, 170.

ATTACHMENT, Writs of, 181.

ATTORNEY, District, Duty of, 182.

ATTORNEY-GENERAL OF U. S., Duty of, 182.

ATTORNEY'S fee to be taxed in every case of recovery, 156, 160.
    Constitutionality of provision, 160.
    Kansas, New Hampshire, and Pennsylvania Statutes, 160-1.
    On appeals to higher courts, 162.
    Practice, 162

ATTORNEY'S FEE—*Continued.*
  Evidence, 163
  Remedial or penal, 163.
AUDITOR, Report of, 176.
AVERAGE weight of truck loads, 91.
BLOCK SYSTEM, 104, 112.
BODY politic may complain to Commission, 170.
BOOK of rates under English statute, 139.
BOOKING, Through, 35, 105.
  Charge for, 62.
  Office accommodations, 102, 107.
BOOKS, Production of, compelled, 164
  Commission may require production of, 168.
BOSTON export trade, 133.
BRADLEY, JUSTICE, Opinions of, as to power of Congress to regulate Commerce, 21.
BREAK OF BULK, 147, 150.
BREWER, J., on attorney's fee to successful plaintiff, 161.
BREWERS, Preferences to, 89.
BRIDGES over navigable streams, 6, 10.
  Used in connection with railroads, 33.
BROKERS, Tax on, 13.
BULK, Difference in, 48, 95.
  Break of, shall not prevent carriage being continuous, 147, 150.
BURDEN OF PROOF, 50, 119.
BUSINESS, DEVELOPING, 77.
  Connecting business with, 115.
CAPITAL, Discriminations in favor of, 54.
CAPITAL invested, Return upon, 39.
CAPITAL STOCK, Reports as to, § 20, 185.
CAR-LOAD lots of freight, 51.
CARRIAGE in different cars, Effect of, 148.
  Continuous, 148.
CARRIERS. See COMMON CARRIERS.

CARS of other companies, Transportation of, 30, 114.
CARS, Use of on other lines is incidental to receiving, forwarding, etc., 38.
  Provide additional, 103, 106.
  Return of, 105.
  Through service, 110.
  Carriage in different, 148.
CASH AND TICKET FARES, 46.
CATTLE. See LIVE STOCK.
CHARGES for transportation, Unjust and unreasonable prohibited, 36.
  Statutes fixing maximum, 38.
  Reasonable, Elements of, 38.
  Equal to all, 40.
  Charter right to fix, 25, 45, 59.
  Undue preferences in, 67.
  Discrimination in between connecting lines, 113.
  Greater for shorter than for longer haul, 120.
  Terminal, 125.
  Schedules of, to be printed and posted, 139.
  Collection and delivery, 141.
  No advance in, except upon 10 days' notice, 145.
  Reductions to be posted immediately, 145.
  All, greater or less than named in schedule forbidden, 145.
CHARITABLE purposes, Carriage, etc., of property for, 187.
CHARTER rights of railroad companies, 25, 45, 59, 169.
  Powers derived from, 103.
CIRCUIT COURTS, Jurisdiction of, 147.
  Suits for damages, 163.
  Criminal cases, 167.
  Aid of, may be invoked by Commission, 168.
  Compel obedience to subpœna, 169.
  Procedure in, to enforce obedience to orders of Commission, 180.
  May appoint persons and prosecute inquiries as it sees fit, § 16, 181.
  Issue writs of injunction and attachment, § 16, 181.
  Order payment of money by carrier not exceeding $500 a day, 181.
  Counsel fees, 182.

CIRCUMSTANCES of transportation, 40, 47.

CLASSIFICATION of traffic, 41, 73, 74.
    Printed schedules to show, 139.

COAL, Transportation of, 46, 54.
    Competition between different kinds of, 46.
    Classification of, 74.

COLLECTING unequal rates forbidden, 40.

COMBINATION for pooling railroad earnings, 134.
    To prevent carriage being continuous, 147.

COMMERCE, Power of Congress to Regulate, 1, 19, 20-24.
    Nature and scope of Power, 1, 20.
    What it includes, 2.
    A natural right, 3.
    With Foreign Nations, 3.
    Among the states, 3, 20.
    With Indian Tribes, 5.
    Acts of Congress held to be valid exercises of power, 6, 26.
    In national matters, power exclusive, 6-9, 21.
    Local nature, When states may regulate, 10.
    Domestic, reserved to states, 11-14, 19, 35.
    "Act to Regulate Commerce," 19.
    Previous Acts of Congress regulating, 23.

COMMISSION. See INTER-STATE COMMERCE COMMISSION.

COMMISSIONERS. See INTER-STATE COMMERCE COMMISSION.
    Salaries of, § 18, 184.
    State railroad, 131.
    Require railroads to erect stations, 131.

COMMON-CARRIERS.
    Actions against, Recovery in, 156-159.
        Where to be brought, 163.
    Accounts, Uniform system of, § 20, 185.
    Business of, Commission authorized to inquire into, § 12, 168.
    Cars of other roads, 114.
    Charges of violations of act to be forwarded to, 170.
    Combinations to prevent carriage being continuous forbidden, 147.

COMMON-CARRIERS—*Continued.*
    Complaints to Commission of violations of Act, § 13, 170.
        Not to be dismissed for want of direct damage, 175.
    Commission, Orders of to carriers found violating the Act, 179.
        Exoneration upon compliance with, 179.
    Contract limiting liability, 40.
    Construction of Act must first be given by, 173.
    Copies of contracts, schedules, etc., to be filed with Commission, 146.
    Damages, Liable in, to persons injured, 156.
    Definitions of, 29.
    Dispatch companies, 31.
    Duty at common law, 37, 172.
    Duties of connecting, 96, 148.
    Equality in rates required, § 2, 40 *et seq.*
    Express companies, 31, 59.
    Facilities and rates to, 83.
    Fast freight lines, 31.
    Interchange of traffic, 96 *et seq.*
    Investigation by Commission, 170.
    Must receive same treatment as other shippers, 59.
    Obligation of, under the Act, 170.
    Penalty for violating the Act, 166.
    Pooling arrangements between, 134.
    Procedure in Circuit Court to enforce obedience to orders of Commission, § 16, 180.
    Railroads are, 30.
    Reparation by, 170.
    Reports, Annual, § 20, 185.
        What to contain, § 20, 185.
        Constitutionality of requirement, 186.
    Shorter and longer distances, 119 *et seq.*
    Subject to the Act, 19, 32.
    Transportation companies are, 31.
    Undue preferences prohibited, 65 *et seq.*

"COMMON CONTROL, Management, or Arrangement," 19.
    Meaning of, 32-35.

COMMON LAW.
    Obligation of common-carriers at, 37, 41, 94, 172.

COMMUTATION TICKETS, 187, 191.

COMPENSATION for transportation must be reasonable, 37.

COMPENSATION, ETC.—*Continued.*
    Greater, in aggregate for short than for long haul, 118.
    Greater or less, than named in schedules, forbidden, 145.

COMPETING LINES, 82.
    Railroads, Earnings of, 134.

COMPETITION between classes of traffic, 46.
    With other lines, 47, 55 *et seq.*, 75 *et seq.*, 127, 133.
    Railroads, 56, 76.
    Water transportation, 57, 75, 129.
    Of interest, 121.
    Pools destroy, 136.

COMPETITORS IN TRADE, 90.

COMPLAINTS of violations of Act, and procedure thereon by Commission, § 13, 170.
    By State or Territorial Railroad Commissioners, 175.
    Not to be dismissed for want of direct damage, 175.
    Orders of Commission when, sustained, § 15, 179.

CONDITIONS of transportation, 40, 47.
    Like, 59.
    Of shipment, 87.

CONGRESS, Power of, to Regulate Commerce, 1-16.
    Purpose of the grant, 1.
    Nature and scope of the Power, 1, 20.
    Acts of, held to be valid exercises of power, 6, 23.
    In national matters, power of, is exclusive, 6-9.
    To make laws carrying out powers granted, 14.
    Can not give preference to one port, 14-16.
    Previous Acts of, regulating commerce, 23.
    Debates in, 29.

CONNECTING LINES, Duties of, 33, 148.
    At common law, 115.
    Under state statutes, 115, 116.
    No discriminations between, 96, 113.

CONSOLIDATION of competing roads, 135.

CONSTITUTION U. S., Art. 1, § 8, cl. 3, 1-14.
—— Art. 1, § 8, cl. 18, 14.

CONSTITUTION, ETC.—*Continued.*
—— Art. 1, § 9, . . 14, 15.
—— Art. 1, § 10, . . 16.

CONSTITUTIONAL LAW, 1-16.
    Act to Regulate Commerce, 19, 22.
    Fourteenth Amendment — Due Process, 24.
    Contracts, Power of Congress to impair, 27.
    Power of Commission to suspend § 4—Nature of, 130 *et seq.*
    Attorney's fee to successful complainant, 160 *et seq.*
    Fifth Amendment, 164.
        Criminating evidence, 165.
    Prima facie evidence statutes, 176.
    Reports of carriers—Domestic affairs, 186.

CONSTRUCTION, Rules of, 29, 67.
    Commission will not give, until complaint made of violation, 170.
    Provisos, 189 *et seq.*

CONTEMPT, Witness may be punished for, 169.

CONTINUOUS CARRIAGE or shipment, 19, 33, 35, 148.
    Lines, 24, 108, 149.
    Joint tariffs on, 146.

CONTRACTS. Of foreign corporations, 9.
    Private — Power of Congress over, 14.
    Existing, 25.
    Special, for rates, etc., 37, 42.
    Furnish shipper's entire freight, 77, 95.
    Pooling, 134.
    With other carriers, copies to be filed with Commission, 146.
    To prevent carriage being continuous, 147.
    Commission may compel production of, 168.

"CONTROL," Meaning of, 19, 32-35.

CONVEYANCE, Maritime, 6.

CONVENIENCE OF PUBLIC, 92, 149.

CORPORATIONS, Foreign, engaged in inter-state commerce, 9
    May complain to Commission, 170.

COST OF SERVICE, 38, 48, 79, 127.
    Difference in rates must bear some proportion to, 49.
    Good faith of company, 49.
    Burden of proof, 50.

COST OF SERVICE—*Continued.*
  Quantity of freight shipped, 50.
  Special service on incline, 79.

COSTS, Under English practice, 157.
  Including, counsel fee, allowed in cases of recovery, 156.

COUNSEL FEE to be taxed in favor of plaintiff in cases of recovery, 156, 160 *et seq.*

CRIMES. See OFFENSES.

CRIMINAL CASE, What is, 164, 165.

CRIMINATING EVIDENCE. See EVIDENCE.

CUSTOMS DUTIES to be collected on freight passing through foreign country, When, 144.

DAMAGE. Special damage, 72, 94.
  Carrier liable in, to persons injured, 156-9.
  Where actions for, to be brought, 163.
  Want of direct, no cause for dismissing complaint, 175.

DAMS across navigable streams, 10.

DELEGATION OF POWER, 131.

DELIVERING GOODS on general orders, 83.

DELIVERING PROPERTY, 19, 37, 38, 83, 94, 96.
  No charge can be made unless service rendered, 60, 62.

DEMAND not necessary before suit, 159.

DEMANDING unequal rates forbidden, 40.

DEMURRAGE, 107, 125, 142.
  Rules or regulations affecting aggregate charge, 139, 142.

DENABY MAIN COLLIERY CO. Cases, 68 *et seq.*

DEPOTS. See STATIONS.
  Schedules of rates, fares, etc., to be posted in, 139.
  What are? 143.

DESTINATION OF GOODS immaterial, 57, 58.
  Place of, 132, 147, 151.

DEVICE affecting charge for transportation, 36, 40.

DEVICE—*Continued.*
  To prevent carriage being continuous, 148.

DEVELOPING NEW TRADE, 47, 57, 77, 128.
  Traffic, 82.

DIRECTION, In same, 119, 130.

DIRECTOR, Compelled to testify, 163.
  Penalty for violating act, 166.

DISADVANTAGE. See UNDUE PREFERENCE.

DISCRETION of the Company, 100.

DISCRIMINATIONS against products of other states, 9.
  In railroad rates, 29, 96.
  Unjust, 40, 94.
  In favor of domestic traffic, 95.
  In charges between connecting lines, 113.

DISEASE, Free transportation to communities scourged by, 188.

DISPATCH COMPANIES are common carriers, 31.

DISTRICT ATTORNEY, Duty of, 182.

DISTRICT COURT, Jurisdiction of, 163.
  Civil, 163.
  Criminal, 166.

DISTRICT OF COLUMBIA, 17, 19.

DISTRICTS, Traffic, 73.

DIVERSION OF FREIGHT, 38, 80.

DOMESTIC COMMERCE, Regulation of, reserved to states, 11-14, 19, 35.
  Traffic, Discriminations in favor of, 95.

DOS PASSOS on Inter-state Commerce Act, 19.

DRAWBACKS FORBIDDEN, 40, 59.

DUE PROCESS OF LAW, 24.

DURESS, 54, 157.

DUTIES on imports and exports, 14, 16.
  Clearance, 15.
  On tonnage, 16.
  New, imposed on company, 98.
  Collected on freight passing through foreign country, When, 144.

EARNINGS OF RAILROADS can not be pooled, 134.

EMPLOYE compelled to testify, 163.
   Penalty for violating act, 166.
   Free transportation to, 187.

EMPLOYMENT of other lines, 78.

ENGLISH STATUTES, 193–208.
   The Railway and Canal Traffic Act, 1854, 193.
   The Regulation of Railways Act, 1868, 197.
   The Regulation of Railways Act, 1873, 198–208.

ENGLISH Statutes and Decisions, 29, 42, 96, 156, 182.
   Equality in rates, 42.
   Undue preferences, 66.
   Weight of English decisions, 29, 67, 97.
   Connecting lines, 96.
   Long and short haul, 120.
   Practice and procedure under, 182.

EQUALITY in rates required, 40.
   At common law, 41.
   Under English statutes, 43 *et seq.*
   State statutes and decisions, 64.
   Mileage rates, 124.

EQUITY, Remedy to recover back excessive charges paid, not in, 159.
   Remedy in Circuit Court, as a Court of, to enforce orders of Commission, 180.

EVIDENCE, Prima facie, 28, 76.
   Lower charge, of unreasonableness of higher, 37.
   Violation of equality statute, 45.
   Long and short haul, 124.
   As to attorney's fee, 163.
   Criminating Evidence, Officers required to give, 163.
      General Rules, 164.
      Pardon—Stat. of Lim., Effect of, 164.
      Statutes requiring the giving of, 165.
      "Furnish evidence against himself," 165.
   Prima Facie—Findings of fact by Commission, 176.
      Constitutionality of such statutes, 176.
      Rules of, 177.
      Railway regulation statutes, 179.

EXCEPTIONS to the Act, 187.

EXCLUSIVE PATRONAGE, No ground of discrimination, 95.

EXCURSION TICKETS, 187 *et seq.*

EXECUTION, Order in nature of, 181.

EXPORTS, Tax or duty on, 14, 16.
   Meaning of, 16.

EXPORT TRADE, 58, 132.

EXPOSITIONS, Property carried to, for exhibition, free or at reduced rates, § 22, 187.

EXPRESS COMPANIES are common carriers, 31.
   Exclusive privileges of, 42.
   Same treatment as other shippers, 59.
   Facilities and rates to, 83, 95.

EXPRESS TRAINS, 59.

FACILITIES between connecting lines, 33, 34, 196.
   Undue preference in, 67.
   To carriers and shippers, 83.
   Omnibus, 88.
   Station, 92, 94, 110.
   Express, 95.
   Interchange of traffic, 96 *et seq.*
   Charges are not, 113.

FACILITIES for receiving, forwarding, and delivering, and interchange of traffic, 96 *et seq.*
   According to powers of company, 103.
   Cars, provide additional, 103, 106.
   Block system, 104, 112.
   Waiting room, 104.
   Can not compel two companies to act jointly, 105.
   Train service, 105, 106, 107.
   Through booking, 105, 108.
   Rates, 109, 116, 117.
   Car facilities, 110.
   Return of cars, 105.
   Off line of railway, 107.
   Continuous line, 108.
   Two lines, longer and shorter, 109.
   Station facilities, 110, 118.
      At common law, 115.
         Establishing new, principles governing, 111.
   Discriminations in charges between connecting lines, 113.
      At common law, 115.
   Drawing cars of other roads, 114.
   At common law and under state statutes, 115.

INDEX. 215

FACILITIES—*Continued.*
  Giving bill of lading, through rate, etc., beyond company's own line, 149.

FACT, Undue preference is a question of, 67.

FAIRS, Property carried to, for exhibition, 187.

FARES, Cash and Ticket, 46.
  Schedules of, to be printed and posted, 139.
  No advance in except upon 10 days' notice, 145.

FEES. See ATTORNEY'S FEE.

FERRIES, Regulation of, 11.
  Used in connection with railroads, 33.

FIELD, JUSTICE, Opinions on power of Congress to regulate Commerce, 4, 20.

FIFTH AMENDMENT to Constitution, 164.

FIRM may complain to Commission, 170.

FLOODS, Communities scourged by, Free transportation to, 188.

FOREIGN CORPORATIONS engaged in inter-state commerce, 9.

FOREIGN NATIONS, Commerce with, 1, 3.
  Transportation to and from, 19.
  Traffic, under English Statutes, 44.
  Shipped through, into U. S., Special provision as to, 144.

FORWARDING of traffic, 96.

FOURTEENTH AMENDMENT, 24

FREIGHT LINES are common carriers, 31.

FREIGHT, Quantity of, 48, 50, 80.
  Contract to furnish all, 58, 77, 95.
  Pools prohibited, 134.
  Shipped through foreign country into United States, 144.
  Devices to prevent carriage of, being continuous, 148.

GEORGIA STATUTES, Connecting roads, 116.
  Railroad commissioners, 131.

GOOD FAITH OF COMPANY, 49,

GOODS being transported between states, 9.
  Delivering on general orders, 83.

GRADES, Steep, 48.

"GROUP RATES," 63, 67.
  Legality of, 68 *et seq.*

HANDLING PROPERTY, 37.
  Cost of, 39.

HARBORS, Improvement of, 10.

HEALTH LAWS, 11, 14.

ILLINOIS STATUTES regulating railroads, 27, 28, 38. 65, 163.
  Long and short haul, 120, 122, 128.
  Pleading under, 159.

IMPORTS, Tax on, 7.
  Duties on, 16.
  Meaning of term, 16.

INDIAN TRIBES, Commerce with, 1, 5.

INDICTMENTS for offenses against Act, 166, 167.
  Remedy for public wrong, 182.

INJUNCTION, Practice as to, 93.
  To enforce filing and publication of rates, 147.
  To enforce orders of Commission, 181.

INSPECTION LAWS, 11, 13, 16.

INSURANCE, Not a transaction of commerce, 14.

INTERCHANGE OF TRAFFIC, 96.

INTERESTS OF COMPANY, 45, 51, 52, 67, 126.

INTERRUPTION must be in good faith and necessary to prevent carriage being continuous, 148.

INTER-STATE COMMERCE, 1, 3–9.
  Tax on, 11.
  When it has commenced, 20, 151.

INTER-STATE Commerce Commission, Constitutionality of, 24.
  May suspend long and short haul section (§ 4), 119 130.
  Nature of power, 119, 130.
  Other features of law remain operative, 132.
  Schedules, contracts, joint-tariffs, etc., to be filed with Commission, § 6, 146.

INTER-STATE, ETC., COM.—*Continued.*
    Persons damaged may make complaint to, § 9, 163.
    Created; appointment; terms, removal and qualification of Commissioners, § 11, 167.
    Vacancy, how filled, § 11, 167.
    Powers of, § 12, 168.
        Inquire into business of carriers, 168.
        Require attendance of witnesses, 168.
        Production of books, papers, etc., 168.
    May invoke aid of U. S. courts, 168.
    Right of Congress to confer such powers, 168.
    Complaints of violations of Act, and procedure thereon, § 13, 170.
    Charges to be forwarded to carrier, 170.
    Reparation by carrier, 170.
    Investigation of charges by, 170.
    Duties of, 170.
    Decisions upon, or construction of law will not be given in advance of complaints, 170 *et seq.*
    Amendment of pleadings and procedings 175.
    Investigation at request of State or Territorial Railroad Commissioners, 175.
    Investigation upon its own motion, 175.
    Written report of investigations, 175.
        Effect of findings of fact therein, 175.
    Reports to be entered of record, and copies furnished, 179.
    Orders to carriers found violating the Act, § 15, 179.
        Copy to be delivered to carrier, § 15, 179.
        Exoneration upon compliance, § 15, 179.
    Procedure in circuit court to enforce obedience to orders, § 16, 180.
    Duty of, to apply to court, 180.
    Regulation of procedings, § 17, 183.
    Majority shall constitute quorum, 183.
    Make and amend general rules or orders, 183.
    Parties may appear in person, or by attorney, 183.
    Votes and official acts to be entered of record, 183.

INTER-STATE, ETC., COM.—*Continued.*
    Official seal to be judicially noticed, 183.
    Any Commissioner may administer oath, 183.
    Secretary of, salary, etc., 184.
    Employes of, salaries, etc., 184.
    Principal office of, 185.
    Sessions elsewhere, 185.
    Annual reports of carriers, What to contain, § 20, 185.
        Commission, § 21, 187.

INVESTIGATIONS by Commission, 170, 175.
    Written report of, 175.
    Effect of findings of fact therein, 175.

IOWA STATUTES regulating railroads, 59, 163.
    Pleading under, 159.
    Counsel fee, 163.

JOINT-TARIFFS. Copies to be filed with Commission, 146.

JURISDICTION of Railway Commissioners under English statutes, 69.
    U. S. Circuit Courts, § 12, 169.
    U. S. District Courts, § 10, 166.

JURY, Trial by, 28, 176.
    Making report *prima facie* evidence, validity of, 176.

KANSAS, Stock law of, 1874, 160.
    Attorney's fee to plaintiff, 160.

LADING, Bill of, Can not compel giving beyond company's own line, 149.

LARCENY of goods, while a part of commerce, 6.

LEGACIES, Tax on, 13.

LEGISLATIVE POWER, Delegation of, 131.

LICENSE LAWS, 13.

LIENS, Maritime, 6, 11.

LIKE CONDITIONS, 59, 159.
    Quantities of freight, 159.

LIKE KIND OF TRAFFIC, 40, 46.
    Property, 118, 126.

LIKE SERVICE, 40.

LINE OF RAILWAY, Over same portion of, 63.
    Over the same, 119, 130.

LINES, Employment of other, 78.
    Two, 81, 82, 109.
    Continuous, 108.

LIQUOR license and tax laws, 13.
    Prohibitory laws, 13.
    Making sales of, *prima facie* evidence, 178.

LIVE STOCK, Transportation of, 23.
    Carriers of, 30.

LOADING, Expense of, 48.

"LOCAL OPTION" LAW, 9.

LOCAL and through traffic, 121, 122, 124.

LOCAL, Subjects of local nature, when may be regulated by states, 10.

LOCALITY, Preference to, 89.

LOCOMOTIVES, Sufficient, 105.

LONG AND SHORT HAUL, 48, 67, 118 *et seq*
    Same charge for short as for longer distance, 67, 68 *et seq.*, 120, 130.
    Greater charge for short than for longer distance, 67, 120.
    Lines, 109.
    Greater compensation in aggregate for shorter than for longer distance forbidden, 118, 125.
    Not authorized to charge same for shorter as for longer distance, 119, 120, 130.
    English decisions, 120.
    Local and through traffic, 121.
    Competition of interest, 121.
    Statutes and decisions in the United States, 122.
        Federal Courts, 122.
        Illinois, 122.
        Massachusetts, 123.
        Oregon, 123.
        Pennsylvania, 124.
    Evidence 124.
    Pleading, 124
    Equal mileage rates, 124.
    "Greater compensation in aggregate," meaning of, 125.
    "Like kind of property," 126.
    "Substantially similar circumstances and conditions," 126.
        Interests of company, 126.
        Cost of service, 127.
        Quantity of freight shipped, 127.
        Competition with other lines, 127.

LONG AND SHORT HAUL.—*Continued.*
    Developing trade, 128.
    "Over the same line," 130.
    "In the same direction," 130.
    Power of Commission to suspend this section, 130.
        Nature of the power, 130.
        Suspension limited to this section, Other features of law remain operative, 132.

MAINE, Statutes regulating railroads, 28, 169.

MALICE, "Willfully" does not imply, 166.

"MANAGEMENT," Common, 19, 32–35.

MANDAMUS, Under English statute, 69.
    To compel carrier to file and publish schedules, etc., 147.
    To redress public wrongs, 182.

MARINE TORTS, 11.

MARITIME conveyance and liens, 6.

MARSHALL, CHIEF JUSTICE, Opinions on power of Congress to regulate commerce, 1–5, 20, 21.

MASSACHUSETTS, Statutes regulating railroads, 64, 169.
    Long and short haul, 120, 122.
    Drawing cars of other companies, 169.

MATERIAL MEN, Liens of, 11.

MEASURE OF RECOVERY, 157.

MILEAGE, Equal or proportional, rates, 124.
    Tickets, § 22, 187 *et seq.*, 191.

MILLER, JUSTICE, Opinions on power of Congress to regulate commerce, 3, 4, 20.

MINISTERS OF RELIGION, Reduced rates to, 187, 191.

MISDEMEANOR, Violations of Act declared to be, 166.

MISSISSIPPI Railroad Commission Act, 179, 186.

MISSOURI RIVER RATES, 68.

MISTAKE as distinguished from design, 166.

MONEY had and received, action for, 157, 158.

MONOPOLIES, 135 et seq

MORMONS, Legislation against, 17.

MUNICIPAL ORGANIZATION, Any, may complain to Commission, 170.
    Governments, carriage, storage, etc., for, 187.

NATURAL ADVANTAGES, Company can not destroy, 74.

NAVIGABLE STREAMS, Bridges and dams, 6, 10.
    Diversion of channel of, 16.

NAVIGATION, Obstructions and burdens upon, 7.

NEW DUTIES or obligations, 98.

NEW HAMPSHIRE, Statute prescribing equality of rates, 54.
    Attorney's fee, 161.

NOTICE, Ten days, of advances in rates, etc., required, 145.
    Reductions may be made without, 145.

OFFENSES, Penalty for violation of Act, 166.
    Indictments, where to be found, 167.

OFFICER compelled to testify, 163.
    Penalty for violation of Act, 166.
    Free transportation to, 187.

OHIO RIVER RATES, 68.

OMNIBUS FACILITIES, 88.

ORDERS, Delivering goods on general, 83.

OREGON, Statutes regulating railroads, 120, 122.
    Long and short haul, 128.
    Railway pools prohibited, 135.

ORIGIN OF TRAFFIC, No discrimination on account of, 133.

OTHER FACTS, Evidence of, 45.

OTHER LINES, Employment of, 78.

OYSTERS, Protection of, 13.

PACIFIC RAILROADS, 18.

PAPERS, Production of, 165.

PARCELS, Small, Cost of handling, 39, 60.
    Packed, 61.

PARDEE, Opinion of Judge, 122, 131.

PARTICULAR descriptio n of traffic, 65, 92.

PASSENGERS, Transportation of, 19.
    Ticket and cash fares, 46.
    Mileage, excursion and commutation, 187 et seq.

PASSES to officers and employes, 187.

PATENTS, Treble damages for infringement, 161.

PEDDLERS, Tax on, 13.

PENALTIES for failing to publish schedules, etc., 147.
    For violations of Act, § 10, 166.

PENNSYLVANIA, Statutes regulating railroads, 65, 124.
    Attorney's fee, 161.

PERSONS, Charges must be alike to all, 40, 41, 47.
    Discriminations against unlawful, 40, 47.
    May make complaint to Commission, 170.

PETITION to Commission for violations of Act, 170.
    Circuit Court to compel obedience to orders of Commission, 180.

PILOTAGE, Regulation of, 10, 16.

PLACE OF SHIPMENT or destination, No discrimination on account of, 58, 74, 133, 151.
    Carriage to be continuous between, 148.

PLEADING, Like Kind of traffic, 47.
    Long and short haul, 124.
    Actions against carriers, 159-160.
    Like conditions, 159.
    Unjust discrimination, 160.
    Amendment of, 175.
    In Circuit Court as a court of equity, 180.

POLITICAL PARTY, No more than 3 commissioners of same, § 11, 168.

POLITIC, Any body, may complain to Commission, 170.

POOLING arrangements prohibited, 134 et seq.
    At common law, 135 et seq.
    English decisions, 136.

POLICE POWERS OF STATE, 14.

POLYGAMY, Legislation against, 18.

POWERS of Corporations, 96, 100, 103 *et seq.*

PRACTICE, 93, 142.
    Under English statutes, 142, 183.
    As to attorney's fee, 162.

PREFERENCE, Congress can not give, to one port, 14–16.
    To localities, 89.
        See UNDUE PREFERENCE.

PREJUDICE. See UNDUE PREFERENCE.

PREMIUM to cover liability of common carrier, 39.

PRIMA FACIE EVIDENCE. See EVIDENCE.

PRINTED SCHEDULES. See SCHEDULES.

PRIVATE CONTRACTS, Power of Congress over, 14.

PRIVILEGE OF WITNESS, 164.

PROCEDURE before Commission, 170.

PRODUCTION of books and papers, 164, 165.

PROFIT OF COMPANY, 39, 45, 51, 52.

PROHIBITORY LIQUOR LAW, 13.

PROOF, Burden of, 50.

PROPERTY, Transportation of, 19.

PROPORTIONAL RATES, 44, 48, 125.

PRO-RATING, 121.

PROTEST not necessary to recovery of damages, 158.

PROVISOS IN ACT, 19, 35, 187.
    Construction of, 188 *et seq.*

PUBLICATION of schedules, rates, tariffs, etc., 139–146.

PUBLIC, Convenience of, 92, 95, 149.
    Duties and remedies unaffected by Act, 182.

PUBLIC USE, Property devoted to, 25.
    Employment of carriers, 30.
    Policy, 136.

PULLMAN CARS, 110.

QUALIFICATIONS of Commissioners, § 11, 167.

QUANTITY of freight shipped, 43, 50 *et seq.*, 80.
    Under statutes, 51.
    At common law, 54.
    Of traffic of a place, 91.

QUARANTINE LAWS, 11, 13, 16.

QUORUM, Majority of Commissioners shall constitute, 183.

RAILROADS.
    Act to regulate Commerce, 19–192.
        Construction of, must first be given by, 173.
        Subject to, 32–35.
    Actions against, Where to be brought, 163.
    Advantages (Natural), Company can not destroy, 74.
    Annual reports, What to contain, § 20, 185.
    Beyond their line, Carrying, 33, 149.
    Bill of lading, Can not compel giving of beyond own line, 149.
    Business, Commission authorized to inquire into, 168.
    Carrying beyond own line, 33, 149.
    Cars, Of other companies, 30.
        Drawing, 114.
        Return of, 105.
        Sufficient for traffic, 106.
        Through, facilities, 110.
    Charter rights of, 25, 45, 169.
    Commission authorized to inquire into business of, § 12, 168.
    Commissioners of, 131.
    Common carriers, 30.
    Competition with other lines of communication, 55 *et seq.*, 127.
    Connecting, Facilities for interchange of traffic between, 96 *et seq.*
        Discriminations between, 113.
    Construction of Act must first be given by, 173.
    Continuous line, 108.
    Damages, Liable in, to persons injured, 156.
        Recovery of, 156–159.
    Defined, 36.
    Delivering goods on general orders, 83.
    Discriminations between connecting, 113.

RAILROADS—*Continued.*
  In rates, 27, 28.
  Drawing cars of other, 114.
  Duties, New imposed on, 98.
  Employes, Passes to, 187.
  Equality of rates required, 40-65.
  Express facilities, 42, 59.
  Evidence. *Prima facie*, 179.
  Facilities for interchange of traffic, 96 *et seq.*
    Off line, 107.
  Instruments of commerce, 2, 21.
  Interchange of traffic between connecting, 96 *et seq.*
    Passes with other roads, 187.
  Interests of, 45, 67, 126.
  Liable in damages to persons injured, 156.
    Recovery of, 156-159.
  Line, Over same portion of, 63.
  Lines, Two, Longer and shorter, 109.
  Locomotives, Sufficient, 105.
  Long and short hauls, 118 *et seq.*
  Natural advantages, Can not destroy, 74.
  Obligations, New, imposed on, 98.
  Officers, Passes to, 187.
  Over same portion of line, 63.
  Pacific, 18.
  Passes to officers and employes, 187.
    Interchange of, with other roads, 187.
  Pooling arrangements prohibited, 134 *et seq.*
  Powers of, 96, 100, 103 *et seq.*
  Preferences, Undue, 65-95.
  Private, 31.
    Side tracks, 48.
  Public carriers for hire, 25, 38.
    Character of, 37, 38.
  Rates, Discriminations in, 27, 28.
    Through, 109.
  Receipts, Tax on, 14.
  Regulation of, 4-5, 12.
  Reports of, Annual, What to contain, § 20, 185.
  Side tracks, Private, 48.
  State statutes regulating, 27.
  Stations, 97 *et seq.*, 110.
    Establishing new, 111.
  Statutes declaring facts *prima facie* evidence, 179.
    Constitutionality of, 176.
  Subject to Act, 32-35.
  Taxation and regulation of, 8.
  Through booking, 105.
    Rates, 109.
    Car facilities, 110.
  Train service, Additional, 105, 107.

RAILROADS—*Continued.*
  Number and times of, 106.
  Two companies, Can not compel to act jointly, 105.
    Lines, Longer and shorter, 81, 109.
  Undue preferences prohibited, 65-95.

RAILWAY and Canal Traffic Act, 1854, 193-197.

RAILWAY Clauses Consolidation Act, 1845, § 90, 42, 43.

RATES, Charter right to fix, 25.
  Discriminations in, 27, 28, 96.
  Special, 37, 40.
  Equality in required, 40.
  Equal mileage, 124.
  Undue preferences in, 67, 68.
  Through, 73, 80, 152.
  Schedules of, to be printed and posted, 139.
  No advance in, except upon ten days' notice, 145.
  Reductions in, to be posted immediately, 145.
  Division of through, 146.

REASONABLENESS of charges, 36-40.
  Elements of, 38.
  Contract limiting liability of carrier, 40.
  Question of fact, not of law, 67.

REBATES forbidden, 40, 59.
  At common law, 41.

RECEIVERS OF RAILROADS, 30.
  Compelled to testify, 163.
  Penalty for violating act, 166.

RECEIVING property, 19, 37,38, 96.
  Unequal rates forbidden, 40.
  Goods, etc., 84.
  Facilities for, 96.

RECOVERY of excessive rates paid, 37, 44, 192.
  Action for money had and received, 157.
  Measure of, 157.

REFRESHMENT accommodations in stations, 102.

REGULATE COMMERCE, Meaning of, 1, 21.

REGULATION of Inter-State Commerce, 21.
  Respecting the Territories, 17.

REGULATION, ETC.—*Continued.*
   Of proceedings before Commission, 183.

REGULATION of Railways Act, 1868 (English), 197.
——, 1873, " 198–208.

RELIGION, Ministers of, Reduced rates to, 187, 191.

REMEDIAL OR PENAL? 147, 163.

REMEDIES for violations of section 6, 147.
   Of Act, 163.

REMOVAL OF COMMISSIONERS, § 11, 167.

REPARATION BY CARRIER, 170,
   Recommendation as to, by Commission, 175.

REPORT OF COMMISSION, Findings of fact therein *prima facie* evidence, 175.
   Auditor. *Prima facie* evidence, 176.

REPORTS, Annual, of Commission, 187.
——, of carrier, 185.
——, Decisions of English Railway Commissioners, 208.

RESTRAINT OF TRADE, Contracts in, 137

RETAIL SHIPMENTS, 50.

RETURN LOADS, 48, 91.
   Of cars, 105.

RIVAL LINE, Threat of building, 58.

RIVERS, Navigable, Power of Congress concerning, 6–8.
   Bridges over, 6, 10.

ROUND TRIP TICKETS, 187 *et seq.*

ROUTE, Through, Principles upon which it is granted, 152.

RULE IS A REGULATION, 1, 21.

RULES of construction, 29, 67.
   Affecting aggregate of charge, 139, 140.
   Of evidence, 177.
   Commission may adopt, 183.
   Adopted by English Railway Commissioners, 208.

SALESMEN, Traveling, Tax on, 13.

SAVINGS from Act, § 22, 187.

SCHEDULES (printed) of freight

SCHEDULES—*Continued.*
   rates and passenger fares to be kept posted, 139.
      Terminal charges and rules affecting the aggregate charge, 140.
      Collection and delivery charges, 141.
      Demurrage, 142.
      Practice under English Act, 142.
      Freight passing through foreign country, Special provision as to, 144.
      No advance in rates, etc., except upon 10 days' notice, 145.
      Reductions to be immediately posted, 145.
      Greater or less compensation than named in schedule forbidden, 145.
      To be filed with Commission, 146.
      Remedies for violations of section 6 as to publishing and posting rates, etc., 147.
      Change of time, 148.

SEA COMPETITION, 57, 75, 133.
   Goods shipped by, 59, 75.

SEASON TICKETS, 89.

SERVICE, Like, 40.
   Cost of, 38, 48.
   Not rendered, No charge for, 62.
   Through, 82.

SERVICES, Terminal, 92.

SERVICE OF PROCESS upon corporation, 147.

SHIPMENT. Place of, 58, 74, 77, 148, 151.
   What is, 151.
   Conditions of, 87.
   Of goods in order of receipt, 95.
   Continuous in same cars, 150,

SHIPPERS, All, must be treated alike, 40, 47.
   Contracting to furnish all their freight, 58, 77, 95.
   Facilities and rates to, 83.
   Motives of, immaterial, 133.

SHORTER than longer distance. See LONG AND SHORT HAUL.

SIDINGS, Shunting on, 93.
   When stations, 144.

SIMILAR CIRCUMSTANCES and conditions, 40, 47 *et seq.*, 118, 126 *et seq.*, 133.
   Cost of service, 48, 127.
   Quantity of freight shipped, 50.

SIMILAR CIRCUMSTANCES—*Continued.*
    Competition with other lines, 55 et seq., 127.
    Developing trade, 57, 128.
    Threat of building rival line, 58.
    Contract to furnish all shippers freight, 58.
    Interests of company, 126.

SLEEPING CAR COMPANIES, Regulation and taxation of, 8.
    Quaere: whether within the Act, 31.

SOCIETY, Mercantile, agricultural or manufacturing, may complain to Commission, 170.

STANDARD OIL COMPANY, Discriminations in favor of, 55.

STATES, Commerce among the several, 1, 3, 19, 20.
    Discriminations against products of other, 9.
    Subjects of local nature, When may be regulated by, 10.
    No tax or duty to be levied on goods exported from the, 14.
    Statutes regulating railroads, held invalid, 27.
    Statutes fixing maximum charges, 38.
    Equality statutes and decisions, 64.
    Railroad Commissioner, Investigation at request of, 175.
    Carriage, storage, etc., for, 187.

STATIONS, Time of closing, 84.
    Facilities, 92–3, 94, 97 et seq., 104, 110.
    Establishing new, 111.
    At common law and under state statutes, 115, 118.
    Printed schedules of rates and fares to be kept posted in, 139.
    What are? 143.

STATUTES fixing maximum charges, 38.
    Constitutionality of, 39.
    Remedial or penal, 147, 163.
    Requiring the giving of criminating evidence, 165.
    Prima facie evidence, Constitutionality of, 176.
    Aimed at individual grievances, 182.
    United States—
        Act of July 20, 1850, Conveyances of vessels, 6.
        Act of July 1, 1862, Union Pacific Railroad, 150.

STATUTES—*Continued.*
    Act of June 15, 1866, Connecting Railroads, 24, 26, 150.
    Act of July 24, 1866, Telegraph Lines, 6.
    Act of February 15, 1868, Criminating evidence, 165.
    Act of March 3, 1873, Alaska, 18.
    Act of March 3, 1873, Transportation of live stock, 23.
    Act of May 2, 1873, Texas and Pacific R. charter, 122, 135.
    Act of February 4, 1887, Regulate commerce, 1–192.
    U. S. Revised Statutes—
        § 860, Criminating evidence, 165.
        § 4386–90, Transportation of live stock, 23.
        § 5257–8, Connecting Railroads, 24, 26, 150.
        § 5263, Telegraph Lines, 6.
    State—
        Colorado—Constitution—Railroads, 94, 115.
        Georgia—February 14, 1874—Connecting Railroads, 116.
        Illinois—July 1, 1871—Railroads—Extortion, 28.
            May 2, 1873—Railroads—Extortion, 26, 38, 123, 128.
        Iowa—Laws, 1874—Railroads—Discriminations, 59.
        Kansas—Stock Law, 1874, Attorney's Fee, 161.
        Maine—March 26, 1858—Railroad Crossings, 28.
            Act of, 1871, Railroad Commissioners, 169.
        Massachusetts—General Railroad Act, 1874—64, 123, 169.
            1817, *Prima Facie* evidence, 176.
        Michigan—Laws, 1873—Railroads—117.
        Mississippi—Railroad Commission Act, 1884—179, 186.
        New Hampshire—December, 20, 1840—Railroads—Attorney's Fee, 161.
        Oregon, February 20, 1885, Railroads—128, 135.
        Pennsylvania—Tonnage Commutation Act, 1861—124.
            May 3, 1866, Corporations—Attorney's fee, 161.
        Tennessee—March 30, 1883, Railroad Commission, 27.
    English Statutes—
        Railway Clauses Consolidation Act, 1845, § 90, 43, 47, 66.

STATUTES—*Continued.*
Railway and Canal Traffic Act, 1854 (in full), 193–197.
—— § 2, 66, 96, 149, 156.
—— § 3, 182.
—— § 7, 40.
Regulation of Railways Act, 1868, § 16, 43, 66, 197.
Regulation of Railways Act, 1873, § 11, 152.
(In full), Appendix, 198–208.

STORAGE, 19, 37.

SUBPŒNA, U. S. courts may issue, 168.
May compel obedience to, 169.

SUITS in equity to enforce orders of Commission, 180.

SUPREME COURT, Appeals to, § 16, 181.

TARIFFS, Joint, to be filed with Commission, 146.
Commission may require production of, 168.

TAX ON IMPORTS, 7.
Railroads, telegraphs, etc., 8.
Inter-state commerce, 11.
Ferries, 12.
Occupations, 13.
Railway receipts, 14.
Articles exported from any state, 14.
In District of Columbia, 17.

TELEGRAPH, Regulation of, Congress, 6.
Taxation and regulation of, by States, 8, 9.

TELEPHONE, Unjust discrimination in use of, 42.

TENNESSEE Railroad Commission Act, 27.

TERMS of Commissioners, § 11, 167.

TERMINAL Services, 92.
Facilities, 96.
Charges, 125, 140.
Printed schedules to show, 139.
When entitled to make, 140.

TERRITORIES, Transportation to and from, 17, 19.
Regulations respecting, 17.
Complaints by Railroad Commissioners of, 175.

TESTIMONY. See EVIDENCE, also, WITNESS.

TEXAS CATTLE LAW, 9.

TEXAS and Pacific Railroad Charter, 114, 122, 134–5.

THROUGH RATES, 73, 80, 109, 116, 117.
Division of, 146.
Principles upon which they are granted, 152.
Service, 82.
Tickets, 82, 149.
Booking, 85, 80, 105, 108.
Car service, 110.
Traffic, 121, 124, 152.
Rate, Giving, does not render Co. liable beyond its own line, 149.
Route, Principles upon which opened, 152.

TICKETS, Discount to passengers purchasing, 45.
Through, 82, 145.
Office accommodations, 102, 107.
See BOOKING.
Third class, 110.
Mileage, excursion and commutation, § 22, 187 *et seq.*
Round trip, 187 *et seq.*
Tourists, 190.

TIME-SCHEDULE, Change of, 148.

TIME when act takes effect, 192.

TONNAGE, Duty on, 16.

TORTS, Marine, 11.

TOURISTS' TICKETS, 190.

TRACKS, Use of, 96.

TRADE, Developing new, 47, 57, 128.

TRAFFIC is commerce, 2.
Like kind of, 40, 46.
Diversion of, 80.
Aggregate, of a place, 91.
Particular description of, 92.
Interchange of, facilities for, 96.
Cars sufficient for, 106.
Local and through, 121, 124.
Through, Defined, 152.

TRAIN SERVICE, Additional, 105, 107.
Number and times of, 106.

TRANSPORTATION, Inter-state, 2–5, 6–9.
Passengers and property, 19, 21.
Live stock, 23.
Companies are common carriers, 31.
Defined, 36.

Transportation—*Continued.*
  Charges for, must be equal, 40.
  Circumstances and conditions of, 40, 133.
  Long and short distances, 118 *et seq.*
  Greater compensation in aggregate for, 125.

TRIAL BY JURY, 28, 176.

TRUNK LINE POOL, 136.

TRUSTEE compelled to testify, 163.
  Penalty for violating act, 166.

TWO LINES, 81, 109.

TYPE, Schedules to be printed in large, not less than ordinary pica, 139.

UNDUE PREFERENCE, Prohibited, 65, 95.
  Reason for this provision, 66.
  Locality, 31, 65, 89.
  Particular description of traffic, 31, 65, 92.
  Inequality of charge may amount to, 44, 49, 56, 66.
  Equality of charge may amount to, 66.
  Person, company, firm or corporation, 65.
  Rates and charges as well as facilities, 67, 68.
  Weight of English decisions, 67.
  Question of fact not of law, 67.
  Interests of company, 67.
  "Group rates," 68.
  Natural advantages, Compan can not destroy, 74.
  Competition with other lines, 75.
  Developing business, 77.
  Contract to furnish shipper's entire freight, 77.
  Employment of other lines, 78.
  Cost of service, 79.
  Quantity of freight shipped, 80.
  Diversion of traffic, 80.
  Through rates, 80.
  Two lines, 81, 82.
  Through tickets, service, etc., 82.
  Facilities and rates to carriers, etc., 83.
  Receiving and delivering goods, etc., 84.
  Conditions of, 87.
  Omnibus facilities, 88.
  Practice, Injunction, 93.
  Damage, 93.
  At common law, 94.

UNDUE PREFERENCE—*Continued.*
  Unjust discrimination, Delivery, 94.
  Station facilities, 94.

UNIFORMITY of regulation, What commerce requires, 6, 21.

UNITED STATES COURTS, Aid of, may be invoked by Commission, 168.
  Compel obedience to subpœna, 169.
  Carriage, storage, etc., for, § 22, 187.

UNJUST discriminations in rates, 28, 40, 94.
  Pleading under statutes against, 160.

USAGE MUST BE UNIFORM, 189.

VACANCY in Commission, how filled, § 11, 167.

VALUE OF GOODS, Difference in rates by reason of, 95.

VIOLATIONS of act declared to be misdemeanors, § 10, 166.
  Complaints of, and procedure thereon by Commission, § 13, 170.

WABASH CASE, Decision in, 19–22.

WAITE, Chief Justice, Opinions on power of Congress to regulate commerce, 2, 20.

WAITING ROOM FACILITIES, 104.

WATER and railroad transportation, 19, 31.
  Transportation, Competition with, 57, 75, 129.

WAREHOUSES, Connecting with railroads, 116.

WEIGHT OF LOADS, 48, 95.

WHARFAGE FEES, 11, 16.

WHOLESALE SHIPMENTS, 50.

WILLFULLY VIOLATING ACT, 166.
  Meaning of, 166.

WITNESS, Compelled to give criminating evidence, 164.
  Privilege of, 164.
  Pardon, Effect of, 164.

WITNESS—*Continued.*
    Statute of limtations, Effect of, 164.
    In criminal case against himself, 164–5.
    "Furnish evidence against himself," 165.
    Commission may require attendance of, 168.

WITNESS—*Continued.*
    Circuit Courts may compel obedience to subpœna, 169.
    May punish for contempt, 169.
    Fees of, ? 18, 184.

WRITS. See ATTACHMENT, INJUNCTION, and MANDAMUS.